THE
wildlife
TRUSTS

NATURE
TALES

COMPILED BY MICHAEL ALLEN AND
SONYA PATEL ELLIS

First published 2010 by Elliott and Thompson Limited
27 John Street, London WC1N 2BX
www.eandtbooks.com

ISBN: 978-1-9076-4221-0

Design copyright: Elliott & Thompson
Text copyright: Michael Allen and Sonya Patel Ellis
Individual Contributions:

Andrew Lack	Gavin Maxwell	Richard Jefferies
Bill Oddie	Geoffrey Grigson	Richard Mabey
Charles Darwin	George Montagu	Robert Macfarlane
Charles Waterton	Gerard Manley Hopkins	Roger Deakin
Chris Baines	Gilbert White	Ronald Lockley
Chris Beardshaw	Henry Eliot Howard	Ruth Padel
Colin Elford	Henry Williamson	Samuel Taylor Coleridge
Colin J. Martin	J. A. Baker	Simon Barnes
Colin Tudge	John Aubrey	Sir Alfred Russel Wallace
David Lack	John Buxton	Sir John Lister-Kaye
Dorothy Wordsworth	John Clare	Sir Joseph Banks
Dominic Couzens	John Woolner	Steve Backshall
Edmund Selous	Jules Pretty	Stephen Moss
Edward A. Armstrong	Kathleen Jamie	Thomas Gray
Edward Grey	Mark Cocker	Tim Dee
Edward Thomas	Miriam Rothschild	William Cobbett
Elizabeth Jane Howard	Nan Shepherd	William Henry Hudson
Eric Ennion	Nick Baker	
Francis Kilvert	Paul Evans	

First published in hardback: 2010
First published in paperback: 2011

9 8 7 6 5 4 3 2 1

A CIP catalogue record for this book is available from the British Library.

Printed in the UK by CPI Cox & Wyman

Typeset in Minion

CONTENTS

CONTENTS

FOREWORD

Britain has a long and remarkable tradition of natural history writing, and this anthology shows just how splendid, perceptive and enjoyable it is.

Its history covers a wide range from entries in field note books and journals kept by scientists, to the imaginative retelling of memorable encounters in the wild. Its practitioners include eighteenth-century parsons, owners of great estates, the labouring poor, academics, travellers and wanderers.

All those included in this anthology have been stirred by their curiosity about the animals and plants with which they shared their lives. They saw a moment in the landscape and recorded its significance to them as a memory of time and place and its dramatic, lasting effect.

We are all part of the natural environment. Its processes provide the air that we breathe, the food and water we eat and drink and the landscapes in which we live. Through the eyes of those that have written these passages, we encounter for ourselves the natural world in all its richness.

I have been fortunate enough to travel widely, but I continue to be inspired by wildlife at home. Reading through this volume I have been reminded that I am not alone. This wonderful collection of some of the greatest nature writers in Britain's history is a pleasure to read from start to finish and a valuable addition to any naturalist's library.

Sir David Attenborough

INTRODUCTION

Some years ago a friend showed me an ancient telescope he had acquired in an antique shop. Three beautiful brass draw tubes made up its full extent. Compared with modern field telescopes it lacked something in brightness and sharpness of image in use; its real delight to me and to the new owner lay in the name engraved on one of the brass tubes:

Thos. Bewick Newcastle.

Thomas Bewick, the incomparable wood engraver and chronicler of the natural world of the late eighteenth and early nineteenth centuries, must have owned and employed the telescope as he sought to get closer to the birds and animals which formed the copy of his natural history books. He may even have watched the small Siberian Swan, named for him, during its winter visits, through this very instrument.

Some of Bewick's engraved images are as memorable as the best prose descriptions, such as those collected in this anthology. One of my personal favourites is of the woodlark, to be found in his *History of British Birds*. The image is set in the bird's typical habitat at the edge of a wood, or maybe in a clearing. The bird is perched confidently and in full song. The delicacy of the monochrome image and the way in which the engraver has produced it, by working away at his block and teasing away the non-essential details, remind me of the essence of good natural history prose. The engraver refines by wasting those elements which are not essential to the image he wants; his creative skill produces the very essence of the bird by such elimination, and yet the decorative art he produces captures the thing itself.

The concentration on the salient elements in the engraver's eye and the detail of what is achieved in the final image could only have been achieved by patient and detailed study of the living bird or animal. The engraver's art, in the paring away of the wooden block, leaves us with an image containing many of the virtues of most of the finest natural history descriptions to be found in this present volume.

Nature Tales is a collection of extracts from the natural history prose of the past three hundred years. Over those years the nature of these British Islands has been the subject of intense investigation by patient and committed observers who have left the record of their discoveries in a wide variety of forms. Above all these passages are linked by the common thread of personal observation. Whether they are the product of a diary, a letter to a friend of similar interests, or of a field notebook whose observations are to be written up later in laboratory or study, they all share the essence of being lived through and of the immediate experience, and those that subsequently were written up for publication still communicate that immediacy, patience and detail.

The tradition of such writing is found throughout the world

but here in these varied islands it has a very long and diverse history. The works which are the product of the late Renaissance curiosity about the natural world range from the early archaeological and natural history interests of Sir Thomas Browne in Norfolk, to those concerned with the listing and classifying of the elements of the natural world, such as John Ray in the late seventeenth century. By the early eighteenth century Carl von Linne in Sweden had produced a system for giving distinct names to different things and the field of natural history observation had a new impetus, as the observers now had an orderly framework in which to set their observations. Gilbert White was able to separate by detailed observation the chiffchaff, willow warbler and wood warbler, three very closely related and, in the field, hard to distinguish species of birds, by detailed observation, and to assign them distinct identities as different things.

From the middle of the eighteenth century the development of ideas of the Sublime and of Romantic sensibility led writers like Thomas Gray, the Wordsworths and Coleridge to travel through these islands and to seek fresh experiences which led to a new level of the appreciation of natural beauty. Man began to measure himself and his feelings in nature and, at the same time as the landscape school of painting of Constable, Turner, Crome, Cotman and Cox was exploring natural forms, so poets and prose writers recorded their own romantic response.

The developing tradition of natural history writing was exposed to two major challenges in the nineteenth century. First there was the challenge to existing orthodoxy, which the theory of evolution appeared to pose to a more conventional theory of natural order and harmony in the natural world, and to man's place in it, from which he could safely draw aesthetic and moral values. Second there was the challenge of increasing urbanisation and the potential destruction of so much natural beauty.

Through these challenges, however, the tradition remained, and the lone amateur naturalist, experiencing and writing about nature at first hand out of doors, ensured the continuity of the tradition. The late nineteenth and early twentieth centuries saw a remarkable development of new societies to protect our landscape and natural history from the worst of the neglect inherent in the apparent estrangement of humanity from nature during the Industrial Revolution and the years of rapid population growth, which accompanied it and was to some extent its cause. These developments began to raise the public consciousness of the need to conserve the natural environment and stimulated a new readership for natural history writing.

In 2012 The Wildlife Trusts, co-sponsors of this anthology, are preparing to celebrate the centenary of the founding of their parent body by Charles Rothschild. Their history is compelling evidence of the valuable role such societies can play in encouraging communities to take responsibility for the natural world and to develop a better understanding of our place in the environment on which we all depend. Such societies, and the other charities which exist to conserve our environment, celebrate and strengthen the tradition of humanity's place in nature. Their amateur naturalist members have taken up the challenge with an impressive commitment to the better understanding of places and the wildlife which thrives in them.

The last century has seen a flourishing of natural history writing as never before in these islands. As the passion to protect the increasingly threatened natural assets grew, so too did the commitment to the diversity of our natural world. Writers like Henry Williamson and Gavin Maxwell created stories of that world in their very different ways, catching the public imagination and helped to add new audiences for the tradition of nature tales.

Ecologists and scientists became familiar to the public through the medium of radio and television, and the Collins *New Naturalist* series of books widened the audience for good scientific writing on habitats and single species or genera.

Meanwhile amidst the development of these new responses to the challenges of the natural world in the late twentieth century, a new generation of creative observers of wildlife and wild places was widening the human understanding of the importance of the environment and of our place within it. Once again, as in the eighteenth century, we were to face with them the excitement of being a part of that world and of measuring ourselves against it and of finding our place within it. We are increasingly challenged to re-engage with the world in which we literally have our being. We must never again lose touch and the new generation of prose writers among our contemporaries are determined that we should feel the force of the natural world and the significance of our encounters with it. The ancients in Proverbs 4:v command us: *Get wisdom, get understanding: forget it not*; if we do learn to understand, we may yet survive the environmental challenges which confront the coming generations.

While I was working on this anthology I reached for my copy of J. A. Baker's *The Peregrine*. As I took it down from the shelves, a book token slip fluttered out, reminding me that the 21 shillings which I paid for this hardback on its publication in 1967 had been a gift from a class to whom I had been teaching a course on William Blake. I am sure that Baker would have approved; his Peregrine is the living incarnation of Blake's assertion: Energy is eternal delight.

The thought takes me back to the sense of excitement I felt at the first reading of this inspirational account of Baker's intense relationship with his falcon. He had seen his first Peregrine in the Essex winter as I was in my last year at school and I was gripped, like so many of his readers, by the account of his obsessive relationship with the bird. A new edition of this remarkable book is now available for the next generation. I hope that many who may meet his work in this volume for the first time will be inspired to buy a copy and make the whole ten-year journey with him, which he first described over forty years ago.

*   *   *

The criteria which were established for the inclusion of a writer in this anthology were tightly drawn. The story was to be based on an encounter in these British islands; it was to be a prose tale and of a length which would allow a wide representation across the centuries. The collection would not be arranged chronologically, but by theme. We hoped to cover a wide diversity of wildlife and to balance the contributions from the historic past with those of a more contemporary flavour. Wherever possible contact was made with living writers, who were invited to contribute an extract from an already published work, or a new piece especially created for the book.

We have been delighted with the response from the living and hope that we will be excused by those who have their own favourites among those from the past, where we may have perversely selected a passage which they may feel does not represent the finest of the writer's published work. It is a very personal selection, eclectic but we hope representative. If it encourages those who meet a new writer or a previously undiscovered passage to go back to the original, then we will have done our work. The tradition is long and distinguished and we can only hint at its enormous richness here.

So what of the future? We are delighted that in association with this publication we have been able to devise a competition to encourage a new generation of natural history writers. The rules established that the prize winner should be an unpublished writer and that the subject should be an encounter with the natural world in these islands, so that the tale created would fit with the criteria for inclusion in this anthology. The prize is inclusion here and we are delighted to have been able to award it to John Woolner. We are grateful to Foyles for their assistance with this and to Simon Barnes who agreed to help us judge the competition. We believe that the great tradition of natural history writing in this country continues to have an exciting future and we feel that the development of the tradition is in good hands.

Michael Allen

CHAPTER 1

IN THE GARDEN

FROM BONSAI TO
BLUE TITS

CHRIS BAINES

Back in 1985, the idea of encouraging wildlife in gardens was very new. Wildlife was classed by most gardeners as a weed, a pest or a disease, while most of the nature conservationists of the day were firmly wedded to exclusive nature reserves for the preservation of precious rarities. When I created the first wildlife garden at the Royal Horticultural Society's Chelsea Flower show, the inscription on my medal read: 'To Chris Baines, for a *Wildfire* garden'. Clearly the words *wildlife* and *garden* had never before been linked positively in the hushed corridors of Vincent Square.

I did have a few acceptable credentials. I had studied horticulture in the late 60s – three years being taught how to kill things, at a time when DDT was still seen as a godsend for gardeners. I had trained as a landscape architect and I had professional experience in public parks and commercial nurseries. Nevertheless, I knew that Chelsea garden plots were like gold dust. My plans for a wildlife garden probably slipped past the Panama-hatted gatekeepers because, a few years earlier, I had designed a successful display of bonsai trees for the Chelsea legend and Second World War hero General Sir Oliver Lease. Perhaps this made me seem safe.

When the formal confirmation of a Chelsea plot arrived, the true enormity of the challenge dawned on me. I had no sponsor. Specialist wildflower nurseries were virtually non-existent and my garden had to stand its ground against some of the most experienced horticultural exhibitors in the world. Chelsea was famous for dramatic displays of exotic flowering shrubs and stately-home-style spectacle. There was no way that primroses, violets and wood anemones could compete head-to-head with big blousy rhododendrons.

From the start I knew my garden had to score points for subtlety and sentimentality. I planned to employ a combination of familiar cottage garden plants and modest wildflowers, all woven into a tapestry of mini habitats that would appeal to gardeners with a small domestic plot and a deep desire to enjoy nature close to home. I was allocated a corner plot, which gave me two edges that could be enjoyed at close quarters, so I opted for a mini-woodland habitat of birch saplings and spring woodland wildflowers on one edge, and a shallow wildlife pool along the other. This meant that I could make the most of such delightful native flowers as lady's smock, brooklime, water forget-me-not and ragged robin by the water's edge, and that the scent of bluebells and the sweet simplicity of primroses and violets would have a chance of rekindling the public's folk memory of landscapes long forgotten.

Most British gardens have a lawn – remember this was in the days before decking – and I wanted to strike a blow for the alternative to stripes and scalping. I wanted daisies. For eleven months of the year, the Chelsea Flower Show site is actually a playing field and I knew that I would be able to utilise the sports turf as my mini-meadow. However, sod's law decreed that mine would be the only patch of grass without a single weed! I did have a very bold white line that marked the corner of a football pitch, but not a single buttercup or daisy. Fortunately, since every other Chelsea gardener was keen to rid their lawn of weeds, I had no difficulty trading turf, and soon acquired a sheet of daisies of my own. This trade in weeds intrigued my neighbours, and in the best spirit of Chelsea, many of them helped me out with words of wisdom, kind encouragement and even the occasional plant. As I enriched my mini-meadow with occasional clumps of snake's head fritillary, bugle and cowslips the penny dropped, and my competitors started to enthuse about the whole idea of gardening for wildlife.

First and foremost, Chelsea is a celebration of horticultural excellence, with thousands paying every year to see the best of garden plants. I knew I had to emphasise the fact that mine was a garden first and wildlife habitat second, and so I used a lot of garden flowers in mixed borders along the two back boundaries. With no big nursery backing me, I found it hard to give the garden the height and maturity that it needed. My former employers were nurserymen and they kindly lent me specimen hollies and hawthorns to make a hedge. Birmingham Parks gave me a few spare ornamental tobacco plants from their municipal display, and I gratefully snapped up a batch of flowering foxgloves that had been rejected because some pest had nibbled at their leaves.

With a couple of days to go, I could see that the back borders were still too sparse to satisfy the judges, but then I had a flash of horticultural inspiration. The previous autumn I had sacrificed my vegetable patch to wildflower production and – more by luck than judgement – I had neglected to remove the lingering remnants of the previous summer's crops. Noticing that a few kale plants of huge proportions were about to flower, I carefully transplanted them to plastic buckets, soaked their roots and drove them down to Chelsea. On press day, the first of the bright-yellow kale flowers opened and they looked magnificent against their grey-green leaves. The sun shone, the kale flowers blossomed and these garden rejects soon became a major talking point. Whatever were these stunning specimens? Clearly no self-respecting gardener at Chelsea Flower Show would admit to recognising vegetable plants that had simply been allowed to run to seed.

The kale plants brought an added bonus to the garden. When the sun shone, the flowers attracted clouds of butterflies. Granted, almost all of them were cabbage whites – perhaps another first for Chelsea – but they really brought the garden to life and gathered the crowds. In the same vein, another success was the big tub of broad beans I positioned by the garden bench. These were familiar plants to almost everyone, but in my wildlife garden they fulfilled a range of roles. They flower profusely and give off a glorious perfume. They are among the best of bee plants; they are guaranteed to demonstrate the scope for using ladybirds to keep control of black-fly; and, of course, they do all that and then provide a tasty crop.

From the start of the opening day there was a striking difference between my wildlife garden and the rest of the exhibits. All of the others were much more spectacular, more dramatic and more impressive than mine, and the public's reaction was every bit as stark a contrast. Most people were awe-struck by the splendour of the orthodox show gardens, but they tended to react in a stunned silence. By contrast the crowds around my much more modest offering talked enthusiastically to one another. They seemed relieved to recognise familiar flowers such as honesty, cranesbill and sweet William, and they seemed thrilled to learn that these were valuable for garden wildlife. The daisies were a triumph. They made people smile and reminisce, and realise that gardening for wildlife could be fun.

A Chelsea Flower Show garden has to be built in a few short days, it lasts a week and then it's cleared away. That makes it difficult to conjure up the very essence of a wildlife garden – the stability and subtlety that comes with time. I used some gnarled old logs to form the boundary, I mulched the woodland edge with leaf mould and I made sure there was mud in the bottom of my shallow artificial pond. These details helped. Beetles emerged from the rotting wood, Blackbirds scratched around among the bluebells and dragonflies patrolling the pond, but the real seal of approval was provided by a family of blue tits.

I clearly had no scope for big old trees and hollow branches in my Chelsea wildlife garden. To compensate I erected a tall, dead, silver birch trunk in one of the back borders, and fixed a birch-bark-covered nest box at the top. This went in at the start and in a day or two the miracle happened. Chelsea blue tits chose my wildlife garden as a place to build their nest. As I dug and built and planted down below, the male blue tit was busy carrying in the grass and feathers for his mate's approval. By the time the show opened, the nest was complete, the female was sitting on eggs and the male was keeping her constantly supplied with food. Those blue tits, more than anything else about my Chelsea garden, persuaded everyone that this idea could work. Plant the right plants, ban pesticides, tolerate a little decay and any garden can attract more wildlife.

I like to think that modest little wildlife garden touched a nerve. At a time when the wider countryside was being farmed to death it helped to give a nation of gardeners real encouragement. It showed that they could make a positive difference and could gain more pleasure from their gardens at the same time. Even the Chelsea groundsman was persuaded. He kept the birch trunk in the corner of his sports field until the blue tits flew the nest.

If you visit Chelsea Flower Show these days, many of the show gardens have a naturalistic feel. Foxgloves, bluebells, pink campion and cowslips have become the plants of choice for many top designers, and commercial nurseries grow them in their tens of thousands. Nest boxes, pond-liners and bird food have all become big business and the RHS is pushing biodiversity for all it's worth. So maybe the inscription on my Chelsea medal was prophetic. Perhaps that little patch of nature in their flower show of 1985 really was a *Wildfire Garden* after all.

Chris Baines

Chris Baines is an independent environmental adviser and an award-winning writer and broadcaster. His book How to Make a Wildlife Garden *is a continuing bestseller and he now works as an adviser to central government, the Heritage Lottery Fund and the development industry. He is a Vice President of the The Wildlife Trusts.*

MY ISLAND IN SUFFOLK

ELIZABETH JANE HOWARD

I have always been fascinated by islands and, as a child, devoured any book about desert islands that I could find. *Adrift in the Pacific, Coral Island, Treasure Island, Masterman Ready,* I read and reread them all – the palm trees that actually had coconuts on them, the white sand, the coral reefs, the sea that seemed always to be turquoise or sapphire; it all made me long to be shipwrecked. For better or worse, this thrilling mishap has never come my way; but, a few years after I came to live in Suffolk, I was able to buy the only island on the river Waveney. It felt like a dream come true, although the Spong – as it is locally named – was no tropical paradise, but a boggy acre with willows that had been regularly coppiced, a few ancient apple trees and the largest ash I have ever seen.

The only access was a rickety bridge, and this had to be rebuilt. We dug a fair-sized pond, and made a canal that ran through the centre of the island to the drain at its end. We cleared the reeds and brambles to make a path round the perimeter, and built three small bridges over the canal. We stocked the pond with suitable fish and planted a couple of water lilies – one white and one red.

My aim was to create a really wild garden that would encourage wildlife. We planted about 30 oaks (my favourite tree and one that sustains more creatures than any other – one or two red, but mostly ordinary English). The water table was so high that they grew at an amazing speed. We planted wild crab apple, a quince, three wych hazels, prunus of varying kinds, and then a number of lilies, buddleia, vibernum and camellias. Roses, Kiftsgate, Veichenblau, Paul's Himalayan Musk and Bobbie James romped up the old apple trees. And, over the years, I have added about a dozen clematis, and a collection of honeysuckle.

I wanted the island to be enjoyable at all times of the year. For the spring, we planted hundreds of bulbs, the little wild daffodil, snowdrops, bluebells, aconites and the little Snake's head lily *Fritillaria meleagris*. I also imported primroses and cowslips (the latter, my favourite wild flower and now growing so thickly that you can hardly put your hand between the plants). Most of the bulbs have naturalised well, but I add to them each year.

At least half the point of this place was to encourage wildlife. I built two owl boxes – Owl Mansions and Owl Court – and a pair of Little Owls has settled in one. We have ducks, a moorhen who built her nest in the middle of the water lilies, willow warblers, a woodpecker, blackbirds, thrush, robins, jenny wrens and a kingfisher who comes to fish the pond that now has newts, frogs and an elegant grass snake that I sometimes see swimming there. There are hedgehogs and the yellow-necked mouse (unseen by me). The most exciting visitor is an otter, and we have had more than one. We know of him or her mostly because of the skeletons of chubb and pike that are left on a grassy bank, but I did once see her slipping across the path a few yards ahead of me into the water. More fortunate people have seen two of them swimming in various parts of the river. There is also a barn owl who hunts in the field across the river, but I have seen him standing on the island at dusk, completely still and majestic, no doubt waiting for me to go so that he can start his evening hunt.

One year a pair of mute swans, who I named Bernard and Dora, built a splendid nest beside the path. I used to feed Dora as she sat faithfully on her nest, while her husband patrolled the area. She was quite friendly, but he was not. One day I encountered him. He stood in the middle of the path before me, his wings spread wide, hissing ominously. This is a test case, I thought, about whether we should share the island or not. So I stood quite still and talked to him in a rather sickening and priggish manner about there 'being room for both of us', 'sharing being a pleasure', and how I'd always been 'nice to them, so why couldn't he be friendly back'? He slowly stopped hissing, and eventually folded his wings and made room for me to pass him on the path. He never menaced me again.

But this tale ends in tragedy. Dora had laid six eggs, but after she had been sitting for a week or so, I went to feed her one morning and found both of them standing by their empty nest. All of the eggs were gone. They must have been stolen by humans, for if an animal had gone for them, there would have been egg shells. There were none. They were both desolate, and kept wandering round the empty nest and then simply staring at it in shock, as though they could not believe what had happened. I put down the food I had brought for them, but they wouldn't touch it. I could only tell them how sorry I was – sorry also that I belonged to a species that would do something so wicked. So then I made an island on the canal where I thought they would be completely safe. They inspected it and turned it down, but built another nest in a slightly safer place, hatching four extremely plain children of whom they were inordinately proud.

No sign of them at present, but nothing on the island is quite the same from year to year. Some springs there are great patches of wild violets, sometimes not. Sometimes in early summer the waters are edged by tall yellow flags; often there are hardly any. Some years the island is hopping with smart little caramel-coloured frogs – this year I have seen only two. Butterflies come and go: the buddleia was planted for them, but they only like the rather shrill mauve kind.

Of course I have had failures. I keep planting anemones and they never come up – the corms eaten by mice, I imagine. I have tried to get foxgloves to flourish and they simply won't. Too wet for them, I fear. Last winter several camellias got eaten to the bone by someone mysterious. Moles are a menace to the young roots of trees and now have an underground system that would do credit to London. On the other hand, wild flowers simply appear: king cups now line the pond – a beautiful sight reflected in the water. The bee orchid sometimes appears – a truly magical sight – but these plants are freakish in their behaviour. They will turn up one year and then disappear and, just as I have given up hope, will appear somewhere quite different. They make plain the fact that wild flowers know what suits them and cannot be tamed into putting up with conditions that garden plants would endure. You win some and you lose some.

But, as my friend Ursula Vaughan Williams said – when she refilled a saucer of milk put out for a stray cat and found three slugs drinking from it – 'There's plenty for all.' I hope my island will continue to be that for everyone who owns or inhabits it in future.

Elizabeth Jane Howard
Elizabeth Jane Howard is an award-winning novelist, best known for her four-novel family saga: The Light Years, Marking Time, Confusion

and Casting Off *(collectively known as* The Cazelet Chronicles*). Her autobiography* Slipstream *tells of her life as an author, her marriages to Peter Scott and Kingsley Amis, and her life in Bungay in Suffolk, where she has created a private and enchanted island nature reserve.*

ON THE ANGER
OF HORNETS

RICHARD MABEY

The hornet burst into the kitchen late one night after one of those interminably wet and cold August days. I had no idea hornets were in any way nocturnal and do not know what drew it towards our open window. But, for a quarter of an hour, its intense presence dominated the room. It thrashed frantically against the walls. It flew so heavily, its segmented body trailing almost vertically downwards, that it looked like two insects clasped together. Close-to, I could see its thorax pulsating like a bellows. It was hyperventilating. This wasn't the furious hornet of popular myth, but one, I think, in the grip of a panic attack. I caught it eventually, with the help of a plastic beer mug and a large birthday card, and put the whole lot out into the drizzle, hoping that at least *that* might be preferable to the cosy prison of our house.

Back in the spring I wrote about how moving to an old house has meant a new intimacy with the mysterious lives of insects. This is partly the result of what an estate agent might call its 'characterful' fabric. It is, forgive the pun, an accommodation with the wild. Beetles sidle in under the ill-fitting doors. Crickets hang out in the lamp-lit corners of the living room. Goodness knows what's going on in the thatch.

But I also have the sense of the house being a kind of squatters' encampment on anciently occupied territory. The emergence of the black ants this year again seemed a ritual of frustration and bewilderment, an awakening into a world turned upside-down. It is supposed to be a brilliant, ephemeral marriage rite, a brief glitter of sequined wings on one special day each year. The winged males and females fly up and mate. The females descend to earth, pull off their wings and begin searching for nesting sites. But in our house, ants poured out of their winter quarters for two months without cease, spilling from alarming new holes in the floor and marching along the tops of my treasured botany books. They shuffled this way and that, across the carpets and up the windows, but seemed desultory and lost, uninterested in getting outside for their nuptial flights. In the evenings they retreated back into their crevices. I helped as best I could, taking ant-covered rugs into the garden and leaving doors and windows open, until the house was over-run by opportunist blackbirds and robins. It was not until mid-August that they finally vanished from the house – or back into it – with, it seemed to me, the next generation unassured.

As I watch our insects as closely as I can, such mysteries proliferate. In June I was mesmerised by the courtship flights of ghost swift moths, in which the males danced and swooped over a patch of reed, with wings vibrating so fast they looked like tiny balls of mist. And just before the farcical hoverfly 'invasion' of the Essex coast in July, when these most benign of pollinators were being vilified as 'pests', I watched hundreds of thin, Latinesque hoverflies feeding on our Polygonums. They were the only species on it, and were nowhere else in the garden. What extraordinary refinements of scent and sight must have brought together those two organisms. Later I tried to capitalise on moths' sense of smell by painting a few trees and posts with that traditional entomologists' mix of beer, brown sugar and black treacle – a potion which seemed, during the brewing, to be rather too tasty to devote to the moths. It was. During the endlessly cool dusks they remained untempted and invisible, hiding out in the herbage. A few – oak rollers, blood-veins, indistinguishable noctuids – hung still and heraldic on the walls, their lives, I felt, only half-lived.

How does one write about creatures whose states of consciousness are so remote from ours, whose lives are so brief and mercurial and full of what we see as the horrors of cannibalism and slavery and living parasitism? Not, certainly, by trying to interpret insects' behaviour in terms of human institutions, as in so much embarrassing writing about social bees and ants. The great Jean Henri Fabre perhaps came close in his intensely observed, empathetic and non-judgemental essays. But perhaps a truly sympathetic approach would need a non-Western mind-set, and a willingness to embrace an idea of consciousness not rigidly welded to the individual organism, and to see insects as subjects not objects.

And yet, when I think of our ants and hornets, I know there are experiences we share, too. The Greek political prisoner George Mangakis befriended three mosquitoes during his long solitary confinement. 'They were struggling hard to resist the cold that was just beginning. In the daytime they slept on the wall. At night they would come buzzing over me. What were they asking from me? Something unimportant. A drop of blood – it would save them. I couldn't refuse. At nightfall, I would bare my arm and wait for them. They would come to me quite naturally, openly. This trust is something I owe them … It shows the solidarity that can be forged between unhappy creatures.'

A few weeks later the hornet returned – upstairs this time. We switched off the light, opened the window, shut the door and left it to its own secret devices.

Richard Mabey

Richard Mabey is a naturalist and author. His acclaimed books include Food for Free, Birds Britannica, Flora Britannica, Beechcombings: The Narrative of Trees, Nature Cure *and* A Brush with Nature.
'On the Anger of Hornets', from 'Nature Cure' *in* A Brush with Nature: 25 Years of Personal Reflections on the Natural World *(BBC Books, 2010).*

HOVERFLY

SIMON BARNES

'I'm starting to come down,' Ralph said.

How many phrases have sounded as sweet? You've passed. I'm not pregnant. I love you. I am pregnant. They want to publish it. It's benign.

Ralph was coming down: that must mean I was coming down. How unspeakably, gloriously wonderful. I made my way, with extreme care, to the hammock. Did I say that we were in a sunny July garden in Fulham? I had only just remembered myself.

I was still as high as a migrating swift, but my journey had in a single phrase become finite. I stretched out luxuriously; the hammock swayed comically but I stayed on board. I'll spare you feeling-the-sun-on-every-individual-pore stuff, because I want to cut straight to the hoverfly.

It was a miracle, you see. It hung in the sky in much the same way that bricks don't, as Douglas Adams was to write of the Vogon Destructor Fleet. Like Adams's hero, I had no idea what I was looking at. I had never noticed one before. Insects, all invertebrate life, was just background stuff, more or less irritating unless it was a butterfly and therefore mildly cosmic. But the hoverfly, for all its defiance of gravity, was not cosmic. It seemed to be a wasp, with its black and yellow stripes, but I knew it couldn't be, because wasps can't manage that bricks-don't stuff. I watched gravely, unalarmed and unharmed as it hung motionless. A bit like time, really. It was like holding infinity in the palm of your hand, like seeing eternity in an hour, only better. It was better because I was Coming Down, and things were becoming less and less cosmic with every slowly passing second.

I had been a boy birder. I had always marvelled at marvellous mammals. But after that, I noticed nothing, was aware of nothing. This hoverfly was a revelation of a new world. It was a world that had existed since the beginning of life on earth: it was a world that didn't have a word yet.

A hoverfly is only pretending to be a desperate character. By dressing up in black and yellow it looks like a dangerous wasp-like creature, but it is nothing of the kind. Much as I was trying to do, by playing the tough-guy acid-head. Batesian mimicry, it's called: I was an expert long before I learnt the term.

To me in my hammock, this hoverfly was a sudden and intensely dramatic revelation of the extraordinary variousness of life: one of the wild world's instantaneous dramas played to an audience of one. I had never before considered that among the wasps and the bumblebees and the houseflies and dragonflies, there existed this extraordinary weightless thing above my hammock. Naturally, I had no idea that there is more than one kind of hoverfly. In fact, there are about 6,000 different species spread out over 200 genera: half as many again as there are species of mammal. One theme: so many variations.

Hoverflies are two-winged flying insects, like houseflies and bluebottles. That makes them Diptera: and there are more than 120,000 species of Diptera already described. Diptera are numbered among the insects: well, estimates vary, but there's probably a million insects described so far.

But I knew nothing of that back then. I was simply aware, in the sun, swaying, coming down, of something extraordinary. I had just realised that there were more kinds of living things than I had ever thought about. Soon enough, I was to find out that there are more than I ever could think about.

I learnt the great museums of London as a child. In the Science Museum I gazed uncomprehending at the big wheels and the shoving pistons of the dinosaur-like engines. It was when I looked at the hoverfly that I had a first dim understanding of the basic mechanism of life. Life works by making more and more and more different kinds of living things.

I was coming down. I was coming down, thank God, and as I did so, I found the truth I had missed when I was at the trip's peak. I realised that the great mysteries and the great truths of life are to be found in ordinary life. I understood that the doors of perception are opened, not by looking into the human mind, but by looking outward: by looking beyond the barriers of species-patriotism, of mammal-chauvinism, of vertebrate-jingoism.

I was at the time a student of connectivity, for that is what literature means. In *Ulysses*, I read of the connections between Bloom, Stephen and Molly, between Joyce and Homer, between the past and present, between the epic and the everyday, between the hero and the humdrum. In my hammock I had my first view of a greater and deeper connectedness: the connections between every living things.

The connectivity was not mystical, not cosmic, not the product of a drug-inspired hallucination. The revelation was humdrum and everyday. It came about because I was coming down, returning to earth, and to earthy and earthly matters. I was conscious of an unimagined connectivity, one of blood and sinew and gut: one of life and of death. Living things: all related: all, ultimately, with a single ancestor. The hoverfly: me: animals both. Hard fact, fact rooted in the earth. I had gone to seek things beyond reality. On the upswing I found only anxiety: but in the downswing, reality was waiting.

There is a name for it now. Biodiversity. It's a rotten word, a rotten word for the greatest miracle you and I will ever be privy to, but it's the word we're lumbered with. But never mind the bloody word: let's savour the fact of it, as I savoured my hoverfly, as Darwin savoured what he called 'endless forms most beautiful'. Let's savour life.

Simon Barnes

Simon Barnes is chief sportswriter for The Times; *he also writes two weekly columns about the wild world. He has written an awful lot of books, including three novels,* How To Be A Bad Birdwatcher *and* How To Be Wild.

THE FORMATION OF VEGETABLE MOULD THROUGH THE ACTIONS OF WORMS

CHARLES DARWIN

Worms have played a more important part in the history of the world than most persons would at first suppose. In almost all humid countries they are extraordinarily numerous, and for their size possess great muscular power. In many parts of England a weight of more than ten tons (10,516 kilogrammes) of dry earth annually passes through their bodies and is brought to the surface on each acre of land; so that the whole superficial bed of vegetable mould passes through their bodies in the course of every few years. From the collapsing of the old burrows the mould is in constant though slow movement, and the particles composing it are thus rubbed together. By these means fresh surfaces are continually exposed to the action of carbonic acid in the soil, and of the humus-acids, which appear to be still more efficient in the decomposition of rocks. The generation of the humus-acids is probably hastened during the digestion by many half-decayed leaves, which worms consume. Thus the particles of earth, forming the superficial mould, are subjected to conditions eminently favourable for their decomposition and disintegration. Moreover, the particles of the softer rocks suffer some amount of mechanical trituration in the muscular gizzards of worms, in which small stones serve as millstones.

The finely levigated castings, when brought to the surface in a moist condition, flow during rainy weather down any moderate slope; and the smaller particles are washed far down even a gently inclined surface. Castings when dry often crumble into small pellets, and these are apt to roll down any sloping surface. Where the land is quite level and is covered with herbage, and where the climate is humid so that much dust cannot be blown away, it appears at first sight impossible that there should be any appreciable amount of sub-aerial denudation; but worm-castings are blown, especially whilst moist and viscid, in one uniform direction by the prevalent winds which are accompanied by rain. By these several means the superficial mould is prevented from accumulating to a great thickness; and a thick bed of mould checks in many ways the disintegration of the underlying rocks and the fragments of rock.

The removal of worm-castings by the above means leads to results that are far from insignificant. It has been shown that a layer of earth, 0.2 of an inch in thickness, is in many places annually brought to the surface per acre; and if a small part of this amount flows, or rolls, or is washed, even for a short distance down every inclined surface, or is repeatedly blown in one direction, a great effect will be produced in the course of ages. It was found by measurements and calculations that on a surface with a mean inclination of 9° 26 , 2.4 cubic inches of earth which had been ejected by worms crossed, in the course of a year, a horizontal line one yard in length so that 240 cubic inches would cross a line 100 yards in length. This latter amount in a damp state would weigh 11 1/2 pounds. Thus a considerable weight of earth is continually moving down each side of every valley, and will in time reach its bed. Finally this earth will be transported by the streams flowing in the valleys into the ocean, the great receptacle for all matter denuded from the land. It is known from the amount of sediment annually delivered into the sea by the Mississippi, that its enormous drainage-area must on an average be lowered .00263 of an inch each year; and this would suffice in four and a half million years to lower the whole drainage-area to the level of the seashore. So that, if a small fraction of the layer of fine earth, .2 of an inch in thickness, which is annually brought to the surface by worms, is carried away, a great result cannot fail to be produced within a period that no geologist considers extremely long.

Archaeologists ought to be grateful to worms, as they protect and preserve for an indefinitely long period every object, not liable to decay, which is dropped on the surface of the land, by burying it beneath their castings. Thus also, many elegant and curious tessellated pavements and other ancient remains have been preserved; though no doubt the worms have in these cases been largely aided by earth washed and blown from the adjoining land, especially when cultivated. The old tessellated pavements have, however, often suffered by having subsided unequally from being unequally undermined by the worms. Even old massive walls may be undermined and subside; and no building is in this respect safe, unless the foundations lay six or seven feet beneath the surface, at a depth at which worms cannot work. It is probable that many monoliths and some old walls have fallen down from having been undermined by worms.

Worms prepare the ground in excellent manner for the growth of fibrous-rooted plants and for seedlings of all kinds. They periodically expose the mould to the air, and sift it so that no stones larger than the particles that they can swallow are left in it.

They mingle the whole intimately together, like a gardener who prepares fine soil for his choicest plants. In this state it is well fitted to retain moisture and to absorb all soluble substances, as well as for the process of nitrification. The bones of dead animals, the harder parts of insects, the shells of land-molluscs, leaves, twigs, &c., are before long all buried beneath the accumulated castings of worms, and are thus brought in a more or less decayed state within reach of the roots of plants. Worms likewise drag an infinite number of dead leaves and other parts of plants into their burrows, partly for the sake of plugging them up and partly as food.

The leaves, which are dragged into the burrows as food, after being torn into the finest shreds, partially digested, and saturated with the intestinal and urinary secretions, are commingled with much earth. This earth forms the dark-coloured, rich humus, which almost everywhere covers the surface of the land with a fairly well-defined layer or mantle. Von Hensen placed two worms in a vessel 18 inches in diameter, which was filled with sand, on which fallen leaves were strewed; and these were soon dragged into their burrows to a depth of three inches. After about six weeks an almost uniform layer of sand, a centimetre (0.4 inch) in thickness, was converted into humus by having passed through the alimentary canals of these two worms. It is believed by some persons that worm-burrows, which often penetrate the ground almost perpendicularly to a depth of five or six feet, materially aid in its drainage; notwithstanding that the viscid castings piled over the mouths of the burrows prevent or check the rain-water directly entering them. They allow the air to penetrate deeply into the ground. They also greatly facilitate the downward passage of roots of moderate size; and these will be nourished by the humus with which the burrows are lined. Many seeds owe their germination to having been covered by castings; and others buried to a considerable depth beneath accumulated castings lie dormant, until at some future time they are accidentally uncovered and germinate.

Worms are poorly provided with sense-organs, for they cannot be said to see, although they can just distinguish between light and darkness; they are completely deaf, and have only feeble power of smell; the sense of touch alone is well developed. They can therefore learn little about the outside worlds, and it is surprising that they should exhibit some skill in lining their burrows with their castings and with leaves, and in the case of some species in piling up their castings into tower-like constructions. But it is far more surprising that they should apparently exhibit some degree of intelligence instead of a mere blind instinctive impulse, in their manner of plugging up the mouths of their burrows. They act in nearly the same manner as would a man, who had to close a cylindrical tube with different kinds of leaves, petioles, triangles of paper, &c., for they commonly seize such objects by their pointed ends. But with thin objects, a certain number are drawn in by their broader ends. They do not act in the same unvarying manner in all cases, as do most of the lower animals; for instance, they do not drag in leaves by their foot-stalks, unless the basal part of the blade is as narrow as the apex, or narrower than it.

When we behold a wide, turf-covered expanse, we should remember that its smoothness, on which so much of its beauty depends, is mainly due to all the inequalities having been slowly levelled by worms. It is a marvellous reflection that the whole of the superficial mould over any such expanse has passed, and will again pass, every few years through the bodies of worms. The plough is one of the most ancient and most valuable of man's inventions; but long before he existed the land was in fact regularly ploughed, and still continues to be thus ploughed by earth-worms. It may be doubted whether there are many other animals that have played so important a part in the history of the world, as have these lowly organised creatures. Some other animals, however, still more lowly organised, namely corals, have done far more conspicuous work in having constructed innumerable reefs and islands in the great oceans; but these are almost confined to the tropical zones.

Charles Darwin (1809–1882)

A world-renowned naturalist, Charles Darwin was educated at Christ's College, Cambridge. In 1831, he embarked on the Beagle, *studying South American geology, and returning in 1836. After retirement through ill-health, his continuing research led to the formulation of his theory of evolution by natural selection in 1844. In 1856 the geologist Lyell urged him to write up the results of his experiments, and two years later Darwin received a manuscript from A. R. Wallace containing an almost identical theory to his own. This he published with his letter containing a sketch of his own theory, and, in 1859, he finally published* On the Origin of Species.

'Earthworms' in 'The Formation of Vegetable Mould Through the Actions of Worms' *(1871).*

CHAPTER 2
ON THE WING

ISLAY

PAUL EVANS

QUEEN OF THE HEBRIDES

'You must never cross the sea,' said the King of the Giants to his daughter Iula. But, as the full moon rose that night, Iula's desire for adventure rose, too. She crept down to the beach and gathered huge rocks, which she placed in front of her as stepping stones and so walked out across the sea. At dawn, exhausted, she came to a dark island. But as soon as Iula stepped ashore, the soft sands gave way, she sank under them and the sea washed over her. The island she discovered took her name – Islay – just as it had taken her body. Daughters, eh? Even giant princess ones, you can't tell 'em anything.

You know you've arrived somewhere interesting when a sign at the airport reads: 'Due to warm weather, there are adders in the terminal car park. Please don't pick them up.' Who does pick up venomous snakes in car parks? The weather is set-fair with hardly a cloud to trouble the bright-blue sky. Gulls hoist themselves over the sea wall at Bowmore. Shelduck drift across calm waters. Oyster-catchers skitter in front of small waves nudging the shoreline below the distillery. Meadow pipits furtle through rocks beyond. Little fishing boats sway on anchors submerged in sleep, nibbled by the dreams of fish.

Bowmore is on the eastern shore of Loch Indaal. I look west to bright hills in the Rhinns of Islay. Behind me, rising high in the northeast, the Paps of Jura are looking particularly glamorous (I've always wanted to say that). A young Portuguese woman talks excitedly about how wonderful the island is – the weather, the whisky. Local people are friendly. Islay is 25 miles long by 20 miles wide and, as the southernmost island of the Inner Hebrides, it is as close to Northern Ireland as it is to mainland Scotland. As far as wildlife habitats go, it's got the lot: sea cliffs, skerries and rocky coves, white-sandy beaches and dunes, machair – coastal grasslands, tidal and freshwater wetlands, streams, peat bogs and tarns, rolling farmland with cereal crops and livestock pasture, hills with heather moorland, some up to 400 metres high. It has very little woodland but, in compensation, there are very few people and very few roads – which all lead to fascinating places.

There would have been much more woodland when the first hunter-gatherers arrived here, around 4500BC, but by 2500BC it was cleared with stone axes for farming. The standing stones, stone circles and burial tombs of the early Bronze Age still exist. Since then, Islay's Celtic and Nordic settlers, together with assorted Sassenachs, have created a poetry of place names: An Sithean (An sheen) is Gaelic for fairy hill; Lyrabus is Norse for muddy farm; Bridgend means ... well, who knows? In the Middle Ages, Islay was the seat of the Lord of the Isles – which sounds a bit Tolkeinesque, but I suspect was more about big blokes with claymores knocking lumps out of each other.

Something about the people, the sound of birds, the quality of the air, leaks into consciousness like a distant memory. But what kind of memory and whose is it? Imagine going back to your old primary school, and the desks and blackboards and smells are exactly as you left them all those years ago. Nothing has changed, except you. That's what Islay feels like: a place recovered from childhood, a fabled island whose landscapes – almost forgotten in most of Britain now – still ring to the cries of lapwings, the haunting song of curlews and the mysterious chanting of corncrakes. This is a shared memory, like a myth, of somewhere we once knew. Just as the giant princess Iula was consumed by her passion in the island she discovered, now called the Queen of the Hebrides, so Islay will absorb me, too.

A PLACE OF BIRDS

A wheatear perches and bobs, dancing on his own little sandcastle in the dunes. His song is a conspiratorial nattering, punctuated by whistling through a missing tooth. He takes off, flashing his white arse, bounding over sandy humps and old wooden posts, leading me on. I follow through shifting waves of marram dunes, to the applause of a flock of rock doves, towards Ardnave Point.

I scramble down shelves of stork's-bill to the warm, still beach to watch Eider ducks with a clutch of 19 ducklings. The dark, piratical form of an arctic skua flies in to harass arctic terns, skimming and twisting over a glassy sea: the sea swallow and her nemesis, the yin and yang of arctic sagas. Between Ardnave Point and Nave Island, grey seals patrol the straights of Na Badagan with a gaggle of moulting grey-lag geese. On the island, behind the ruined chapel, are cliffs where peregrine falcons nest. A buzzard traces a thermal above the rabbit-scurrying dunes. There are lawns of blue speedwell or yellow cinquefoil and, in wet flushes, redshank and lapwing tread with a nervousness that, at times, overcomes them and they launch skywards, calling plaintively before settling again, in their own unsettled way. And all the while, larks are powering skyward, propelled by song.

Suddenly, from the corner of my eye, I see something black lob over a dune. As I follow it, two umbrella-handle heads poke from the marram grass and shout a challenge. They are a pair of young chough, their beaks still orange instead of red, and they are watching me intently. Then two adult birds swerve through the air and land nearby. Their glossy black plumage, and pillarbox-red curved beaks and legs, give them a heraldic elegance. In fact, choughs appear on the Cornish coat of arms and there's a legend that King Arthur's soul migrated into one of these birds when he died. Watching them close up – the airy grace of their flight, the swaggering walk, the tribal black and red costume – it's easy to imagine the traffic of spirits between ancient heroes and choughs. They're iconic birds of the western sea cliffs and hills, a tribe of crows that share that dark-yet-playful Corvid intelligence, but have evolved a lightness of being. 'Chough' is perhaps an approximation of their call. It's a sharp, ominous exclamation, but with a lyrical twist; at this moment, it's aimed at me.

Well choughed, I follow them through the dunes – a pair here, a chattering (the collective noun for chough) there. Four young choughs sit on an old wire fence, calling into the air; then a parent bird swoops down and lands a few paces in front of them, and the youngsters cluster round. It all seems part of a timeless conversation – a living mythology tied to the margins of the western lands, to the sun and the sea.

THE NIGHT CRAKE

South from Ardnave, along the western edge of Loch Gruinart, the light is fading as I arrive at the RSPB visitor centre at the Gruinart nature reserve. Here, the scented white flowers of burnet rose, or Scotch briar, are beginning to glow in the gloaming. Rooks gathering in windblown sycamores rattle out their good-night calls like a huge, insane Waltons family. I walk out onto Gruinart

Flats, an expanse of wet meadows spangled with northern marsh orchid and heath-spotted orchid; fens and marshes with rude tufts of sedge and rush, cut through with a grid of drainage ditches and water channels.

Dusk, at this latitude in summer, becomes a lavish and baroque affair. Day slides towards night with ceremony. Clouds create glowing structures of light as the sky darkens and it really doesn't feel dark until after midnight. Even then there are glowing curls and luminous streaks above, as the first stars appear. By then, everything has changed. The mood has altered. Meanings shift. The nocturnal life of the place has become metaphysically different from daytime. Wildlife that was furtive and muted by day takes on a confidence of spirit, as if evolving into other species. The darker it gets, the wilder it becomes.

A sedge warbler hiding in scrub cranks his gramophone apprehensively, until it busts into a scratchy old 78 song from the bygone shadows of his willow parlour. As grey and pink shreds trail across the dark sky, lapwings make their last wheeling calls; redshank ring like a street full of bicycles; there's a strange five-note call, perhaps a moorhen, and the haunting sweet-sorrowful cries of curlews quiver across the wetlands.

Suddenly, around silver grey reeds edging a ditch, there's the sound of two notes played by a violin bow. It's an Eristalis drone-fly, whose sonic whine changes pitch as he rises and falls in altitude. Speeding up, the drone-fly fiddles furiously, like Black Jack Davy himself, as the object of his desire approaches. A distant humming and popping begins like tinnitus, but gets louder. I can't see a thing, only thousands of ripples on the water's surface. If these were midges, I should be eaten alive by now, but they are. This is the night an entire species of Corenomids (*Chironomid*) – non-biting midges – hatch at once. The larva pushes through the water's surface, splits down the thorax and out pops the midge to set the pitch of its tiny wings against the mass of others – there must be millions of them.

Darkness brings the orchestral midge manoeuvres and an intensity of bird sounds creating a nocturnal aural landscape that could never be experienced in daylight. The stars of this landscape have come out to play.

The first is snipe, drumming. This eerie sound is not produced by the snipe's voice but by its tail feathers as air rushes through them when it dives earthwards from up in the sky. At first it sounds like a pantomime ghost – *whooooo* – but with repetition and intensity under the still night sky, the dark wetlands become haunted by a clan of aerial spectres.

In the distance, but moving closer, comes a sound like waterproof trousers swishing together, walking across the Flats. But, as it approaches, each swish becomes a whip crack, fizzing with energy and mystery. It's the call of the spotted crake – a bird rarely seen or heard. But tonight belongs to the other crake, the corncrake. Up until a hundred years ago, the corncrake – a migrant from Africa – was known throughout Britain as a spirit of summer: heard but hardly ever seen. The poet John Clare, who called this bird the landrail, wrote:

'A mystery still to men and boys
Who know not where they lay
And guess it but a summer noise
Among the meadow hay.'

But over the years, this summer noise has been lost from Britain and the corncrake is heard in just a handful of places. Islay is its stronghold. The modern way to describe the corncrake's call, and to imitate it, is to scrape a credit card up and down the teeth of a comb. That might work during the day, but the credit card and comb trick – symbols of personal wealth and vanity that they are – are wholly inadequate when the corncrake really comes alive at night.

I can hear dozens of corncrakes going for it all across the Gruinart Flats and I home in on one of them. Letting myself through a gate into a field, I stand a couple of paces from a nettle-clump, no bigger than a small chair, from which comes an astonishing sound. The bird is hidden, invisible; my guess is that even if I kicked the nettles, my boot would connect with nothing. The call is mesmerising. I try to get inside it: four breaths out – *crake-crake, crake-crake* – one breath in: a mantra for deep meditation, even if the bird breathes very differently. After a few minutes inwardly chanting, I am lost in a summer night's dream, in a space between continents and times, a dummy for the ventriloquist crake magician.

What shatters this altered state wells up somewhere at the base of the cerebral cortex, and then floods through my brain like cold water; the screech of a barn owl snaps me out of it, back to the vast shuddering night.

Paul Evans

Paul Evans is a writer and broadcaster, a country diarist for the Guardian, *a contributor to environmental periodicals, a presenter of natural history programmes for BBC Radio 4, an author and narrator of radio dramas, and a lecturer in nature writing at Bath Spa University. He holds a PhD in philosophy from Lancaster University and has a background in nature conservation and horticulture, including the British Association of Nature Conservationists, Plantlife, the National Trust and a botanical garden in America. He lives in Much Wenlock, Shropshire with his family.*

SWIFTS AT NEST

DAVID LACK

Nest-building often starts on the day that the second member returns from the south, though sometimes not until several days afterwards. Both male and female collect material and both build it into the nest. They work independently and do not help each other. Thus if one bird is on the nest when the other arrives with material, the sitter merely moves off to let the other build. On two occasions when both adults arrived together with material, there was some display and even a brief scuffle before each independently built it.

Unlike what happens in most birds, building does not stop when the eggs are laid, but continues right through incubation. As a result, the nest is larger and neater at the end than the start of incubation. An adult leaving its mate on the eggs often enters with new material, and the incubating bird spends much of its time pecking around the outside of the nest and sticking down loose bits. So soon as the young hatch, building stops, but parents which lose their eggs continue building until late in the summer. Likewise the non-breeding pairs, mainly yearlings, continue building right through the summer. They spend much less time than the incubating birds in sticking down, so that, in comparison, their nests are larger but less tidy. Although the yearlings do not lay eggs, they usually return to the same nesting hole in the following year, so that the time spent in building is not wasted.

The swift normally collects all its nesting material on the wing. Hence building occurs irregularly, being most frequent when there is enough wind to carry material up into the air. Dead grass, hay, straw, dead and also green leaves, flower petals, winged seeds, seed fluff, bud sheaths, cocoons, feathers and scraps of paper, including a bus ticket, have been found in the tower nests. The birds have sometimes brought fresh poppy petals, which made a vivid splash of red in the nest. One bird even brought a cabbage white butterfly, not as food, for it did not try to eat it, but as nesting material, which it tried to stick to the side of the nest. This it found hard to do as the butterfly was still partly alive and started a reflex jerking of its wings, but eventually it succeeded.

In collecting nest material, as in feeding, swifts are great opportunists, using whatever happens to be common. We knew when a grass field near the tower was being cut, as the birds were soon bringing hay for their nests. Again, just after two pigeons had fought on the roof of the tower, a swift entered with a pigeon's feather in its bill. In the war both in Italy and Denmark, nests were sometimes built of the shreds of tinfoil dropped by the R.A.F to confuse enemy radar.

The swift carries nesting material chiefly across its mouth, from which feathers or straw often project out sideways, but it brings smaller objects inside the mouth. It sticks this material to the nest with saliva, which is used from the start of the building. When producing saliva, it sometimes continues to hold the material in its bill, but at other times it first lays it down. It crouches with the head held low, and sometimes it nods its head or quivers its body, with wings held partly out. Bill and throat can be seen moving, and saliva appears in sticky threads. The bird usually does this for three or four minutes after bringing material into the box, with pauses of up to half a minute rest, when it often lays its head on the side of the nest. It shapes the nest by turning round in it and scrabbling with its feet, eventually making a shallow cup.

All other swifts, like our bird, have to solve the problem of a nesting place, which is safe from enemies and has a clear space in front for flying in at high speed. The means that the different species use are varied and it is hard to know which to admire most.

David Lack (1911–1973)

David Lack was a naturalist, ornithologist and author who wrote a number of landmark works on nature. His most influential and celebrated works include Darwin's Finches, The Life of the Robin *and* Swifts in a Tower. *He was a Fellow of Trinity College, Oxford, Director of the Edward Grey Institute of Ornithology and, in 1972, was awarded the Darwin Medal of the Royal Society.*

'Swifts at Nest', from Swifts in a Tower *(Methuen, 1956).*

ROOKS

CHARLES WATERTON

There is no wild bird in England so completely gregarious as the rook, or so regular in its daily movements. The ring-doves will assemble in countless multitudes, the finches will unite in vast assemblies, and waterfowl will flock in thousands to the protected lake during the dreary months of winter; but when returning sun spreads joy and consolation all over the face of nature, their congregated numbers are dissolved, and the individuals retire in pairs to propagate their respective species. The rook, however, remains in society the year throughout. In flocks it builds its nest, in flocks it seeks for food, and in flocks it retires to roost.

About two miles to the eastward of this place are the woods of Nostell Priory, where, from time immemorial, the rooks have retired to pass the night. I suspect, by the observations that I have been able to make on the morning and evening transit of these birds, that there is not another roosting-place for, at least, 30 miles to the westward of Nostell Priory. Every morning, from within a few days of the autumnal to about a week before the vernal equinox, the rooks, in congregated thousands upon thousands, fly over this valley in a westerly direction, and return in undiminished numbers to the east, an hour or so before the night sets in. In their morning passage, some stop here; others, in other favourite places, farther and farther on – now repairing to the trees for pastime, now resorting to the fields for food, till the declining sun warns those which have gone farthest to the westward, that it is time they should return.

They rise in a mass, receiving additions to their numbers from every intervening place, till they reach this neighbourhood in an amazing flock. Sometimes they pass on without stopping, and are joined by those that have spent the day here. At other times they make my park their place of rendezvous, and cover the ground in vast profusion, or perch upon the surrounding trees. After tarrying here for a certain time, every rook takes wing. They linger in the air for a while, in slow revolving circles, and then they all proceed to Nostell Priory, which is their last resting-place for the night. In their morning and evening passage, the loftiness or lowliness of their flight seems to be regulated by the state of the weather. When it blows a hard gale of wind, they descend to the valley with astonishing rapidity, and just skim over the tops of the intervening hills, a few feet above the trees; but, when the sky is calm and clear, they pass through the heavens at a great height, in regular and easy flight.

Sometimes these birds perform an evolution, which is, in this part of the country, usually called the shooting of the rooks. Farmers tell you that this shooting portends a coming wind. He who pays attention to the flight of birds has, no doubt, observed this downward movement. When rooks have risen to an immense height in the air, so that, in appearance, they are scarcely larger than the lark, they suddenly descend to the ground or to the tops of the trees exactly under them. To effect this, they come headlong on pinion a little raised, but not expanded in a zigzag direction (presenting alternately their back and breast to you), through the resisting air, which causes a noise similar to that of a rushing wind. This is a magnificent and beautiful sight to the eye of the ornithologist. It is idle to suppose for a moment that it portends wind. It is merely the ordinary descent of the birds to an inviting spot beneath them, where, in general, some of their associates are already assembled, or where there is food to be procured. When we consider the prodigious height of the rooks at the time they begin to descend, we conclude that they cannot effect their arrival at a spot perpendicular under them by any other process so short and rapid.

Charles Waterton (1782–1865)

Charles Waterton was a naturalist and pioneer in conservation. Descended from an ancient landowning family, he inherited Walton Hall in Yorkshire, which he subsequently turned into a wildlife sanctuary. He developed an adventurous passion for natural history and became an outstanding taxidermist. Travelled extensively in Europe, South America, the US and West Indies, he published an account of his travels, Wanderings *(1825), and three series of essays in natural history in 1838, 1844 and 1857.*

'Rooks', *from* Essays in Natural History 1838–1857.

FROM *THE NATURAL HISTORY OF SELBORNE*

GILBERT WHITE

SELBORNE, JUL. 8, 1773

We have had, ever since I can remember, a pair of white owls that constantly breed under the eaves of this church. As I have paid good attention to the manner of life of these birds during their season of breeding, which lasts the summer through, the following remarks may not perhaps be unacceptable. About an hour before sunset (for then the mice begin to run) they sally forth in quest of prey, and hunt all round the hedges of meadows and small enclosures for them, which seem to be their only food. In this irregular country we can stand on an eminence and see them beat the fields over like a setting-dog, and often drop down in the grass or corn. I have minuted these birds with my watch for an hour together, and have found that they return to their nest, the one or the other of them, about once in five minutes; reflecting at the same time on the adroitness that every animal is possessed of as far as regards the well-being of itself and offspring. But a piece of address, which they show when they return loaded, should not, I think, be passed over in silence. As they take their prey with their claws, so they carry it in their claws to their nest; but, as the feet are necessary in their ascent under the tiles, they constantly perch first on the roof of the chancel, and shift the mouse from their claws to their bill, that their feet may be at liberty to take hold of the plate on the wall as they are rising under the eaves.

White owls seem not (but in this I am not positive) to hoot at all; all that clamorous hooting appears to me to come from the wood kinds. The white owl does indeed snore and hiss in a tremendous manner; and these menaces well answer the intention of intimidating; for I have known a whole village up in arms on such an occasion, imagining the churchyard to be full of goblins and spectres. White owls also often scream horribly as they fly along; from this screaming probably arose the common people's imaginary species of screech-owl, which they superstitiously think attends the windows of dying persons. The plumage of the remiges of the wings of every species of owl that I have yet examined is remarkably soft and pliant. Perhaps it may be necessary that the wings of these birds should not make much resistance or rushing, that they may be enabled to steal through the air unheard upon a nimble and watchful quarry.

While I am talking of owls, it may not be improper to mention what I was told by a gentleman of the county of Wilts. As they were grubbing a vast hollow pollard-ash that had been the mansion of owls for centuries, he discovered at the bottom a mass of matter that at first he could not account for. After some examination he found that it was a congeries of the bones of mice (and perhaps of birds and bats) that had been heaping together for ages, being cast up in pellets out of the crops of many generations of inhabitants. For owls cast up the bones, fur, and feathers of what they devour, after the manner of hawks. He believes, he told me, that there were bushels of this kind of substance.

When brown owls hoot their throats swell as big as a hen's egg. I have known an owl of this species live a full year without any water. Perhaps the case may be the same with all birds of prey. When owls fly they stretch out their legs behind them as a balance to their large heavy heads, for as most nocturnal birds have large eyes and ears they must have large heads to contain them. Large eyes, I presume, are necessary to collect every ray of light, and large concave ears to command the smallest degree of sound or noise.

SELBORNE, JAN. 2, 1769

As to the peculiarity of jackdaws building with us under the ground in rabbit-burrows, you have, in part, hit upon the reason; for, in reality, there are hardly any towers or steeples in all this country. And perhaps, *Norfolk* excepted, *Hampshire* and *Sussex* are as meanly furnished with churches as almost any counties in the kingdom. We have many livings of two or three hundred pounds a year, whose houses of worship make little better appearance than dovecots. When I first saw *Northamptonshire, Cambridgeshire* and *Huntingdonshire*, and the fens of *Lincolnshire*, I was amazed at the number of spires which presented themselves in every point of view. As an admirer of prospects, I have reason to lament this want in my own country; for such objects are very necessary ingredients in an elegant landscape.

What you mention with respect to reclaimed toads raises my curiosity. An ancient author, though no naturalist, has well remarked that: '*Every kind of beasts, and of birds, and of serpents, and things in the sea, is tamed, and hath been tamed, of mankind*'.

It is a satisfaction to me to find that a green lizard has actually been procured for you in *Devonshire*, because it corroborates my discovery, which I made many years ago, of the same sort, on a sunny sandbank near *Farnham* in *Surrey*. I am well acquainted with the south hams of *Devonshire*; and can suppose that district, from its southerly situation, to be a proper habitation for such animals in their best colours.

Since the ring-ousels of your vast mountains do certainly not forsake them against winter, our suspicions that those which visit this neighbourhood about *Michaelmas* are not *English* birds, but driven from the more northern parts of *Europe*, by the frosts, are still more reasonable; and it will be worth your pains to endeavour to trace from whence they come, and to inquire why they make so very short a stay.

In your account of your error with regard to the two species of herons, you incidentally gave me great entertainment in your description of the heronry at Cressi-hall; which is a curiosity I never could manage to see. Fourscore nests of such a bird in one tree is a rarity which I would ride half as many miles to have a sight of. Pray be sure to tell me in your next whose seat Cressi-hall is, and near what town it lies. I have often thought that those vast extents of fens have never been sufficiently explored. If half a dozen gentlemen, furnished with a good strength of water-spaniels, were to beat them over for a week, they would certainly find more species.

There is no bird, I believe, whose manners I have studied more than that of the *caprimulgus* (the goat-sucker), as it is a wonderful and curious creature: but I have always found that though sometimes it may chatter as it flies, as I know it does, yet in general it utters its jarring note sitting on a bough; and I have for many an half hour watched it as it sat with its under mandible quivering, and particularly this summer. It perches usually on a bare twig, with its head lower than its tail, in an attitude well expressed by your draughtsman in the folio *British Zoology*. This bird is most punctual in beginning its song exactly at the close of day; so exactly that I have known it strike up more than once or twice just at the report of the *Portsmouth* evening gun, which we can hear when the weather is still. It appears to me past all doubt that its notes are formed by organic impulse, by the powers of the parts of its windpipe, formed for sound, just as cats purr. You will credit me, I hope, when I assure you that, as my neighbours were assembled in an hermitage on the side of a steep hill where we drink tea, one of these churn-owls came and settled on the cross of that little straw edifice and began to chatter, and continued his note for many minutes: and we were all struck with wonder to find that the organs of that little animal, when put in motion, gave a sensible vibration to the whole building! This bird also sometimes makes a small squeak, repeated four or five times; and I have observed that to happen when the cock has been pursuing the hen in a toying way through the boughs of a tree.

*   *   *

SELBORNE, FEBRUARY 28, 1769

… It gave me satisfaction to find that we accorded so well about the *caprimulgus*: all I contended for was to prove that it often chatters sitting as well as flying; and therefore the noise was voluntary, and from organic impulse, and not from the resistance of air against the hollow of its mouth and throat.

If ever I saw any thing like actual migration, it was last Michaelmas-day. I was travelling, and out early in the morning: at first there was a vast fog; but, by the time that I was got seven or eight miles from home towards the coast, the sun broke out into a delicate warm day. We were then on a large heath or common, and I could discern, as the mist began to break away, great numbers of swallows (*Hirundines rusticae*) clustering on the stunted shrubs and bushes, as if they had roosted there all night. As soon as the air became clear and pleasant they all were on the wing at once; and, by a placid and easy flight, proceeded on southward towards the sea: after this I did not see any more flocks, only now and then a straggler.

I cannot agree with those persons that assert that the swallow kind disappear some and some gradually, as they come, for the bulk of them seem to withdraw at once: only some stragglers stay behind a long while, and do never, there is the greatest reason to believe, leave this island. Swallows seem to lay themselves up, and to come forth in a warm day, as bats do continually of a warm evening, after they have disappeared for weeks. For a very respectable gentleman assured me that, as he was walking with some friends under *Merton-wall* on a remarkably hot noon, either in the last week in December or the first week in January, he espied three or four swallows huddled together on the moulding of one of the windows of that college. I have frequently remarked that swallows are seen later at *Oxford* than elsewhere: is it owing to the vast massy buildings of that place, to the many waters round it, or to what else?

When I used to rise in the morning last autumn, and see the swallows and martins clustering on the chimnies and thatch of the neighbouring cottages, I could not help being touched with a secret delight, mixed with some degree of mortification: with delight, to observe with how much ardour and punctuality those poor little birds obeyed the strong impulse towards migration, or hiding, imprinted on their minds by their great Creator; and with some degree of mortification, when I reflected that, after all our pains and inquiries, we are yet not quite certain to what regions they do migrate; and are still farther embarrassed to find that some do not actually migrate at all.

These reflections made so strong an impression on my imagination, that they became productive of a composition that may perhaps amuse you for a quarter of an hour when next I have the honour of writing to you.

Gilbert White (1720–1793)

Born at Selborne, Hampshire, Gilbert White was a naturalist and fellow of Oriel College, Oxford. Circa 1758, he was curate of Faringdon, near Selborne. His correspondence with Thomas Pennant, *from 1767, formed the basis of* The Natural History and Antiquities of Selborne, *one of his best-known works. A series of letters written to Daines Barrington between 1769 and 1787 are contained in the second part of his* Natural History. *The book, published by his brother Benjamin in 1789, was soon highly valued by naturalists.* A Naturalist's Calendar, *extracted from his papers after his death, appeared in 1795.*

From The Natural History of Selborne *(1789).*

RAVENS

HENRY ELIOT HOWARD

Those who have studied wildlife on one of the rocky headlands, which are so numerous around our coasts, will probably be familiar with the rivalry that exists between the Raven and certain birds of prey. Where the Raven finds shelter for its nest, there, too, the Peregrine has its eyrie – and so it happens that these two species are continually at war. Now the warfare occurs not only during the season of reproduction but continues throughout the greater part of the year, and can even be observed in the late summer or early autumn – the period when we should expect to find the instinct less susceptible to appropriate stimulation. But it is of a more determined kind early in the spring, and it is then that we witness those remarkable exhibitions of flight, the skill of which excites our imagination.

The Falcon rises above the Raven, stoops at it, and when it seems no longer possible for a collision to be avoided, or, one would imagine, for the Raven to escape destruction, the Raven skilfully turns upon its back and momentarily faces its opponent, and the Falcon with equal skill changes its course, passing upwards and away. The attack however is soon repeated, and though no collision may actually take place, yet the fact that the Raven, when it turns to face its adversary, is obliged to drop the stick which it carries, is not only an indication of the character of the struggle, but it shows that a definite end is gained – that the efforts of the Raven to build in that particular locality are hampered. But the Falcon is not the only enemy that the Raven has to face; Buzzards are just as intolerant of the presence of Ravens in the neighbourhood as the Ravens are of them, and consequently there is incessant quarrelling wherever the same locality is inhabited. As a rule, the fighting occurs whilst the birds are on the wing; the Buzzard rises to a considerable height, and, closing its wings, stoops at the Raven below, and when within a short distance of its adversary, swerves upwards and gains a position from which it can again attack.

The Buzzard, however, is by no means always the aggressor; I have watched one so persistently harassed by a Raven that at length it left the rock upon which it was resting and disappeared from view, still followed by its rival. Thus it seems as if they were evenly matched, and, when they occupy the same locality, it is interesting to notice how the initiative passes from the one to the other according to the position occupied by the birds in their respective territories.

Henry Eliot Howard (1873–1940)

A Midlands steelmaster, Henry Eliot Howard's earliest interests in ornithology lay in the close observation of individual birds and their behaviour. While clearly an amateur who gave his spare time to his studies, he was a voracious reader and student of scientific research in the field of animal behaviour. Territory in Bird Life *(1920) is a classic*

in its field, and established the framework in which subsequent studies of bird behaviour developed the modern science of ethnology.
'Ravens', from Territory in Bird Life *(1920)*.

TRUNK CALLS

DOMINIC COUZENS

You make a mistake by going out to seek Lesser Spotted Woodpeckers. These birds are only ever a gift. Scan the small twigs of the canopy if you must – but never expect to see them. You'll be disappointed. But if you go into their habitat in a spirit of serendipity, with half an ear for a ringing series of 'peeps', and half an eye for a treetop waif, then there are few more magical birds with which you can spend your birding time.

Fifteen years ago, leading a bird group, I must have got the mood right. It was March and our location was Cassiobury Park, near Watford. It was blustery and hardly ideal for birding, and there were plenty of people around. But remember – none of that mattered. Our mood was right. We were ripe to be bowled over.

Of course, we heard the Lesser Spot first. You almost always do. From the treetops came that loud peeping, like an overenthusiastic electronic alarm clock. Hearing the sound always makes the heart miss a beat. The senses sharpen. There's the tense wait, hoping that the bird will deign to show itself.

But this time there wasn't a wait. Almost immediately the midget came into view and settled on a large oak just above our heads. Binoculars rose in one movement, conducted by the new arrival. I had expected our bird to be a male, with the crimson cap, since only the males give the peep call. But this was a female. Nonetheless I garbled the usual instructions about the bird's black-and-white ladder on the back, its fine streaks on the front and the lack of red at the base of the tail – standard Lesser Spotted commentary, a spoken sprint for a bird always about to dash away.

It soon became apparent, though, that this individual had things on its mind other than persecuting birders, and it clung to its vertical hold mid-oak with a certain statuesque defiance. It soon became obvious why. Within moments a second Lesser Spotted Woodpecker floated in close to the top of the tree, amidst a tangle of dead branches. The first bird didn't flinch, but the brisk March air warmed up with the tension. What was the second bird doing? Was this a pass, perhaps? Or a trespass?

For a few moments the two birds did nothing, but then our first individual suddenly rose effortlessly to the treetops with a few fluent wing-beats. Now the woodpeckers were almost on the same level, but on opposite sides of the trunk. This looked like a challenge. From our position the stand-off didn't look friendly, but with woodpeckers you can never tell; their displays mix aggression with lust, and the birds probably often don't know themselves which one is their primary motivation.

What followed next was spellbinding, but also comical. Little by little, the two rivals or mates began climbing up the dead branch, on opposite sides. First one made a few upward hops, then the second did the same. They did this several times, each climb a little incremental challenge, a few hops of insult – or titillation (we still couldn't establish the sex of the second bird). It was obvious where this was going. In a few woodpecker quick-steps they would reach the top of the branch and meet face to face.

But High Noon had to wait, because the two Lesser Spotteds above us were suddenly interrupted. Incredibly, this was by a third Lesser Spotted Woodpecker – a year's worth of sightings! The interloper left no doubt as to its gender. It perched prominently lower down on the main tree trunk, peeping loudly, and showing off its smart crimson crown. With the male's theatrical arrival, the dynamic of the encounter now suddenly became obvious. The male was there to cheerlead his mate, who was in dispute with a trespassing female. In woodpecker conflicts, territorial rights are always settled gender to gender. For whatever reason, the morning's challenge was a feminine one.

The battle shifted to a neighbouring tree, and it now took on a higher intensity amidst the denser latticework of branches. The females, on different boughs, began making ritualised sprints towards the top of their chosen tree. They raced in this way again and again, one branch to another, for minutes on end, as if involved in some bizarre game in a reality quiz show.

But after much chasing, one leg up a limb suddenly halted. You could almost see the dust blowing off the woodpeckers' feet. Both birds fixed their gaze towards each other and their fuses suddenly went. The two set upon each other, and, for a moment, the branches played host to a whirr of woodpeckers and it was impossible to be sure what was going on.

You rarely ever see a woodpecker fight, let alone one between two minors. But for a while we watched as the birds lost their dignity and their reticence. No feathers flew, but the birds chased wildly, several times spiralling around the trunk of our first tree, one on the other's tail, as if out of control on a helter-skelter. These were woodpeckers unveiled, birds without an eye to the outside world, in the red mist where winning is more important than survival.

However, unsatisfying for the story, we never did find out who won. After almost an hour, both birds chased away to the other side of the canal. The male followed and, little by little, his excited peeps faded away into the no-person's-land of the woodland canopy.

Probably the incumbent was victorious; in bird disputes, trespassing rarely produces an overthrow. But we never worked out why this single intruder was so boldly making a challenge. Was she really trying to usurp the pair from their patch, against the odds? Or, more mischievously, trying to lure the male away? Intriguingly, ten per cent of Lesser Spotted Woodpecker females actually hold two mates concurrently. Perhaps she was making a trunk call?

In truth, the best encounters with birds leave you not just reeling from the thrill, but puzzling for explanations. With three stars in our drama, we were always trying to interpret behaviour on the hoof, and confusion was part of the overall overwhelming experience.

I never saw a Lesser Spot at Cassiobury Park again, despite several repeat visits. And that, of course, was my mistake. After the display we had been treated to, future expectations at this same site would always have undermined the serendipity. There are some moods that you just can't manufacture.

Dominic Couzens

Dominic Couzens is the author of more than 20 books on birds and wildlife, including the Secret Lives of Garden Birds, The Secret Lives of Garden Wildlife, Top 100 Birding Sites of the World *and the travelogue:* My Family and 50 Other Animals. *He writes for numerous magazines and gives regular talks. Visit his website at: www.birdwords.co.uk.*

A NATURAL
AMPHITHEATRE

EDMUND SELOUS

FEBRUARY 23RD

Walking over the downs, this afternoon, I saw large numbers of black-headed gulls and rooks feeding together. Never once was one of the latter chased and made to give up its prey by any gull, in the way in which the pewits are made to, or otherwise in any way molested. One must suppose that the gull is not the master of the rook, as it is of the peewit. The beak of the latter, indeed, is not formidable, but it can strike hard with the wing both on the ground and in the air, and in the nesting season will drive any rook from its haunts. As, also, all the gulls, with the doubtful exception of the great black-backed, are forced to deliver to the Arctic skua, a bird much inferior, both in size and beak, to both the herring and the lesser black-backed kinds, such considerations do not probably affect the question. Perhaps the difference is to the credit of the rook's superior intelligence or more robust character, but this explanation does not satisfy me either. A greater intermingling between these gulls and the pewits would, for me, be a much more likely reason, but whether or to what extent this is the cause I do not know.

In feeding thus over the land, the gulls hovered, as is their wont, coming down at intervals on anything that they saw. The rooks more commonly walked – which is *their* wont – but they, too, frequently rose, more frequently, I think, than they would have done had they been alone. Afterwards, indeed, when they were so, this was confirmed. When, looking up, I caught the gulls against the brow of a hill, it was difficult to imagine that this was not the sea, for hundreds of them were alternately hovering over and descending upon it, exactly as though they were fishing amongst a shoal of herrings. So I ponder upon the retention, by these properly marine birds, of their marine habits, even whilst feeding over the land surface, of their rising from and descending upon it as upon the sea, and not walking about as do rooks and starlings, when left to themselves – for, under their influence, the former had acted much in the same way, rising and hovering with them.

But, coming back, a surprise was in store for me, from which I either learnt or wrongly concluded that the time of the day had a good deal to do with the terrestrial habits of these gulls; and, besides this, I saw a very wonderful thing. On one side of the road, which wound over the downs, was a large and very beautiful natural amphitheatre formed by the intersection of some of the slopes of these, and upon its smooth-swept sides and terraces a very large number of black-headed gulls – upwards of a thousand, I should say; at the least – were walking and feeding. They passed rapidly along, searching the sward and appearing to pick something off it with their bills at very frequent intervals, insomuch that they resembled fowls or pigeons feeding on grain. It was a beautiful sight to see them in such great numbers and so thickly clustered; and, by the aid of a hedge and bank; I watched them for some time from a very near distance – those, that is to say, that were nearest to me, for they covered a wide area. The light was now greatly faded, and it occurred to me that they could no longer see to hawk comfortably on the ground, as their custom is during the daytime.

It was, in fact, upon the verge of dusk, and two rabbits shortly ran out upon the turf, as though for the business of the night. They ran all about amongst the gulls, and these flew up or jumped into the air and came down again, as though annoyed and embarrassed by them. A third rabbit now ran out; and as it did so the wonderful thing I have alluded to took place, for a few of the gulls nearest to it rising, at once, and as upon a signal, the entire number; distributed as they were in various bodies over the whole expanse of the amphitheatre, rose also; and, drawing together from all points, swept swiftly and silently down the short green valley out of which it opened; and were lost round the smooth shoulder of the hill which on one side bounded it. The effect was as though the rabbit had had something to do with it; as it certainly would have had; though only by accident; if we can suppose that the going up of these few birds instantaneously influenced a great multitude of others busily feeding over a wide space; not any of whom had been in the least degree affected by the similar rising, only just before, of some of their number on account of two other rabbits.

This I can hardly credit; but find it more reasonable to suppose that the universal flight-impulse happened almost to synchronise with the going up of these few birds – almost to catch them in the air. Whatever the cause, the same idea of departure seems at the same moment of time; or so near it as to have had that effect, to have swept through the minds of a great number of widely though not thinly distributed gulls. The way in which from every part of the amphitheatre they all swept together and instantly departed, all one way, vanishing in a flickering, ghostly manner; leaving the great, silent amphitheatre amidst the hills empty and lonely, as though they had never been upon it, was most impressive – the very rabbits seemed impressed by it. How their going sunk upon me! How their absence was felt! How lonely; how dreary it became!

When they were gone I walked all over the slope near me where they had been feeding; and also over parts near it where they had not been, to see if worms were laying out on the grass or anything else that would explain the quick and constant way in which they had seemed to be picking things up – there was just sufficient light to see this. There appeared, however, to be nothing living; and the only substance that was sufficiently plentiful to have allowed the birds to feed so continuously was rabbits' dung, with which the turf was thickly scattered. I am half inclined to think it was this they had been getting. Both jackdaws and ravens seem to affect it. Moreover, it explains why they had walked and not hovered. No need to descry what was everywhere.

Edmund Selous (c.1860–c.1933)

Pioneer of behaviour studies of the birds of the British Islands, Edmund Selous remains one of the least understood British ornithologists because of the confused arrangement of the material in his books. A lone wolf, he did not belong to clubs or publish much in the scientific journals. His best-known work is Realities of Bird Life *(1927), and his passion was for the birds of the wild, northern places.*

'A Natural Amphitheatre', from Realities of Bird Life (1927).

THE CALL OF
THE WILD

MARK COCKER

'This is really the best place to see lions. Where you can see
them how they're meant to be. Where they're in their true
state. Here the lions are really wild.'

I remember the words clearly. They were English words but
pronounced in that rather exotic, somehow awkward, chiselled
tone of the Afrikaans speaker. He was a South African professional
big game hunter, working in a part of a Botswanan national park
that was licensed for sportsmen to come to shoot wild animals,
including a small number of lions. The licence fees were extremely
high and the hunting strictly regulated, so that the revenue
derived from the death of a few lions, however distasteful that may
seem to many of us, helped to finance the wider conservation of
Botswana's wonderful wildlife. To me it seemed a reasonable
argument, especially in a country as relatively poor as Botswana.

But the part of the professional hunter's case, which I queried
then, and challenge now, was the notion that only in his sector of

the park were the lions really wild. I think we know what he meant. In the protected areas where they are not hunted, the lion prides become habituated to a constant wagon train of land cruisers, and eventually they behave as if the intruding humans never existed, no matter how closely they approach. Yet in the shooting concession areas the lions run away at the merest glimpse of humans. However, my point would be that the lions aren't wild. In shrinking from contact with humans, the big cats are not expressing some innately hostile spirit that is fundamental to their nature. They are simply frightened – frightened for their lives. But fear and wildness are not the same things.

I'm reminded of that conversation every time I visit north Norfolk in winter because, in a way, the same scenario is played out on the grazing marshes around the coast. Head down the track known as Lady Ann's Drive at Holkham Beach and you cannot fail to notice the huge flocks of wild geese that are spread across the fields on both sides. Or, perhaps, I should rephrase that, because the geese look so contented, so nonchalant about the human traffic, that a visitor could easily overlook them – assuming that they were merely wildfowl in an ornamental collection. But the pink-footed geese that are so abundant on that part of the coast are as wild as they get.

They come to us in late autumn from their breeding grounds on the east coast of Greenland, but especially from the dark lava fields of central Iceland, where they nest in sometimes dense colonies close to the mountain ice caps. Frequently they like to build their circular nest mounds of breast down and vegetation, which build up year on year, by the edge of a cliff, where the gander keeps tight watch on his brooding partner to protect her from Arctic foxes.

So when the great dark skeins of geese arrive in Norfolk I find the clamour of their beautiful, resonant, dog-like calls filled with a sense of northern wilderness. They are, it is true, without fear of the humans with whom they share the Norfolk coast because they are no longer hunted in protected areas like Holkham National Nature Reserve. But I like to think that it is not the geese who have lost their wildness; it is we who have acquired it. Or, rather, we have acquired a passionate commitment to their wildness. It appeals to and fulfils something within us. The geese are, in a sense, a symbol of a reawakened reverence for life beyond our own species and outside our prescription.

The human-tolerant goose flocks of north Norfolk – no less than the sleepy and complacent lions of the Okavango national parks – express at least one success of our conservation policies. There are now 150,000 pink-footed geese wintering in Norfolk and every season those dark skeins across the sky spread their calls ever wider, partly helped by fields full of harvested sugar-beet tops, which have become a major part of their diet. Some of the single roost flocks coming for the night to Scolt Head Island have numbered 80,000. Imagine it. 200 tonnes of feather and sinew all descending in one great rush of powerful wings and hammering hearts. The county has become the setting for one of the great wildlife spectacles in Britain, if not all Europe. Norfolk as a whole is now the winter destination for about half the entire global population of pink-footed geese.

The other day I caught just a small fraction of this magnificent concentration of birds as the geese came into roost on the marshes to the west of Lady Ann's Drive. Some were already landing in front of us and were joining the ever-expanding mass, which spread across the fields as a solid carpet of long-necked birds. But across the heavens through the entire 180-degree panorama we could see skein after skein, the nearer birds superimposed upon the more distant flocks so that the bare sky was crazed with the sequence of their lines. Order was shattered and that ever-changing vision of wing-quickened chaos was matched by a glorious recessional of their calls fading back into the sour sound of the wind.

Those birds of the far north have the power to transform the atmosphere of the entire landscape. They made north Norfolk – that fundamentally humanised place – a more interesting and fulfilling country. They brought some other rare and wonderful element to it. And they aroused in me some additional and richer sense of what life can be. Perhaps it is the meeting of these two elements – the outer and the inner life – which we should really call 'the wild'.

Mark Cocker

Mark Cocker is an author and naturalist. His eight books include Birder: Tales of a Tribe *and* Crow Country, *which won the New Angle Prize for Literature (2009) and was shortlisted for the Samuel Johnson Prize (2008).*

THE GAMEKEEPER
AT HOME

RICHARD JEFFERIES

Twice a year the hawks and other birds of prey find a great feast before them; first, in the spring and early summer, when the hedges and fields are full of young creatures scarcely able to use their wings, and again in the severe weather of winter when cold and hunger have enfeebled them.

It is difficult to understand upon what principle the hawk selects its prey. With apparent disdain, he will pass by birds that are within easy reach. Sometimes a whole cloud of birds will surround and chase him out of a field; and he pursues the even tenor of his way unmoved, though the sparrow and finch almost brush against his talons. Perhaps he has the palate of an epicure, and likes to vary the dish of flesh torn alive from the breast of partridge, chicken or mouse. He does not eat all he kills; he will sometimes carry a bird a considerable distance and then drop the poor thing. Only recently I saw a hawk, pursued by 20 or 30 finches and other birds across a ploughed field, suddenly drop a bird from his claws as he passed over a hedge. The bird fell almost perpendicularly, with a slight fluttering of his wings, just sufficient to preserve it from turning head-over-heels, and on reaching the hedge could not hold to the first branches, but brought up on one near the ground. It was a sparrow, and was not apparently hurt – simply breathless from fright.

All kinds of birds are sometimes seen with the tail feathers gone: have they barely escaped in this condition from the clutches of a hawk? Blackbirds, thrushes and pigeons are frequently struck: the hawk seems to lay them on the back, for if he is disturbed that is the position in which his victim usually remains. Though hawks do not devour every morsel, as a rule nothing is found but the feathers – usually scattered in a circle. Even the bones disappear; probably ground vermin make away with the fragments.

The hawk is not always successful in disabling his prey. I have seen a partridge dashed to the ground, get up again, and escape. The bird was flying close to the ground when struck; the hawk alighted on the grass a few yards further in a confused way, as if over-balanced, and before he could reach the partridge the latter was up and found shelter in a thick hedge.

Richard Jefferies (1848–1887)

A naturalist and novelist, Richard Jefferies was the son of a Wiltshire farmer. He contributed to local papers before moving to London, where he wrote for the Pall Mall Gazette, *which first published his* Gamekeeper at Home *(1877) and* Wildlife in a Southern County *(1879). He subsequently returned to the country. Edward Thomas called* The Gamekeeper at Home, *'The first thoroughly rustic book in English, by a countryman and about the country, with no alien savours whatever.'*
'The Hawk', from The Gamekeeper at Home (Pall Mall Gazette, 1878).

CUCKOO

MIRIAM ROTHSCHILD

There are about 200 different species of cuckoo, but only one breeds in Britain – The European cuckoo. The ancient Hebrews were possibly deceived by its hawk-like appearance and, for this reason, may have prohibited it, along with the nightjars and owls, as an article of diet.* Today, most casual observers who catch sight of a cuckoo beating along open hedgerows, or gliding out of a thicket or copse, mistake it for a bird of prey. It must be admitted that in silhouette, colouring, size and flight it is superficially very like a sparrow-hawk. Compared with some of its foreign relatives it is a drab bird. The upper parts and breast are blue-grey and the remaining under-parts whitish with dark bars. The legs and feet are yellow. In Asia, India and Africa many cuckoos are brilliantly coloured – bright metallic green, purple, bronze, golden and pied. Quite a large proportion of the American species – most of which are not parasitic – are terrestrial birds, who rarely use their wings,

*According to the authorised version.

but can put on an amazing turn of speed running across country or through dense undergrowth.

The song of the male cuckoo is too well known to require description, but in these days of specialisation many naturalists are unaware that the female of the species does not 'Cuckoo' at all, but has a soft bubbling call – rather like a sudden rush of water through a narrow-necked bottle. Almost everything about the European cuckoo is peculiar, even its diet. Hairy caterpillars constitute its favourite food – a form of nourishment that no other bird would touch – and their hairs become embedded in the cuckoo's gizzard so that it appears to be lined with dense fur. This diet is an inherited rather than acquired taste, which develops once the cuckoo has left the care of its foster-parents – no matter what form of food it has previously received from them.

When the cuckoo returns from its winter quarters in Africa, the female selects a territory for herself, preferably in rather open country. Sometimes she returns to the same area several years running. In the case of the European cuckoo, the territory is a few acres in extent, but in some African species – such as the small golden cuckoo (*Lampromorpha caprius*), which victimises colonial nesting-nesting weavers – it may be restricted to one tree. She defends this territory against all other female cuckoos parasitising the same fosterer as herself. Although successful invasions sometimes occur it is unusual to find two female cuckoos in the same area laying in the nests of the same species of small bird. Individuals parasitising other hosts are tolerated. Occasionally a young bird who has failed to establish a territory of her own will roam across country, laying at random in any available nest she can find.

The male cuckoo also establishes a territory, but in the case of the British species it rarely coincides with the territory of any particular female. He favours wooded areas or the edge of small copses rather than open country. The cuckoo's relations with the opposite sex are distinctly casual and very promiscuous. Sometimes numerous males gather when they hear a female's amorous bubbling and she may copulate with one, two, or all of them. At other times one particular male may seek her out persistently and thus give the impression that they are permanently paired. Again, a male bird may haunt several adjacent territories, bestowing his favours freely on all the female owners.

The female cuckoo hunts systematically for the nests of her victims, which are generally small passerine birds – chiefly those who feed on insects. Quite often though, the linnet, which is a seed-eater, is chosen. When she locates a pair building, she begins a careful and prolonged vigil, observing the behaviour and movements of the future fosterers from a point of vantage and sometimes gliding down to examine the nest at close quarters. The visual stimulus thus received appears to excite ovulation and the cuckoo's egg reaches maturity and is ready for laying about five days later – in fact, shortly after the fosterers themselves have begun to lay. Most birds deposit their eggs early in the morning, but the cuckoo does so in the early afternoon, a period at which the parent birds – providing their clutch is incomplete – are most likely to be absent. She glides over the selected nest several times and then quickly alights in it and lays one egg directly in the nest – the entire action occupying no more than five seconds. Subsequently she destroys one or more of the fosterers eggs, either by throwing them out or by crushing and eating them.

Sometimes she carries one a considerable distance in her beak before disposing of it. When the cuckoo deposits her egg in a small domed nest with a side entrance, it is impossible for her to enter and lay in the usual manner. The egg is then forcibly projected into the aperture from the bird's cloacae, while she hovers immediately over the nest. Whether this sometimes happens is a matter of acute controversy. The majority of eggs (if not all) which are seen being carried by cuckoos are not their own, but eggs of the fosterers which they are about to destroy.

Miriam Rothschild (1908–2005)

Dame Miriam Rothschild was born in Ashton Wold in Northamptonshire, the daughter of Charles Rothschild, who founded The Society for the Promotion of Nature Reserves in 1912. Both her father, who had described 500 new species of fleas, and her uncle Walter, who built a private natural history museum at Tring, were profound influences on her and the development of her interest in natural history. She became a leading authority on fleas and her study of parasitism, Fleas, Flukes and Cuckoos, was widely acclaimed. She published over 300 papers on entomology and zoology, was elected an FRS in 1985 and continued her studies to the very end of her life. She was a Vice President of The Wildlife Trusts.

'Cuckoo' from Fleas, Flukes & Cuckoos *(St. James's Place, 1952).*

THE PEREGRINE

J. A. BAKER

November 28th. Nothing was clear in the tractor-echoing dreariness of this misty day. The thin and faltering north-west wind was cold.

At eleven o'clock a peregrine flew up to one of the line of tall pylons that extends across the valley. He was blurred in mist, but the deft bowing and fanning of his wings was instantly familiar. For 20 minutes he watched the plover feeding in the surrounding fields, then flew west to the next pylon. There he was silhouetted in an owl shape against the white sky, his sunken head rounding out into high curved shoulders and tapering down to a short blunt-ended tail. He flew north again, moving up above the shining mist-coils of the river, the red-gold burnish of his plumage glowing into dimness. His wings rowed back with powerful strokes, sweeping him easily, majestically forward.

I could not follow him in such poor light, so I went down to the brook, thinking that later he might come there to bathe. Blackbirds and chaffinches were scolding in the hawthorns by

North Wood, and a jay was perching in alders and looking down at something. Keeping in the cove of the hedges, I went slowly along to the thick mass of hawthorns. I forced my way into them till I could see the fast-moving water of the brook, which the jay had been watching. Through the dark mesh of thorny twigs, I saw a peregrine falcon standing on stones, a few inches from the water, looking intently at her own reflection. She drank a few sips, dipped her head beneath the surface repeatedly, splashed, dowsed and flapped her wings. Blackbirds and chaffinches stopped scolding, and the jay flew off.

She stayed in the water for ten minutes, gradually becoming less active; then she waddled heavily ashore. Her curious parrot-like amble was made even more ungainly by the weight of water in her feathers. She shook herself a great deal, made little jumps into the air with flailing wings, and flew cumbersomely up into a dead alder that overhangs the brook. Blackbirds and chaffinches started scolding again, and the jay came back. The peregrine was huge with water, and did not look at all happy. She was deeper-chested and broader-backed than the tiercel, with a bigger hump of muscle between her shoulders. She was darker in colour and more like the conventional pictures of young peregrines. The jay began to flutter around her in an irritating manner. She flew heavily away to the north, with the jay screeching derisively in pursuit.

I found her in a dead oak to the north-east of the ford. The tree stands on higher ground, and from its topmost branches a hawk can see for several miles across the open river plain to the west. After looking all around, and up at the sky, she began to preen. She did not raise her head again until she had finished. The breast feathers were preened first; then the undersides of the wings, the belly, and the flanks, in that order. When the preening was done, she picked savagely at her feet, sometimes raising one to get a better grip on it, and cleaned and honed her bill upon the bark of the tree. She slept fitfully till one o'clock, then flew quickly away to the east.

*   *   *

March 5th. The snow is neolithic, eroded by the warm south wind. Snow tumuli crumble where the great drifts rose against the sky. The whole valley ripples with running water. Ditches are streams, streams brooks, the brook a river, the river a chain of moving lakes. Lapwings and golden plover have come back. All day the lapwing flocks were passing over to the north-west. I looked at them in binoculars and found larger flocks above them, flying much higher, invisible to the unaided eye.

By half-past three I had given up searching for the peregrine and was sitting glumly on a gate near the dead oak. When he suddenly flew past me, I was lifted to joy on the surge of his wings. There was a zestful buoyancy, a lilting eagerness in his rushing-past, boring, dipping, swaying, curving-up flight. He perched in a tree to the east and looked back at me. I felt that I had been found. He crouched on a low branch in the crabbed, uneasy, sidling stance that means he is hunting. Among the many gnarled branches of the oak he was hard to pick out. After five minutes desperate rest he flew off to the eastern orchard. Rising and falling, he went switchbacking over the wind, and dashed down at fieldfares that rose from the trees. I followed him through the long orchard aisles. Blackbirds were still scolding, and hundreds of fieldfares were skirmishing, but the hawk had gone. I went back to the gate.

At half-past four the jackdaw cloud above the brook lifted and scattered as the peregrine came through. Sweeping down wind, he sailed splendidly up from the south, wings help high in a 'V', swaying and gliding at speed. He was all wind-borne and flowing. He swept on towards the north orchard, skimmed over the boundary poplars, curved down in a tremendous wing-lit parabola. I did not see him again.

During the day's long tramp I found 49 kills: 45 woodpigeons, two pheasants, a red-legged partridge and a blackbird. Only the last two were recent; the rest had been hidden under snow for a long time.

March 6th. Still the warm south wind renewing, the sun warm, the air light and clear. Yellowhammers sang in the lanes and there were chaffinch flocks in the orchards. Black-headed gulls came into the valley from the south, and soared above the river. They turned where the river turns, spiralled high above the ridge, and floated away north-east. They circled higher than the lapwing flocks, which were again moving in from the coast. Some lapwings flew down to join the large numbers that have gathered now in the valley fields, but most went steadily north-west.

By two o'clock I had been to all the peregrine's usual perching places, but had not found him. Standing in the fields near the north orchard, I shut my eyes and tried to crystallise my will into the light-drenched prism of the hawk's mind. Warm and firm-footed in long grass smelling of the sun, I sank into the skin and blood and bones of the hawk. The ground became a branch to my feet, the sun on my eyelids was heavy and warm. Like the hawk, I heard and hated the sound of man, that faceless horror of the stony places. I stifled in the same filthy sack of fear. I shared the same hunter's longing for the wild home none can know, alone with the sight and smell of the quarry, under the indifferent sky. I felt the pull of the north, the mystery and fascination of the migrating gulls. I shared the same strange yearnings to be gone. I sank down and slept into the feather-light sleep of the hawk. Then I woke him with my waking.

He flew eagerly from the orchard and circled above me, looking down, his shining eyes fearless and bland. He came lower, turning his head from side to side, bewildered, curious. He was like a wild hawk fluttering miserably above the cage of a tame one. Suddenly he jerked in the air as though shot, stalled, wrenched himself violently away from me. He defecated in anguish of fear, and was gone before the white necklace of sun-glittered faeces reached the ground.

March 7th. A day of endless wind and rain, which I wasted away in the lee of hollow trees, in sheds and barns, and under broken carts. I saw the hawk once, or thought I saw it, like a distant arrow flicking into a tree, blurred and distorted by the million shining prisms of the rain.

All day the unquenchable skylarks sang. Bullfinches lisped and piped through the orchards. Sometimes a little owl called lugubriously from its hollow tree. And that was all.

March 8th. I went out at four o'clock. The evening of the night was dark, and the warm west wind blew wet. Owls were calling in the long dim twilight before dawn. At six o'clock the first lark sang, and soon there were hundreds of larks singing up into the brightening air. Straight up from their nests they rose, as the last stars rose up into the paling sky. Rooks cawed as the light increased, and gulls began to fly inland. Robins, wrens and thrushes sang.

In the flat fens near the coast I lost my way. Rain drifted softly through the watery green haze of fields. Everywhere there was the sound and smell of water, the feeling of a land withdrawn, remote, deep sunk in silence. To be lost in such a place, however briefly, was a true release from the shackles of the known roads and the blinding walls of towns.

By seven o'clock the sky was clear again. I climbed on to the coast wall just as the sun was rising. Quickly it pierced the rim of the sea; a huge, red, hostile, floating sun. As it lifted heavily off into the sky, light flashed and shattered from it, and it was a globe no longer.

A hen-harrier rose from its roosting place on the saltings and flew to the wall. It hovered low above the withered grass, which moved dryly in the draught from its wings. It was coloured like the waving grass: grey-brown and fawn and reddish-brown. The ends of its wings were black, and its long brown tale was barred and mottled light and dark. At the base of its tail the brilliant white splash of its upper tail coverts shone in the sunlight. It flew slowly into the wind, keeping low, beating its wings twice and then reaching them above its back in a 'V' as it glided forward with the dark primaries splaying open and curling upward. It hovered again, and glided down over the steep sides of the wall in long banking curves. It crossed from side to side, drifting over the grass still glittering with rain, lightly, softly, silently riding over the bending grass and looking down through the parting stems for prey. Imperceptibly it drifted away and was lost as suddenly as a shadow is lost when the sun goes in.

Slowly the wind dropped, and the air became warmer. The sun shone through a thin parchment of high cloud. Distance lengthened. Horizons sharpened as the morning grew. The grey sea dwindled out, mumbling with a line of foam at the far edges of the shining mud beyond the vast moorland of the saltings. The remote farms and villages clustered up along the top of the empty inland fields. Redshanks chased and fretted over the broad dyke that runs beside the wall. More rain was coming, but for the moment all was still.

At half-past ten, clouds of small birds sprayed up from the fields and a Merlin cleaved through them like an arrow, dipping and darting. It was a thin narrow falcon, flying low. It swept over the sea-wall, curved out across the saltings, and swung up into steep spirals, its long sting-like body swaying in the blur of its jabbing, flicking wings. It flew fast, yet its wide circling seemed laborious and its rising slow. At 300 feet it came round in a long curve, and poised, half-hovering. Then it flew forward into the wind towards a skylark singing high above the fields. It had seen the lark go up, and had circled to gain height before making an attack. From behind, the Merlin's wings looked very straight. They seemed to move up and down with a shallow flicking action, a febrile pulsation, much faster than any other falcon's. It reached the lark in a few seconds, and they fell away towards the west, jerking and twisting together, the lark still singing. It looked like a swallow chasing a bee. They rushed down the sky in zigzags and I lost them in the green of the distant fields.

Their rapid, shifting, dancing motion had been so deft and graceful that it was difficult to believe that hunger was the cause of it and death the end. The killing that follows the hunting flight of hawks comes with a shocking force, as though the hawk had suddenly gone mad and had killed the thing it loved. The striving of birds to kill, or to save themselves from death, is beautiful to see. The greater the beauty, the more terrible the death.

March 9th. The morning sun was low and dazzling, and the wind cold, as I walked along the sea-wall by the north shore of the estuary. A peregrine falcon startled me by her sudden upward leap from the lee of the wall, where she had been hidden. I was directly above her, looking down at the long tapering span of her wings and the humped width of her back. She rose quite silently, like a short-eared owl, and flitted away across the marsh, rocking violently from side to side, tilting between two vertical planes, standing in air on the tips of each wing in turn. When a long way off, she glided slowly down into the grass. I could not find her again. She had been sleeping in the sun – perhaps after bathing – and had not heard me coming.

Heavy rain fell in the afternoon. The falcon flew up to a dead oak, near the sea-wall, and watched the waders gathering on the saltings at high tide. She was still there when I left, huddled and sombre in the pouring rain, as whistling wigeon drifted in with the tide and the babble of waders grew louder.

March 10th. Towering white clouds grew in the marble sunlight of the morning. The wind eroded them to falling weirs of rain. The estuary at high tide brimmed with blue and silver light, then tarnished and thinned to grey.

A falcon flew low across the marsh, weaving through the wind with sudden dips and swerves, as though moving under invisible branches and twisting between invisible trees. She flew like a big, sleepy Merlin. The sun shone on the splendid burnish of her back and wings. They were a deep roan colour, the colour of a redpoll steer, like the patches of red soil that stain the ploughlands to the north. The primaries were black, with a tint of blue. The comma-shaped curl of the dark-brown moustachial mark gleamed like a nostril on the white face. The hump of muscle between her wings rose and fell under the feathers as the wings moved forward and back. She looked docile, yet menacing, like a bison. Redshanks stood sleekly in the grass and watched her go by. They were quite still, save for the nervous bobbing and twitching of their bright-orange legs.

An hour later, from a flurry and cry of curlew, the falcon lifted clear and circled slowly up above the marsh. She glided in a thermal of warm air that bent its white bloom of cloud before the strong north wind. With rigid wings outstretched, she rose in a trance of flight, wafted upon air like a departing god. Watching the falcon receding up into the silence of the sky, I shared the exaltation and serenity of her slow ascension. As she dwindled higher, her circles were widened and stretched out by the wind, till she was only a sharp speck cutting across white cloud, a faint blur on blue sky.

She drifted idly; remote, inimical. She balanced in the wind, 2000 feet above, while the white cloud passed beyond her and went across the estuary to the south. Slowly her wings curved back. She slipped smoothly through the wind, as though we were moving forward on a wire. This mastery of the roaring wind, this majesty and noble power of flight, made me shout aloud and dance up and down with excitement. Now, I thought, I have seen the best of the peregrine; there will be no need to pursue it farther; I shall never want to search for it again. I was wrong of course. One can never have enough.

Far to the north the falcon tilted downward and slid slowly through sun and shadow towards earth. As her wings swept up and back, she glided faster. And then faster, with her whole body flattened and compressed. Bending over in a splendid arc, she plunged to earth. My head came forward with a jerk as my eyes followed the final vertical smash of her falling. I saw fields flash up behind her; then she was gone beyond elms and hedges and farm buildings. And I was left with nothing but the wind blowing, the sun hidden, my neck and wrists cold and stiff, my eyes raw, and the glory gone.

J. A. Baker (1926–1987)

Baker's life is something of a mystery. He was born in 1926 and died at the age of 61. Born in Essex he spent his life in the country, wrote two books and left a collection of diaries. Much the best known of his works is The Peregrine (1967), increasingly acknowledged as a masterpiece of 20th Century natural history writing. The book largely takes the form of a diary as Baker enters the Peregrine's world day after day, from Autumn to Spring each year, following the birds and observing the intimate relationship they have with their winter landscape.

'The Peregrine', from The Peregrine *(Collins, 1967).*

FROM *THE NATURAL HISTORY OF WILTSHIRE*

JOHN AUBREY

CHAPTER XII. BIRDS.

We have great plenty of larkes, and very good ones, especially in Golem-fields and those parts adjoyning to Coteswold. They take them by alluring them with a dareing-glasse*, which is whirled about in a sun-shining day, and the larkes are pleased at it, and strike at it, as at a sheepe's eye, and at that time the nett is drawn over them. While he playes with his glasse he whistles with his larke-call of silver, a tympanum of about the diameter of a threepence. In the south part of Wiltshire they doe not use dareing-glasses but catch these pretty ætheriall birds with trammolls.

The buntings doe accompany the larkes. Linnets on the downes. Woodpeckers severall sorts: many in North Wilts.

Sir Bennet Hoskins, Baronet, told me that his keeper at his parke at Morehampton in Hereford-shire, did, for experiment

---

*'Let his grace go forward, and dare us with his cap like larks.'
Shakspere, *Henry VIII*. Act III. sc. ii.

sake, drive an iron naile thwert the hole of the woodpecker's nest, there being a tradition that the damme will bring some leafe to open it. He layed at the bottome of the tree a cleane sheet, and before many houres passed the naile came out, and he found a leafe lying by it on the sheete. Quaere the shape or figure of the leafe. They say the moone-wort will doe such things. This experiment may easily be tryed again. As Sir Walter Raleigh saies, there are stranger things to be seen in the world than are between London and Stanes.

In Sir James Long's parke at Draycot Cerne are some wheat-eares; and on conie warrens and downes, but not in great plenty. Sussex doth most abound with these. It is a great delicacie, and they are little lumps of fatt.

On Salisbury plaines, especially about Stonehenge, are bustards. They are also in the fields above Lavington: they doe not often come to Chalke. (Many about Newmarket, and sometimes cranes.) On Salisbury plaines are gray crowes, as at Royston.

'Like Royston crowes, where, as a man may say,
Are friars of both the orders, black and gray.'
J. CLEVELAND'S POEMS

'Tis certain that the rookes of the Inner Temple did not build their nests in the garden to breed in the spring before the plague, 1665; but in the spring following they did. Pheasants were brought into Europe from about the Caspian sea. There are no pheasants in Spaine, nor doe I heare of any in Italy. Capt. Hen. Bertie, the Earle of Abingdon's brother, when he was in Italy, was at the great Duke of Tuscany's court entertained with all the rarities that the country afforded, but he sawe no pheasants. Mr Wyld Clarke, factor fifteen yeares in Barberie, affirmes there are none there. Sir John Mordaunt, who had a command at Tangier twenty-five yeares, and had been some time governour there, a great lover of field sports, affirmes that there are no pheasants in Africa or Spaine.

Bitterns in the breaches at Allington, &c. Herons bred heretofore, sc. about 1580, at Easton- Piers, before the great oakes were felled down neer the mannour-house; and they doe still breed in Farleigh Parke. An eirie of sparrow-hawkes at the parke at Kington St. Michael. The hobbies doe goe away at..... and return at the spring. Quære Sir James Long, if any other hawkes doe the like?

Ganders are vivacious animals. Farmer Ady of Segary had a gander that was fifty yeares old, which the soldiers killed. He and his gander were both of the same age. (A goose is now living, anno 1757, at Hagley hall in Worcestershire, full fifty yeares old.)

Sea-mewes. Plentie of them at Colern-downe; elsewhere in Wiltshire I doe not remember any. There are presages of weather made by them.

'The seas are ill to sailors evermore
When cormorants fly crying to the shore;
From the mid-sea when sea-fowl pastime make
Upon dry land; when herns the ponds forsake,
And, mounted on their wings, doe fly aloft.'
Virgil's *Georgics*, lib. i. Englished by Mr. T. May

John Aubrey (1626–1697)

An antiquary, John Aubrey revealed the megalithic remains at Avebury, Wiltshire, in 1649. He was made a Fellow of the Royal Society in 1663, and went on to make antiquarian surveys under the Crown by patent, in 1671. He created large topographical collections, including a number of observations on natural history in Wiltshire and Surrey. He is best known as the author of a collection of short biographical pieces, usually referred to as Brief Lives.

'Miscellany', from The Natural History of Wiltshire *(1847).*

THE REDSTART

JOHN BUXTON

I have suggested that 600 visits may be the normal minimum required by the hen redstart to build a nest; but it is obvious that in some sites far fewer will be needed. For no broad and deep foundation will be possible in a narrow chink in a wall, or where the nest is built on the remains of an old nest. And one nest which I found in Buckinghamshire was in a crevice in a willow-tree, where the eggs were laid on the fine soft fragments of rotten wood which were in the hole, so that I suppose the hen had had no need to carry any material there, but had simply made a cup with her legs and breast and so laid her eggs in a mere scrape. But such a nest is clearly exceptional.

The redstart's nest is large but not very well made: there is no need for the skilled architecture of a chaffinch or a goldcrest or a wren, since the nest is supported by the tree or wall or ground where it is built. It is nothing more than a lining to insulate the eggs from contact with the cold earth or stone. (The clutch of six eggs that I have just described as laid on the rotten wood of a willow all hatched successfully, for the soft wood was sufficient insulation.) And since the hen needs only to lay the material down and shape it into a cup, but not to weave it together as does a chaffinch, her visits to the nest are normally very brief – not more than five or six seconds. Occasionally she will stay as long as half a minute, and then perhaps she is turning about to shape the cup.

But for all her hurry to finish the nest the hen remains cautious as she leaves it, and almost always will peer out of the hole for a moment before flying away for the next load. When she returns she is less cautious, and will often fly straight up to the hole trailing a long, conspicuous straw, or carrying a white feather in her beak. Sometimes she will be more circumspect, and will perch on a branch close by before entering the nest; but since, before she will first begin to build, the site of the nest must be advertised to any curious eye by the cock's antics, her attempting now to conceal it would be rather absurd. Her caution on leaving the nest is on her own behalf, to enable her to see that no enemy is awaiting her, and is not a means of protecting the nest. And after all, the narrow entrance admits few enemies into the nest, to destroy the eggs or the chicks. As Lack has recently pointed out, birds that nest in holes tend to have larger clutches than birds with open nests; also their chicks tend to stay longer in the nest. The protected nest is safer, and a large family may therefore be raised in the longer time required.

While the hen is building, the cock is rather inconspicuous, and, as already has been mentioned, he scarcely ever sings: indeed most days at this stage pass without a single phrase of song being given. But he generally remains in the neighbourhood of the hen and of the nest, following her on trips to collect material, and returning with her towards the nest. Yet the two birds show very little interest in one another: the cock does not assist in any way, and copulation seldom occurs once the nest is started. However, in one pair Ruiter records that on the day on which the nest was begun the cock sang quite frequently in the morning, visited the box, and even entered it after the hen. He also perched on the box, fluttering his wings repeatedly. But he very soon quietened down, and his interest in the hen had very much lessened within a few hours of her beginning the nest. The cock has indeed almost nothing to do, but he rests after the strenuous days that have just passed when he was establishing his territory, inducing the hen to enter the nest, and mating. And for the hen, the quiet days of egg-laying and incubation will soon ensue.

John Buxton (1912–1989)

Poet and Fellow of New College, Oxford, where he was Tutor in English literature, John Buxton made an intensive study of the breeding redstarts in the surroundings of the prisoner-of-war camp where he was held in Germany for five years during the Second World War. His work was published as a New Naturalist Monograph in 1950 and remains the classic study of the species.

'Redstarts at nest', from The Redstart *(Collins, 1950).*

TAWNY OWL

EDWARD A. ARMSTRONG

Four days later, a misty morning did not deter us from setting forth at five a.m. By the time we were tramping through the wood along the lode, which led to the owl's haunt, a glorious day was coming to birth. Light filaments of brightest green decked the birch woods; in their midst stood tasselled oaks clothed in russet hues, stained to pink by the slanting sunlight. The ash-trees were just acquiring their light, stippled cloud of greenery, and the beeches were already thick with vivid foliage. At our feet the sapphire blossoms of the speedwell glimmered amongst the grass, and beneath the trees the bluebells lay in misty pools as if the azure skirts of Heaven had trailed across the woods that night. Bracken crosiers, thrusting up through the sere brown debris of yester-year seemed almost to writhe with sudden life. The full dawn-chorus had already subsided, but such a joyous company of birds sang on that the woods were full of melody. As we approached a dark pool a teal shot vertically from the water, and a jay, screeching hideously, made off with guilty flight and a glitter of blue-enamelled wings.

The owl was sitting, squatting low and looking rather like a frightened cat; but when my camera shutter clicked, off she went. I was soon concealed in a bower of branches that the keeper had prepared, and my pleasant vigil began. Before half an hour had elapsed, the owl, which I had caught sight of now and then swinging past at a great speed, appeared with magical suddenness a few feet from the nest. She had arrived with no more noise than a puff of thistledown or dandelion globe. Never before nor since have I sat by the nest of a bird that gave no audible indication of its approach or presence; usually some note, a swish of wings, a twig gently moves, the light patter or a scratch of alighting feet, announces that the owner of the nest is coming or has arrived. Even a nightjar may make some slight sound. One whose close acquaintance I made uttered a note rather like *phut* when anxious or suspicious. On these occasions one's senses are abnormally alert, for there is sometimes intense excitement and nervous strain as one waits for one's quarry, and the faintest noise seems portentous. But the owl's downy wings make no sound at all; the bird comes with gossamer softness; a moment ago she was not and now she is. The effect is as if one had been smitten with a sudden deafness. There were times when I forgot to concentrate on the nest, letting my wits wander, and when I looked again I was astonished to find her already there; but her startling materialisations out of the void gave an additional charm to my sojourn on the bird's doorstep.

The owl stands gazing about her for a few moments, turning her large brown head as on a pivot. When she looks away, a great, broad, speckled neck is to be seen, but as she turns her face all is changed. The large, yellow, saucer-eyes are almost terrifying at this short distance and she seems to stare me through and through. Surely she sees me and my camera's glass eye gazing at her! Happily I am mistaken; she obviously suspects danger no more in one direction than in another for she searches the landscape from side to side and all around. As she stands there she looks like an old, old woman – Oh so old! – withered up and shrouded in a speckled, brown shawl. It is a thrilling moment.

Edward A. Armstrong (1900–1978)

A parson in a Cambridge parish, Edward A. Armstrong received the Honours MA of the University of Cambridge for his scientific and literary work; the Stamford Raffles Award of the Zoological Society of London and the medal of the John Burroughs Association for his book Birds of the Grey Wind *(1942). Widely travelled in the world on birding expeditions, he is best known for his books on bird behaviour and the New Naturalist Monograph on* The Wren *(1955). Published many papers on historical, literary and theological themes, including* Shakespeare's Imagination *(1946).*

'Tawny Owl', from Birds of the Grey Wind *(Oxford, 1940).*

THE ITCHEN VALLEY

EDWARD GREY

In one mile of the Itchen Valley that had much rough tussocky ground, too rough and coarse to be mown, there used always to be two, and sometimes three, pairs of grasshopper-warblers; and just when the even-song of birds had ceased in the warm dusk of June and July evenings, the grasshopper-warblers would begin to sing. Thus to me the song became associated with failing light and the end of a day's fishing. The territory of each bird became familiar to me, the presence of each was greeted every year and noted evening after evening on the way home in the quiet twilight: my waders, brushing through the lush, soft growth on the river bank, made a sound not out of keeping with that of the bird. Apart from the act of singing, the grasshopper-warbler is not seen: its small dark form is as unobtrusive in its ways as a mouse in the thick rough herbage, where the bird nests. The sound it makes suggests dryness; as if there were no moisture in the palate. Its manner is very quiet, but the length of time for which the song is sustained gives the impression that the bird takes exceeding pleasure in it.

April 28 to 30 (E.)

I came by the last train on Friday night the 27th and walked out from Winchester, at midnight. It was warm and soft: I heard a nightingale, and one sedge warbler was singing within hearing of the road, just where a piece of the river could be seen, light at the end of a little dark path. I walked with my hat off and once felt a little soft rain fell amongst my hair: there were great forms of leafy trees and a smell and spirit everywhere and I felt the soft country dust about my feet.

... A nightingale's song is the most wonderful, but the most imperfect, of songs. The long notes are divine, but they come seldom, and never go on long enough: the song continually breaks out with a burst, which promises a fine full spell, but it is always broken off in the most disappointing way. A blackcap's song, which comes next in quality, is short enough, but it seems finished in a way that no part of a nightingale's ever does, and one can't help thinking with some satisfaction of a good, steady old thrush singing right through from the beginning of February to the middle of June.

July 1 (E.)

Two hot days. We have enjoyed both days immensely. When we arrived there was one wren singing most noticeably round the cottage; as I looked out it flew happily over the cottage from the poplars to the limes, singing as it passed over the roof: 'like a blessing' D. said when I told her. It sang nearly all day yesterday and to-day, always near us somewhere. To-day as I was waking the first thing I was aware of was the blackcap's song: I knew of it for some time before I was properly awake: it too sang nearly all day close round us. Both these birds were still in full song, and it seemed as if they were a special gift to us – a parting one perhaps before all songs cease for the season. The woods are nearly silent, and it was very strange and sweet to have these two birds singing as loud and more constantly than any birds had been noticed to sing before. We sat out the whole day, till sunset, when we went for a walk in the meadows. D. planted some Test musk which F. Lubbock had sent her, and I bathed. The spotted flycatchers really have turned the old chaffinch nest into a spotted flycatcher's: there are four eggs and the bird is sitting, but flies off whenever we look round the corner.

Sir Edward Grey, Viscount Grey of Fallodon (1862–1933)

Statesman and bird-lover, Sir Edward Grey was brought up at Fallodon, Northumberland, where, from boyhood, he watched birds, fished and developed his love for country life. Liberal MP for Berwick on Tweed, and Foreign Secretary between 1905 and 1916, he was created a viscount in July 1916. Fly Fishing (1899), Fallodon Papers (1926) and The Charm of Birds (1927), demonstrate his love of country pursuits and gifts as a nature writer.

THE RUNNING SKY

TIM DEE

Dusk on the winter solstice: the shortest day and longest night of the year. I was cold and alone on a track on the Somerset Levels, looking towards the dying light in the west. Moving across the sky in front of me, like the breath of the earth, were thousands of birds – starlings arriving to roost, to put away their day, and so, too, on this day, the year. From the next dawn the glorious creep towards spring would be under way: more light; a future; repairs; song, nests and eggs.

The year had drained to this pinching day and its paltry hours of watery sun. In the middle of the afternoon, a cold, iron-hard dark arrived from the east and pushed all the light away to a buckling golden foil fussing on the western horizon. There the day launched a last flare like a crack of magmas seamed through lava. The year was burning down.

It was freezing on the old track across the peat moor at Westhay. Last night's unmelted ice thickened and reached towards tonight's dewfall. It frosted the tiny flashes of the puddles, the lank grass around them, and my boots. Molehills along the track had frozen mountain-hard with little ice caps on their summits. The sky was clear and harsh. High ice crystals prinked its blue like a snowfield. Night was coming and I shivered, but from all the points of the evening skies the starlings came over me like warmth.

Westhay is part of the watery grid of the Somerset Levels. They are level or flat only relative to the hills that rim them on three sides. Their flatness is like the flatness of the sea out to their western edge. The land buckles as if it remembers it came from this sea. Around 10,000 years ago, at the end of the last Ice Age, when the sea rose, Westhay became a salt marsh. Six and half thousand years ago, as the sea receded, the marsh silted up and became, in slow succession, a freshwater reed swamp, then wet fen woodland, and then a raised bog.

Millennia of rot laid down peat that cloaked these new flatlands with a deep black soil. More than 5000 years ago, people built the first trackways – like the one I stood on – across the spongy soak so they could pass to and from adjacent higher ground, the hills of the Mendips and the humps and mounds of Glastonbury. At Shapwick, near Westhay, in the spring of 3806 BC, the Sweet Track – a wooden road – was laid, using cut (and probably coppiced) oak, ash, lime, hazel, alder and holly. It is amongst the earliest pieces of woodmanship in the world. Later, people began to dig the peat. Walking on the track, I could feel the earth's plastic bounce, its five-thousand-year-old give.

Nowadays, something of an old, low-intensity life lingers on the Levels in the slow suck and churn of mud and grass, in the drip and spread of water and sunlight. I could see where an abandoned orchard's unpicked cider apples fermented beneath the skeletons of their trees, red globes of bright treasure in a damp grave. In the fields, bullocks chewed an endless cud. Their hot breath hung at their nostrils, as they breathed out their own local weather systems, making clouds from a cast of their lungs.

People, starlings, cattle and peat-cutting lived side by side until the recent past. In the last few years, commercial digging finished, and the gouges cut into the land were abandoned and allowed to fill with water and new vegetation. At Westhay, the old peat workings left flooded mires and swampy pools with reeds growing across them, making a perfect night-time sanctuary for roosting birds.

Every evening, through the winters of the past few years, thousands, even millions, of starlings have come to sleep here. Eight million were counted, somehow, in one roost here a year or so ago. This may be the largest ever gathering of birds in Britain. Imagine Hyde Park Corner in failing light and the entire population of London arriving there from all points across the city.

At Westhay, some starlings were local birds, others flew in from miles away. Arrow-headed echelons of them had shot south above me as I drove to the Levels hours before. Starlings are sharp and pointed, and the first flocks they form on their way to their roosts are sharp and pointed too. They were already heading purposefully towards Westhay, raking the sky. In midwinter the starling's day is even shorter than the few hours of light. Not long after midday they are thinking of bed and their assembly flights begin.

Other starlings spend their winter days in fields adjacent to the reed-beds where they will roost. Flocks of 100 or more were already out on the Levels. Local birds and arriving birds mixed, squabbling, feeding and talking. In the fields they looked older and more purposeful than they did as village starlings an hour before. They seemed to be joining some necessary action. A call-up was under way.

That evening, summer was further off than it would ever be. Stowed sunshine from months ago was rationed, like the last grains of sugar in a siege. Its light and heat survived only the flimsiest of things: the feathered seed heads of the reeds that engraved fine scratches onto the plate of the sky, and the tiny contact calls swapped between parties of long-tailed tits as they moved through the willow tops, living in the warmth of their own talk. Everything else was, or soon would be, a shade of black.

The light had nearly gone. All that was moving looked shadowed: the great spotted woodpecker whose bouncing flight ahead of me echoed the folds and dips of the fen path appeared to have lost its white and red; the buzzard that planed alongside the ditch looked so dark I thought at first it was a melanistic bird; the gulls beating north were as drained of colour as the cormorants flying the other way.

Black had overtaken the starlings too. If I could separate just one bird from the lines flying above me, or the legions in the fields, I could find their daytime sheen of pearl-spotted oily iridescence, but the massing birds took on a generic darkness. It was not the furred black of wet peat; that came later. For now, the starlings' black was the feathered brown-black of drying peat, the soil at the surface, not the buried earth.

From all sides there were lines of starlings, in layers of about 15 birds thick stretching for three miles back into the sky and coming towards the reed beds that surrounded me. They came out of the furthest reaches of the air, materialising into it from far beyond where my eyes or binoculars could reach in the murk. All flew with a lightly rippling glide, as if the net they were making of themselves was being evenly drawn into a single point in the reed bed.

Their arrival and accumulation had been eerily silent. From the early afternoon, first in the villages and then in the staging fields, there had been a great noise. A collective telling and retelling of starling life rose through those hours of pre-roost talk to a complicated but loquacious rendering of all things – idiomatic adventure, mimetic brilliance and delighted conversational murmur. Once this annotation of the day was done, the birds grew quiet and lifted up and off to begin their thickening flights towards the roost.

There were thousands of mute birds around me, their wheeze and jabber left behind. Many thousands more were too far away to hear, but their calm progress towards the roost suggested they flew in silence. Closer, the only noise was of the flock's feathers. As they wheeled and gyred *en masse*, the sound of their wings turning swept like brushes dashed across a snare drum or a Spanish fan being flicked open. The air was thick with starlings, inches apart and racked back into the darkening sky for a mile. Every bird was within a wing stretch of another. None touched.

A rougher magic overtook them as they arrived above the reeds. Great ductile cartwheels of birds were unleashed across the sky. Conjured balls of starlings rolled out and up, shoaling from their descending lines, thickening and pulling in on themselves – a black bloom burst from the seedbed of birds. One wheel hit another and the carousels of birds chimed and merged, like iron filings made to bend to a magnet. The flock – but *flock* doesn't say anything like enough – pulsed in and out.

I could feel my eyes being forced to deepen their field of view to take in birds behind birds behind birds; I could feel my brain slowing as it tried to compute the organising genius of what was in front of me. Floating above a peat bog in the dark, I was to sit a maths exam in a room drawn by Escher. I couldn't do it. I failed O-level maths twice and optical illusions make me feel sick. To describe the flock is like trying to hold on to a dream in daylight – it slips from me, It cannot be summoned except in fragments, and they cannot be transcribed. Try singing it.

I thought of Thomas Tallis's 40-part devotional motet *Spem in alium* from 1570. For as long as I have known it I have loved this piece, especially the recording made in 1962, in King's College Chapel, Cambridge. Could its 11.5 minutes of singing light the black midwinter night and the black midwinter starlings?

Spem in alium doesn't describe what the flock does. It is the flock. The music – unaccompanied singing, or rather singing that only accompanies itself – comes in, opening its throat before us, beginning with some tentative note on some frontier of sound, arriving into a space from a place without space, from far away. It might be one bird flying, or the sound of a wave beginning far out in the Atlantic. The sound catches and swirls towards us, becomes a striving, and folds into itself and floats and opens further with a beautiful frail young solo which twists away my ears and then gives onto a landscape like the great heave of an abstract painting, making me think of Peter Lanyon's sky masterpieces, as well as starlings hatching from the evening. It is huge and everywhere, but tilted and very close. And all along there is the strangest of pulses, a breathing, flexing continuo, that rises into the heights of the chapel at King's College, climbing around the stone like a filling bath.

The voices arrive from all corners, unfolding and bending, in relay and alone. Forty throats open. They sing together and against one another, and then against one another and together again. It is a wind blowing out of paradise. It is a vast river of warm stone and dark skies, of sea silver, of black sheen and matt and dust and lisping and echoes and news and pain, and it deepens beyond voices until the great stone room is singing its own song, and its sound goes brightly down beneath the building into the earth and then rebounds, coursing up the vaulting out into the winter night. There are snake whispers and dead leaves rustle; there is music for outriders and prophets, songs for latecomers and dreamers. It is a coffin and a bed. Then: a resolution, the first song of many sung 'Domines', that wrestles with the flex of moving song, which wants to gather the word in right away and take it home, but cannot; the word repeats and rises and wanders beautifully out into terraced voices, with vistas that stretch as far as the mind can go, pushing back the night, opening the earth, and then the lit dark comes, its stars thrown over you the moment the sun goes, the soil sings. And big and kind and at the right time it ends, calming to begin with, an embrace and a decision, and then the wild shriek of a single young voice climbing and breaking back out into the sky for one last flight, loud, and screaming, and elated.

Tim Dee

Tim Dee was born in Liverpool in 1961. He has worked as a BBC radio producer for 20 years and divides his life between Bristol and Cambridge. His first book The Running Sky: A Birdwatching Life *tells of his bird-watching past and was published to great acclaim. He also compiled* The Poetry of Birds *with Simon Armitage.*
'Winter solstice', from The Running Sky *(Jonathan Cape, 2009).*

GOLD-CRESTED WREN

GEORGE MONTAGU

This elegant little species is the smallest British bird. Its weight seldom exceeds 80 grains; length three inches and three quarters. The bill is slender and black; irides hazel. The crown of the head is singularly beautiful; the crest is composed of a double series of feathers, arising from each side, and almost meeting at their points; the exterior are black, the interior bright yellow; between which, on the crown, the feathers are shorter, and of a fine deep orange; the forehead, chin, and round the eyes, whitish; the hind part of the head, neck, and back, green; the two first dashed with ash-colour; quills dusky, edged with green; at the base of the secondary quills is a black bar, above which the coverts are tipped with white, lightest on the belly, a little tinged with yellow; the tail is somewhat forked, the feathers dusky, edged with yellowish green.

The female has the head rather less crested, and the crown is bright yellow where the male is orange.

The young birds do not possess the crest and yellow feathers till autumn.

The nest is not made with an opening on one side, as described by some, but is in form and elegance like that of the chaffinch, composed of green moss, interwoven with wool, and invariably lined with small feathers, with which it is so well bedded as to conceal the eggs. It is sometimes placed against the body of a tree covered with ivy, but most times underneath a thick branch of fir.

Albin, on the authority of Derham, and most of the common authors, describe this nest as having a side entrance. The truth seems to be that this bird, like many other species, appears to know how to accommodate its nest to the locality chosen. When it selects a spot where there is a natural canopy, it does not take the trouble to build one; but when this is wanting, it forms as neat a dome, with a small side entrance, as any of the other British Wrens. It is the only native bird, I believe, which ever suspends its nest like so many of the tropical birds, for though it is said not unfrequently to build against the trunk of a tree covered with ivy, I have always found it hanging under the broad bough of a spruce fir, or cedar, or a yew-tree, the thick, flat disposition of the leaves forming a sort of umbrella over the opening. The materials of the nest are the same as those of the goldfinch and chaffinch, namely, green moss, (*hypnum tenellum,* &c.) or lichens, felted together very neatly with wool, and lined with the down of willows and other plants, or very soft feathers. The eggs are from seven to ten in number, of a brownish white; rather darker at the larger end; their weight nine or ten grains.

A pair of these birds, who took possession of a fir tree in my garden, ceased their notes as soon as the young were hatched; and as this beautiful little family caused me much delight and amusement, some observations thereon may not be unacceptable to the curious reader. When I first discovered the nest, I thought it a favourable opportunity to become acquainted with some of the manners of this minute species, and to endeavour to discover whether the male ever sung, by way of instructing the young ones. Accordingly, I took the nest when the young were about six days old, placed it in a small basket, and by degrees enticed the old ones to my study window; and after they became familiar with the situation, the basket was placed within the window; then at the opposite end of the room. It is remarkable that although the female seemed regardless of danger, from her affection to her young, the male never once ventured within the room; and yet would constantly feed them while they remained at the outside of the window: on the contrary, the female would feed them at the table at which I sat, and even when I held the nest in my hand, provided I remained motionless. But on moving my head one day, while she was on the edge of the nest, which I held in my hand, she made a precipitate retreat, mistook the open part of the window, knocked herself against the glass, and laid breathless on the floor for some time*. However, recovering a little, she made her escape, and in about an hour after I was agreeably surprised by her return, and she would afterwards frequently feed the young while I held the nest in my hand.

The male bird constantly attended the female in her flight to and fro, but never ventured beyond the window-frame; nor did he latterly ever appear with food in his bill. He never uttered any note but when the female was out of sight, and then only a small chirp. At first there were ten young in the nest, but, probably for want of the male's assistance in providing food, two died. The visits of the female were generally repeated in the space of a minute and a half or two minutes, or, upon average, 36 times in an hour; and this continued full 16 hours in a day, which, if equally divided between

---

*It is probable that the focal distance of such minute animals' eyes is very near, and that large objects are not represented perfect on the *retina*; that they do not seem to see such distinctly is certain, unless in motion.

the eight young ones, each would receive 72 feeds in the day; the whole amounting to 576. From examination of the food, which by accident now and then dropped into the nest, I judged from those weighed, that each feed was a quarter of a grain upon average; so that each young one was supplied with 18 grains weight in a day; and as the young birds weighed about 77 grains as the time they began to perch, they consumed nearly their weight of food in four days at that time**. I could always perceive by the animation of the young brood when the old one was coming; probably some low note indicated her near approach, and in an instant every mouth was open to receive the insect morsel. But there appeared no regularity in the supply given by the parent bird: sometimes the same was fed two or three times successively; and I generally observed that the strongest got most, being able to reach farthest, the old one delivering it to the mouth nearest to her, and after each feed she waited a while to see if any *muted*. The lesser species of birds, who are so frequently fed, seldom or ever mute but immediately after they are fed, by which means the *fæces* are never left in the nest, but are instantly carried away by the parent bird.

This minute species braves the severest winters of our climate, being equally found in all parts during that rigorous season, and is by no means so scarce as it is supposed to be, but, from its diminutive size, it is seldom noticed. It would in all probability be much more plentiful, but from some cause which we have not been able to discover, the female is frequently destroyed at the time of its incubation, and the nest with the eggs left to decay.

**This extraordinary consumption seems absolutely requisite in animals of such rapid growth. The old birds of this species weigh from 80 to 90 grains.

George Montagu (1751–1815)

Writer on natural history, and Captain in the British Army during the war with the American colonies, George Montagu retired to Easton Grey in Gloucestershire, where he devoted himself to scientific study. His Ornithological Dictionary *was published in 1802, in the same year that he distinguished the Montagu's Harrier from the Hen Harrier. Other publications include* The Sportsman's Dictionary (1792) *and* Testacea Britannica *(1803).*

'Gold-crested Wren', from Ornithological Dictionary *(1802).*

ADVENTURES AMONG BIRDS

WILLIAM HENRY HUDSON

Then, after a few minutes, from a great way off in the sky came the sounds of approaching geese, and the wounded bird turned his breast towards the land and stood with head held high to listen to and see his fellows returning uninjured with crops full of corn, boisterous in their happiness, to the roosting place. The sound grew louder, and presently the birds appeared, not in a compact body, but in three single lines or skeins of immense length, while between these widely separated lines were many groups or gaggles of a dozen to 40 or 50 birds arranged in phalanx form.

I had been witnessing this evening return of the geese for a fortnight, but never, as now, united in one vast flock, numbering at least 4000 birds, the skeins extending over the sky for a length of about a third of a mile. Nor had the conditions ever been so favourable; the evenings had been clouded and it was often growing dark when they appeared. On this occasion the heavens were without a cloud or stain and the sun still above the horizon. I could see it from the flat marsh like a great crimson globe hanging just above the low, black roofs of Wells, with the square church tower in the middle. The whole vast aerial army streamed by directly over me and over their wounded fellow below, still standing statuesque and conspicuous on the brown, level marsh. In two or three minutes more, the leading birds were directly above the roosting-place on the flat sands, and at this point they paused and remained stationary in mid-air, or slowly circled round, still keeping at the same height; and as others and still others joined them, the whole formation was gradually broken up, skeins and phalanxes becoming merged in one vast cloud of geese, circling round like a cloud of gulls. Then the descent began, a few at a time detaching themselves from the throng and sweeping obliquely downwards, while others, singly or in small parties, with half-closed wings appeared to hurl themselves towards earth with extraordinary violence. This marvellous wild-wing display continued for four or five minutes before the entire multitude had come to the ground. Altogether it had been the most magnificent spectacle in wild-bird life I had ever witnessed in England.

It was not until all were down and invisible, and the tumult of the multitudinous cries had sunk to silence, that the wounded bird, after some moments of indecision, first taking a few steps onwards, then returning to the side of the redshanks, as if reluctant to part from those little unhelpful friends lest he should find no others, finally set off walking towards the sea.

William Henry Hudson (1841–1922)

Born near Buenos Aires, William Henry Hudson was a naturalist and writer who grew up watching the birds of the great plains on the farms and ranches of the Rio de la Plata. At the age of 15 he contracted a fever that affected his heart, and moved to London at the age of 28. A free spirit and an apostle of the back-to-nature movement, he did not insist that knowledge is the essence of understanding nature. He is best remembered for short pieces that communicated visions of natural events in great personal detail.

'Geese – North Norfolk', from Adventures among Birds *(1923).*

CHAPTER 3

BY RIVER AND SEA

BASS ROCK

ERIC ENNION

We run out from the pleasant little harbour of North Berwick in a fishing yawl, out into the Forth, the Bass four miles ahead and looking very much nearer than it really is in the clear morning sunlight. Tourists in launches circle it but may not land there. For a long while, it does not seem to change and then suddenly enlarges. The white points scintillating round it resolve into hundreds of white gannets, gliding in the air-lifts due to its presence. A little nearer and the faint murmur one had been hearing for some minutes resolves into a medley of harsh rattling cries and wailings. Never still and all at once, it seems, the rough grey cliffs are towering high above you, every ledge and niche crowded with breeding seafowl: gannets, guillemots, razorbills, kittiwakes, with shags on their seaweed nest-piles on the rocks at the base – but well above eye-level from the yawl – puffins in holes in the old fort masonry, herring gulls and an occasional pair of graceful lesser black-backs parading on the grassy slopes ... The yawl puts out her fenders and edges alongside the landing for us to go ashore: she slips away with a promise to be 'back at fourrr'.

Up the long flights of concrete steps past the lighthouse, through the dark alleyways of the ancient fort – a shag's neck thrusts snakily out of a ruined port – up again alongside the huge pipe that leads compressed air to the foghorn; and a scramble up the last 50 feet to the top. Nothing maybe to compare with the great cliffs of St Kilda or Foula, but looking across to the misty Isle of May, to the far Fife shore, to ships steaming up and down the Forth no bigger than toy boats in a baby's bath, to the white specks of gulls and gannets resting below on a wrinkled sea, there is a feeling of height and remoteness far in excess of the actual truth: a feeling almost of translation into the *corps élite* of this great white host soaring for ever above and wheeling around the Bass; tailing off in an endless stream of comings and goings down the Forth and out beyond to fishing grounds as far away maybe as Whitby, Lowestoft or the Dogger Bank.

Every so often a gannet glides in, checks, furls its six-foot wingspan away and rubs bills in noisy greeting with its mate: it has come home laden, perhaps after a two- or three-hundred-mile flight, with a dozen fair-sized herrings, or four or five big fat mackerels, in its crop. It preens and dozes until its mate suggests it is time to take over – or the chick that it is time to be fed. By now most of the nests are flattened and set solid with dried white excrement: an acrid incense, peculiarly the gannets' own, wafts to high heaven, especially on a warm day – a stench which presently fades as your nose grows weary of registering it. From time to time a parent will fly in with a sprig of campion or fresh bunch of seaweed, laying it on the nest as rushes were once strewed on a medieval dining floor: the main difference is that, unlike human beings, the seafowl themselves contrive to stay immaculately clean despite the slum conditions of their surroundings.

A few late nests may still hold single newly hatched chicks, naked reptilian little objects with shiny, pimply, smoke-pink skin. But most of them, though varying in size, are covered in thick white cotton-wool down, their dark-grey bills and naked faces giving a golliwog effect in reverse. In some the flecked juvenile plumage is beginning to appear patchily in the down. They lie each on its nest, sprawling in full-fed abandon – in so far as anything as tubby as a gannet chick can be said to sprawl – with always one parent on guard, brooding or standing by. Where level space permits the overall pattern of the pairs and nests is as regular as the intersections of a net, governed as it is by the range of beak-thrust from one to the next all round. Off-duty adults, however, club together sociably on neutral ledges and uncommonly handsome they look.

Eric Ennion (1900–1981)

Doctor and artist, Eric Ennion was educated at Gonville and Caius College, Cambridge. After nearly 20 years of general practice in the Cambridge Fens, he became Warden of the Flatford Mill Field Study Centre in 1945, and moved to become Director of the Monk's House Bird Observatory in Northumberland in 1950. He was the author of six books, including Adventurer's Fen *and* The House on the Shore *(1959). In later life, he was best known for his charismatic bird paintings and sketches.*

'Bass Rock', from The House on the Shore *(Routledge and Kegan Paul, 1959).*

FISH-WATCHING

COLIN J. MARTIN

I became a fish-watcher in Cyprus. From afternoon swims in the warm blue sea, it was a short step to an underwater mask and fins: a short step, but one I shall remember all my life. Words are not enough to describe the thrill of first coming into contact with the underwater world. It is not so much being able to see all that is going on below the surface, although that is wonderful enough; it is the sense of being part of the sea – of being accepted in a new element.

From the moment I first ducked my masked head I was an addict. I learned how to use the aqualung and was soon spending every available moment underwater. Different people have different ideas about how to spend their time there. Some explore wrecks. Others develop an interest in archaeology, bringing pottery and implements of incredible antiquity to the surface. The more aggressive become hunters and stalk fish through the rocks with a spear gun. I felt no desire to kill fish; they were so beautiful alive that I just wanted to watch them.

The diver has the great advantage over, say, the bird-watcher; he can move about freely without disturbing the fish. They have no fear of man, provided that he does not harm them; one shot of a spear gun will clear an area in seconds. On a single dive it is possible to see a variety of fish behaving quite normally. As behaviour in their natural habitat has been little explored by scientists, the observant amateur can contribute greatly to knowledge in this field.

*   *   *

All good things come to an end; but when I had to exchange the sunny Mediterranean for our own cold shores, to my great surprise I found opportunities for fish-watching here, too. True, it is even more difficult – it is colder and a diving suit is essential. Even so, the fish are just as varied in our sea as in the Mediterranean.

My real discovery came one weekend when, for lack of something better to do, I decided to dive in our local river. It was another new world – not as clear as the sea and, of course, not at all deep. Diving acquaintances look at me pityingly and say, 'The river? You'll be lucky if you get seven or eight feet of water.' But the thrill is being under the surface, whether it is two or two hundred feet above you.

I go down in this stretch of river nearly every weekend now; it has become something of a Sunday afternoon stroll. I even know some of the fish personally. There is the old salmon no one can catch, though they have been trying for years. He does not go out to sea, but just stays in his pool getting older and wiser and more battle-scarred. He does not even glance at me now, though last year he did take exception when I tried to stroke him. There is a big eel, too, and I must admit to being rather scared of him. He has only one eye and moves with such ruthless purpose that I prefer to keep out of his way.

The river teems with trout and grayling. Trout are dull. Grayling are much more fun – the gossips of river life, always darting about in shoals, never still, keeping to the faster waters. They are also the most handsome of the river fish. Salmon are lordly, and trout garish; but grayling, with delicate striping and patterned fins, are truly beautiful. Unfortunately, they are rather shy and difficult to approach, but I found a way of getting among them. I would go upstream, dive in and let the current carry me silently towards them. Suddenly, if I was lucky, I would burst into the middle of the shoal, catching them completely unawares. But it would be a very short glimpse, for the current would carry me inexorably on. Then came the slog upstream to get above them once again.

Strangers visit the river from time to time. Sometimes I meet a flounder, all the way from the sea, flapping lopsidedly over the riverbed. They come up to feed themselves into breeding condition. Most unusual and interesting are the lampreys, which come up the river to spawn in April and May. They are among the most primitive backboned animals known, having an ancestry going back more than three hundred million years. They look pretty primitive, too, without paired fins and having a row of small openings in place of the usual covered gills. Strangest of all, they have no jaws. Instead they have a toothed sucker with a hole in the middle, and behind it a rasping tongue, which moves backwards and forwards over whatever the fish is grasping with its sucker. Unfortunately they often prey on other fish, especially salmon, attaching themselves to, and eating into, the living flesh. This parasitic habit has inevitably earned them the hatred of anglers.

Last year I arrived in the river when the lampreys were spawning. A mass urge seemed to descend on a whole group of them at precisely the same moment, and they congregate to scoop out with their suckers a shallow trench in the gravel, into which they individually deposit their eggs. As with salmon, spawning exhausts the lampreys, and most of them die. The young are small worm-like creatures quite unlike the adults and take up to five years to develop.

Lampreys are supposed to make good eating, but they look so revolting that I have not dared to stomach a dish. King Henry apparently had no such scruple when he polished off the famous 'surfeit' that killed him. I did catch one to have a close look at it. It fastened its mouth on to my wrist and refused to let go until I raised it out of the water. The feel of the rasping tongue was most unpleasant.

Now I have built an underwater camera, and this summer I hope to get some really good action shots to prove to disbelievers that my fish stories are true. To any naturalist in search of adventure my advice is: 'Get underwater'.

Colin J. Martin

Colin J. Martin wrote for The Countryman *magazine during the 1960s, one of the oldest, most respected countryside magazines in the world and revered by those who share its concerns for the countryside, the people who live and work in it, and its wildlife.*
'Fish-watching', from The Countryman Wild Life Book *(The Countryman/David & Charles Ltd, 1969).*

DOLPHINS

GAVIN MAXWELL

The porpoises, six-foot lengths of sturdy grace, are the commonest of all the whale visitors to the Camusfearna bay. Unlike the rumbustious dolphins, they are shy, retiring creatures, and one requires leisure and patience to see more of them than that little hooked fin that looks as if it were set on the circumference of a slowly revolving wheel; leisure to ship the oars and remain motionless, and patience to allow curiosity to overcome timidity. Then the porpoises will blow right alongside the boat, with a little gasp that seems of shocked surprise, and at these close quarters the wondering inquisitiveness of their eyes shows as plainly as it can in a human face, a child's face as yet uninhibited against the display of emotion. The face, like the faces of all whales but the killer, appears good-humoured, even bonhomous. But they will not be stared at and, after that quick gasp, they dive steeply down into the twilight; they go on about their own business, and will not linger to play as do the dolphins.

One summer a school of 17 bottle-nosed dolphins spent a whole week in the Camusfearna bay, and they would seem almost to hang about waiting for the boat to come out and play with them. They never leapt and sported unless the human audience was close at hand, but when we were out among them with the outboard motor they would play their own rollicking and hilarious games of hide-and-seek with us, and a sort of aquatic blind-man's-buff, in which we in the boat were all too literally blind to them, and a target for whatever surprises they could devise. The beginning followed an invariable routine; they would lead, close-packed, their fins thrusting from the water with a long powerful forward surge every five or ten seconds, and we would follow to see how close we could get to them. When we were within 50 feet or so there would be a sudden silence while, unseen, they swooped back under the boat to reappear dead astern of us. Sometimes they would remain submerged for many minutes, and we would cut the engine and wait. This was the dolphins' moment.

As long as I live, and whatever splendid sights I have yet to see I shall remember the pure glory of the dolphins' leap as they shot up a clear ten feet out of the sea, one after the other, in high parabolas of flashing silver at the boat's very side. At the time it gave me a *déjà-vu* sensation that I could not place; afterwards I realised that it recalled irresistibly the firing in quick succession of pyrotechnic rockets, the tearing sound of the rockets' discharge duplicated by the harsh exhalation of air as each dolphin fired itself almost vertically from the waves.

In this school of dolphins there were some half a dozen calves, not more than four or five feet long as against their parents' twelve. The calves would keep close alongside their mothers' flanks – the right-hand side always – and I noticed that when the mothers leapt they kept their acrobatics strictly within the capabilities of their offspring, rising no more than half the height of those unencumbered by children.

The members of this school of dolphins spoke with voices perfectly audible to human ears; rarely when they were very close to the boat, but usually when they were heading straight away at a distance of a hundred yards or two. As they broke the surface with that strong forward-thrusting movement, one or more of their number would produce something between a shrill whistle and a squeak, on a single note held for perhaps two seconds. It seems strange that I can find no written record of any whale-sound as plainly and even obtrusively audible above water at this.

Gavin Maxwell (1914–1969)

Gavin Maxwell was brought up in the isolated moorlands of Galloway, where he learned to love the wild land and the creatures which inhabited it. Later in his life he wrote about those years in The House of Elrig *(1965). In 1945 he bought the small Hebridean Island of Soay and tried to establish a Basking Shark fishery, of which he wrote in* Harpoon at a Venture *(1952). His most famous book is* Ring of Bright Water, *published in 1960, an autobiographical account of his pioneering days in Camusfearna in the Western Highlands, featuring his famous otters, Mijbil and Edal.*

'*Dolphins', from* The Ring of Bright Water *(Penguin, 1960).*

SHELLS AND OTHER BEACH OBJECTS

GEOFFREY GRIGSON

Collecting shells may be a kind of false natural history. A marine biologist prefers his shells to be tenanted, to contain the living creature, cockle, mussel, scallop, etc.; in which case tenant and shell have a double fascination. But that does not prevent the rest of us behaving like men for many thousands of years, and enjoying the single, easier fascination of shells without their tenants. They are the best of all objects of the beach – of the right beach, sandy, not too steep, and on a lee shore. Long open sand beaches are often disappointingly but inevitably devoid of shells or exceedingly thin in shells, in contrast, for example, with the low-tide sands of the north coast of Norfolk, an excellent extent for tiny scallops or queens of all shades from orange to deepest claret, or the low-tide lagoon of the Isles of Scilly, an area for seaweed species and sand species, where you find abundance of pink cowries, wentletraps, top-shells, dog-whelks, cockles, tellins, queens, and a most colourful miscellany of periwinkles washed out of the seaweed. At low tide on the Scillonian cockle bars you crush shells as you go –

violet, white, pink, yellow, the colours of the sunsets away across Tresco and Bryher. But this – like others – is rather a dangerous shelling area, where as you walk and search you have to remember the swiftness and depth of the returning tide.

It is true that shells around the British Coast are not spectacular in form or tint. There is no kind, for instance, as shimmering, as opaline and oriental on a large scale as the shell of the Ormer, with its row of holes, from the Channel Isles. Yet even limpets of different kinds are less dull in their iridescence *inside*, when they are fresh, than one would think from the old tide-line specimens. The cowries, auger shells, tops, periwinkles, queens and scallops offer an education in tint and form, especially the queens and scallops, which have been an ancient motif in the arts of Europe and the arts of Mexican and South American Indians. Also there is variation around the coasts, some shells being local – such as the Wide-mouthed Whelk of the north-east, a larger relative of the Buckie or Common Whelk, or the Spiny Cockle, the Red Nose of the Devonshire beaches, in contrast to the smooth ridged shells of the Common Cockle. Some are uncommon, particularly shells of the Violet Sea-Snail, stranded now and again on ocean beaches around Land's End or along the south-west of Ireland – shells of a mollusc which lives in the Atlantic upheld by a float of its own mucus, eating miniature jelly-fish. These violet shells, though, are frail and easily broken.

Scallops have an extraordinary book to themselves, with learned and exquisite illustrations – *The Scallop: Studies of a Shell and its Influence on Humankind* edited by Ian Cox, and published in 1957 to mark the diamond jubilee of the Shell Company. In general the best book for identifying shells and those objects of the beach among which the oyster-catchers run and peer and peck in their search for food is Collins *Pocket Guide to the Sea Shore,* by John Barrett and C. M. Yonge. It deals with shells, stranded jelly-fish, sea urchins, starfish, with the soft 'bones' of cuttlefish (which used to be made into tooth powder), with seaweeds, with the blackish horny egg capsules – or 'Witches' Purses' or 'Mermaids' Purses' – of dog-fish and Common Skate and other kinds of ray (dog-fish purses have curly tendrils, instead of points or horns), with the egg capsules of the whelk, which blow around like hardened froth. It deals with everything, I nearly wrote, forgetting those other *objets trouvés* of the tide line, *objets involuntaires* or *perturbés* which a scientific handbook has to overlook – from the glass balls or floats from a trawler net to every object washed ashore and rolled back and forth and moulded and transformed by sea-action, the sea being a sculptor bizarrely gifted. Sea-moulded and blunted shapes of bottle glass of every colour, of ornamental earthenware, or red brick and tile, sea pebbles, sea-moulded pieces of branch or wood, can all prove objects of valid fantasy. To be mentioned among them are the lumps of amber occasionally washed ashore on the beaches and shingle bars of North Norfolk and elsewhere along the east coast – not yellow translucent bits like necklace beads, but little knobs battered, scratched, and dulled (but still amber) in long transit across the North Sea; also – I do not know that they have a name, though they are among the oddest objects of natural sculpture – the fish-shaped lengths or rolls of clay to be found where the sand of very active open beaches is backed by fine shingle in a coloured mosaic, blue, yellow, purple, white, orange, red, on a pottery background, Assyrian clay tablets of the shore.

Along western beaches from Orkney to Cornwall, beach debris may contain the beans of two climbers of the pea family, which currents have floated across the Atlantic – shiny, flattish, hard beans up to two inches across, brown, of the West Indian *Entada gigas*; and much prettier, the beans of the tropical climber *ucuna urens*, smaller brownish-purple except for a rim marking of café au lait and black, which nearly encircles the bean. I have always found that a few of these various beach objects consort very well with human products – with china, earthenware, silver etc, the miscellaneous decoration of table, shelf and mantelpiece.

For beach pebbles, in their mineral variety, see a curious recent book, Clarence Ellis's *Pebbles on the Beach*.

Geoffrey Grigson (1905–1985)

Geoffrey Grigson was a prolific poet, author, editor, critic and broadcaster, who wrote on art, travel, the British countryside and botany. His many influential books that brought nature to the public include The Englishman's Flora, The Shell Guide to Flowers of the Countryside, The Shell Guide to Trees and Shrubs, The Shell Guide to Wild Life *and* Country Writings.

'Shells and Other Beach Objects', The Shell Country Book *(Phoenix House, 1962)*.

THE LIVING
MOUNTAIN

NAN SHEPHERD

I have written of inanimate things, rock and water, frost and sun; and
it might seem as though this were not a living world. But I have
wanted to come to the living things through the forces that create
them, for the mountain is one and indivisible, and rock, soil, water
and air are no more integral to it than what grows from the soil and
breathes the air. All aspects of one entity, the living mountain. The
disintegrating rock, the nurturing rain, the quickening sun, the seed,
the root, the bird – all are one. Eagle and alpine veronica are part of
the mountain's wholeness. Saxifrage – the 'rock-breaker' – in some of
its loveliest forms, *Stellaris*, that stars with its single blossoms the
high rocky corrie burns, and *Azoides*, that clusters like soft sunshine
in their lower reaches, cannot live apart from the mountain. As well
expect the eyelid to function if cut from the eye.

Yet in the terrible blasting winds on the plateau one marvels
that life can exist at all. It is not high, as height goes. Plants live far
above 4000 feet. But here there is no shelter – or only such shelter
as is afforded where the threads of water run in their wide sloping

channels towards the edge of the cliffs. Whatever grows, grows in exposure to the whole vast reach of the air. From Iceland, from Norway, from America, from the Pyrenees, the winds tear over it. And on its own undulating surface no rocks, or deep ravines, provide a quiet place for growth. Yet the botanist with whom I sometimes walk tells me that well over twenty species of plant grows there – many more, if each variety of moss, lichen and algae is counted. He has made me a list of them, and I can count them. Life, it seems, won't be warned off.

The tenacity of life can be seen not only on the tops but on the lower shoulders where the heather has been burnt. Long before the heather itself (whose power to survive fire as well as frost, wind, and all natural inclemencies is well known) shows the least sign of life from the roots beneath its charred sticks, or has sprouted anew from seeds hidden in the ground, birdsfoot trefoil, tormentil, blaeberry, the tiny gestina, alpine lady's mantle, are thrusting up vigorous shoots. These mountain flowers look inexpressibly delicate; their stems are slender, their blossoms fragile; but burrow a little in the soil, and roots of a timeless endurance are found. Squat or stringy, like lumps of dead wood or bits of sinew, they conserve beneath the soil the vital energy of the plant. Even when all the upper growth is stripped – burned or frosted or withered away – these knots of life are everywhere. There is no time nor season when the mountain is not alive with them. Or if the root has perished, living seeds are in the soil, ready to begin the cycle of life afresh. Nowhere more than here is life proved invincible. Everything is against it, but it pays no heed.

The plants of the plateau are low in stature, sitting tight to the ground with no loose ends for the wind to catch. They creep, either along the surface, of under it; or they anchor themselves by a heavy root massive out of all proportion to their external growth. I have said that they have no shelter, but for the individual flower there is the shelter of its group. Thus the moss campion, *Silene*, the most startling of all the plateau flowers, that in June and early July amazes the eye by its cushions of brilliant pink scattered in the barest and most stony places, has a habit of growth as close-set as a Victorian posy. Its root too is strong and deep, anchoring it against the hurricane, and keeping its vital essence safe against frost and fiery drought, the extremes and unpredictable shifts of weather on the exposed plateau. In these ways this most characteristic of the plateau flowers is seen to be quite simply a part of the mountain. Its way of life lies in the mountain's way of life as water lies in a channel.

Even its flamboyant flowers are integral to the mountain's way of life. I do not know how old the individual clumps may be, but judging from the size to which those close-knit cushions grow, some must have endured the commotion of many winters. Most of the mountain flowers are long livers. The plant that races through its cycle in a single season could never be sure, up here, of fruition – there might be no successors. Death would dog, not only the individual, but the species. Yet even the long livers must renew themselves at times, and it is on only some of the summer days that insects can fly to the mountain top. So the *Silene* throws this ardent colour into its petals to entice the flies.

Lower on the mountain, on all the slopes and shoulders and ridges and on the moors below, the characteristic growth is heather. And this too is integral to the mountain. For heather grows in its most profuse luxuriance on granite, so that the very substance of the mountain is in its life. Of the three varieties that grow on these hills – two Ericas and the ling – the July-blooming bell heather is the least beautiful, though its clumps of hot red are like sun-bursts when the rest of the hills are still brown. The pale cross-leaved heath, that grows in small patches, is an exquisite, almost waxen-still, with a honey perfume. But it is the August-blooming ling that covers the hills with amethyst. Now they look gracious and benign. For many miles there is nothing but this soft radiance. Walk over it in a hot sun, preferably not on a path ('I like the unpath best,' one of my small friends said when her father called her to heel), and the scent rises in a heady cloud. Just as one walks on a hot day surrounded by one's own aura of flies, so one walks with one's own aura of heather scent. For as the feet brush the bloom, the pollen rises in a perfumed cloud. It settles on one's boots, or if one is walking barefoot, on feet and legs, yellowy-fawn in colour, silky to the touch, yet leaving a perceptible grit between the fingers. Miles of this, however, stupefies the body. Like too much incense in church, it blunts the sharp edge of adoration, which, at its finest, demands clarity of the intellect as well as the surge of emotion.

To one who lives the hills at every season, the blossoming is not the best of the heather. The best of it is simply its being there – is the feel of it under the feet. To feel heather under the feet after a long abstinence is one of the dearest joys I know.

Scent – fragrance, perfume – is very much pertinent to the theme of life, for it is largely a by-product of the process of living. It may also be a by-product of fire, but then fire feeds on what lives, or what has lived. Or of chemical action, but if there are obscure chemical processes at work in the dead stuff of the mountain, they give little indication to my nose. The smells I smell are of life, plant and animal. Even the good smell of earth, one of the best smells in the world, is a smell of life, because it is the activity of bacteria in it that sets up this smell.

Plants then, as they go through the business of living, emit odours. Some, like the honey scents of flowers, are an added allurement to the insects; and if, as with heather, the scent is poured out most recklessly in the heat of the sun, that is because it is then that the insects are out in strength. But on other cases – as the fir trees – the fragrance is the sap, is the very life itself. When the aromatic savour of the pine goes searching into the deepest recesses of my lungs, I know it is life that is entering. I draw life in through the delicate hairs of my nostrils. Pines, like heather, yield their fragrance to the sun's heat. Or when the foresters come, and they are cut, then their scent is strong. Of all the kinds that grow on the low reaches of the mountains, spruce throws the strongest perfume on the air when the saw goes through it. In hot sun it is almost like a ferment – like strawberry jam on the boil, but with a tang that tautens the membranes of nose and throat.

Of plants that carry their fragrance in their leaves, bog myrtle is the mountain exampler. This grey-green shrub fills the boggy hollows, neighboured by cotton-grass and sundew, bog asphodel and the spotted orchid, and the minute scarlet cups of the lichens. Its fragrance is cool and clean, and like the wild thyme it gives it most strongly when crushed.

The other shrub, juniper, is secretive with its scent. It has an odd habit of dying in patches, and when a dead branch is snapped, a spicy odour comes from it. I have carried a piece of juniper wood for months, breaking it afresh now and then to renew the spice. The dead wood has a grey silk skin, impervious to rain. In the wettest season, when every fir branch in the wood is sodden, the juniper is crackling dry and burns with a clear heat. There's nothing better under the girdle when scones are baking – unless perhaps small larch twigs, fed into a fire already banked. Once, striking thick loose snow from low juniper bushes before walking through them, I surprised myself by striking from them also a delectable fragrance, that floated on the wintry air.

Birch, the other tree that grows on the lower mountain slopes, needs rain to release its odour. It is a scent with body to it, fruity like old brandy, and on a wet warm day, one can be as good as drunk with it. Acting through the sensory nerves, it confuses the higher centres; one is excited, with no cause that the wit can define.

Birch trees are least beautiful when fully clothed. Exquisite when the opening leaves just fleck them with points of green flame, or the thinning leaves turn them to a golden lace, they are loveliest of all when naked. In a low sun, the spun silk floss of their twigs seems to be created out of light. Without transfiguration, they are seen to be purple – when the sap is rising, a purple so glowing that I have caught sight of a birchwood on a hillside and for one moment thought the heather was in bloom.

Among drifts of these purple glowing birches, an occasional rowan looks dead; its naked boughs are a smooth white-grey, almost ghastly as the winter light runs over them. The rowan's moment is in October, when even the warmth of its clustering berries is surpassed by the blood-red brilliance of its leaves. This is the 'blessed quicken wood', that has power against the spirits of evil. It grows here and there among birches and firs, as a rule singly, and sometimes higher than either, a solitary bush by the rivulet in a ravine.

October is the coloured month here, far more brilliant than June, blazing more sharply than August. From the gold of the birches and bracken on the low slopes, the colour spurts upwards through all the creeping and inconspicuous growths that live among the heather roots – mosses that are lush green, or oak-brown, or scarlet, and the berried plants, blaeberry, cranberry, crowberry and the rest. Blaeberry leaves are a flaming crimson, and they are loveliest of all in the Rothiemurchus Forest, where the fir trees were felled in the 1914 War, and round and out of each stump blaeberry grows in upright sprigs; so that in October a multitude of pointed flames seem to burn upwards all over the moor.

This forest blazed with real fire in the early summer of 1920. One of the gamekeepers told me that forty of them were on the watch for ten days and nights, to keep the fire from spreading. And by night, he said, the tree trunks glowed like pillars of fire.

Not much is left now of this great pine forest. Yet in the glens that run up into the mountain, there are still a few of the very old firs that may have been the original Caledonian forest. Old trees still stand in Glen Einich, as they do at Ballochbuie on the other side of the mountain; and by the shores of Loch an Eilein, are a scatter of enormous venerable Scots firs, their girth two and a half times the span of my (quite long) arms, the flakes of their bark a foot and a half in length and thick as books, their roots, exposed where the soil has been washed away above the path, twisted and intertwined like a cage of snakes. Here and there also, notably by the sluice gates at the exit of Loch Einich, can be seen, half-sunk in the bog, numbers of the roots of trees long perished.

This sluice dates, like those on other of the lochs, to the late eighteenth century, when the ancient wood rang with the activity of the fellers. The trunks ready, the sluices were opened, and the trees guided down on the rush of water to the Spey. There is a vivid description of it, as a child remembered it, in Elizabeth Grant of Rothiemurchus's *Memoirs of a Highland Lady*. When the timber was first realised to be a source of wealth, and felled, small sawmills were erected on the various burns – tiny clearings, with the saw, a but and a ben and a patch of corn; but soon it was found more profitable to float all the timber downstream to the Spey, where it was made into rough rafts and so carried to Fochabers and Garmouth. The very sites of these ancient sawmills are forgotten. Today come the motor lorries, the sawmill and all its machinery making a compact township for the time that it is required; and outsiders, not the men of the place, fell and lop and cut. Only the old ways still linger here and there as where a native horse, tended by a man deep-rooted in the place, drags the chained trunks down from inaccessible corners, and is led back for the night to one of the ancient farms on the edge of the moor.

The first great cutting of the forest took place during the

Napoleonic wars, when home-grown timber was urgently required. A century later we have seen the same thing happen. In 1914 and again, and more drastically, in 1940, the later wood has gone the way of the former. It will grow again, but for a while the land will be scarred and the living things – the crested tits, the shy roe deer – will flee. I tremble especially for the crested tit, whose rarity is a proud distinction of these woods.

I have heard people say that they have watched in vain for these exquisite tits, but, if you know their haunts (I shall not give them away), they can be conjured easily from a tree by simply standing still against its trunk. You have heard the stir and small sound of tits, but at your approach they are gone, there is not a bird to see. But stand quite still, and in a minute or two they forget you, and flit from branch to branch close to your head. I have seen a crested tit turn itself around not a foot from my eye. In the nesting season, however, they will scold like fishwives. I have been scolded at by a pair of them with such vehemence that in pure shame for them I have left their tree.

How fierce was the rush of water when the ancient sluices on the lochs were opened, an eighty-year-old woman made plain to me when she told me how it was once used to outwit the gauger. For a drop of the mountain dew was made on the far side of the Beinnie, in a thick place beneath Carn Elrig where I once lost my path; and when the man who made it had the word passed to him that the gauger was on the way, he had no time to hide the stuff. Indeed, then, when the word came to him, he was nearer the sluice than the still, and to the sluice he went – I can see him *spangin'* on, heel to the ground, with the loping stride of the Highlander bent on business. So when the exciseman came, turbulent water raced between him and the drop whisky. And no crossing it that day at the least. Nor perhaps the next.

Gaunt remains of pine trees high on the mountain sides show

that the earlier forest went further up than the present forest does. Yet here and there a single seed, wind borne or dropped by a bird, has grown far above the main body of the trees. Some of these out-liers show the amazing adaptability of this tree. They can change their form at need, like any wizard. I know one, rooted a few paces from a 2900 feet summit, a sturdy plant but splayed to the mountains and almost roseate in structure, three feet across and not more than five inches in height. There it clings, plastered against the arid ground. I shall watch with much interest to see how much larger it will grow, and in what direction.

Dead fir roots, left in the soil long after the tree is gone, make the best kindling in the world. I know old women who look with the most utter contempt on paper as a fire-lighter and scorn to use more than one match to set a fire going. I know two such old women, both well over eighty, both living alone, one on the Spey side of the mountains and one on the Dee, who howk their fir roots on the moor, drag them home and splinter them. Then you may watch them, if you visit their frugal homes when the fire is out, build the *rossity reets* (we call them that on the Aberdeenshire side) into a pyramid with their brown hard wrinkled fingers, fill the kettle with a cup from a pail of well water, hang it on the *swye* and swing it over the blazing sticks. And before you have settled to your *newse* the tea is made, and if the brown earthenware teapot has a broken spout ('my teapot has lost a tooth'), and tea splutters from it on to the open hearth and raises spurts of ash and steam, you can call it a *soss* or a libation to the gods as you feel inclined, but it will not make the tea less good nor the talk less racy.

Of the inconspicuous things that creep in heather, I have a special affection for stagmoss – nor the hard braided kind but the fuzzy kind we call 'toadstails'. I was taught the art of picking these by my father when I was a small child. We lay on the heather and my fingers learned to feel their way along each separate trail and side branch, carefully detaching each tiny root, until we had thick bunchy pieces many yards long. It was a good art to teach a child. Though I did not know it then, I was learning my way in, through my own fingers, to the secret of growth.

That secret the mountain never quite gives away. Man is slowly learning to read it. He watches, he ponders, patiently he adds fact to fact. He finds a hint of it in the 'formidable' roots of the moss campion and in the fine roots that the tiny eyebright sends into the substance of the grass to ease its own search for food. It is in the glaucous and fleshy leaves of the sedums and the saxifrages, through which they store the bounty of the earth against the times when the earth is not bountiful. It is in the miniature size of the smallest willow, whose woolly fluff blows about the bogs. And in the miniature azalea that grows splayed against the mountain for protection, and lures the rare insects by its rosy hue, and flourishes, like the heather, on granite; whereas granite cannot meet the needs of many of the rare mountain flowers, that crave the streaks of limestone, or the rich humus of the micaschist – like that rarest of all, found in only one spot in the Cairngorms, the alpine milk-vetch, its delicate pale bloom edged with lavender, haunted by its red-and-black familiar the Burnet moth: why so haunted no one knows, but no milk-vetch, no Burnet moth. On a wet windy sunless day, when moths would hardly be expected to be visible at all, we have found numbers of these tart little creatures on the milk-vetch clumps

The more one learns of this intricate interplay of soil, altitude, weather, and the living tissues of plants and insect (an intricacy that has its astonishing moments, as when sundew and butterwort eat the insects), the more the mystery deepens. Knowledge does not dispel mystery. Scientists tell me that the alpine flora of the Scottish mountains is Arctic in origin – that these small scattered plants have outlived the Glacial period and are the only vegetable life in our country that is older than the Ice Age. But that doesn't explain them. It only adds time to the equation and gives it a new dimension. I find I have a naive faith in my scientist friends – they are such jolly people, they wouldn't fib to me unnecessarily, and their stories make the world so interesting. But my imagination boggles at this. I can imagine the antiquity of rock, but the antiquity of a living flower – that is harder. It means that these toughs of the mountain top, with their angelic cunning and the effrontery to cheat, not only a winter, but an Ice Age. The scientists have the humility to acknowledge that they don't know how it has been done.

Nan Shepherd (1893–1981)

A novelist and lecturer, Nan Shepherd was born in Deeside. She graduated from Aberdeen University and lectured in English at what is now Aberdeen College of Education. An enthusiastic gardener and hill-walker, she was a keen member of the Deeside Field Club and made many visits to the Cairngorms. Though widely travelled in Europe and South Africa, she remained devoted to the house in which she grew up and spent most of her adult life, three miles from Aberdeen. The Living Mountain *was published in 1996 as part of* The Grampian Quartet. *'Life: The Plants',* The Living Mountain *(Canongate Books, 2008).*

THE STREAM

HENRY WILLIAMSON

Away from the last house – West End Farm, where I made my first and last barrel of cider – the stream became wild again, marked by the green growth of rushes, meadowsweet, yellow flag-lilies, and umbelliferous plants. On the north-west slope sheep fed on very green grass growing below the duct or ditch which led from the village cesspool. Above the duct could be seen another field, and then the village school, built above the lane which leads down to Vention Sands.

Sometimes a heron stood on the rushy ground, overlooking the stream, which now in places was a yard wide. The water was clear in the sunshine. Children coming home from school wandered by the banks, plucking flowers of ragged robin, and yellow irises; gathering watercress, too, the leaves of which were not so strong and dark as those growing under the sinister patch of green grass higher up the valley side. Queer little fish with big heads and fore-fins like arms clung to the stones of the bed, coloured pale brown like the algae – mullheads, or loach, which ate the dead-leaf-nibbling grubs whose coverings of stick and stone fragment were gummed to their bodies. Trout and eels eat the loach; and one summer evening, while wandering down the 'river' (as Ernie called it), exploring it from source to sea, I saw a satisfying sight. An eel even longer than Revvy's arm was waving in the bright shallow water, waving and sinuating from its head buried under a stone.

I imagined the mullhead wriggling its way under a stone, following a stick-caddis grub; the eel, smelling the mullhead down the stream, moving up silently, following the scent washed down. I had seen eels moving up a brook to the entrails of a rabbit, thrown away by someone in Ham whose house was near the stream, probably Mrs Revvy Carter, or Alice of Hole Farm, or Clib the grave-digger and postman.

The eel quested like a mute hound in the water. Slowly it burrowed under the stone, its body rippling with the strength of eagerness. I had been dozing on the bank, freeing myself from village confinements into the light and warmth of one of the rare and lovely west-wind days, when time is truly the sunshine; and keeping very still, was watching the behaviour of the fishes. Then, above the idle murmur of the stream in the hovers of the banks, I heard a noise as of a dog shaking its coat, followed by the sound of a heavy animal rolling in the rushes just below me. The west wind blew up the valley, otherwise the otter would not have been so careless. Wondering when he would see me, I kept as still as I could: it seemed that he must detect my body swaying from the waist, hear the breath in my mouth, and certainly start and sink away silently in the water at the noise of my swallowing. But no, he leaned down to drink. I saw alertness come into the loose brown form. The head appeared to sharpen from the nose, the whiskers sensitive to the water-writhing of the eel; for the otter, at the low angle, could not have seen it in the water beyond the cattle-broken bay where it stood on its low webbed feet.

It slipped so silently into the water, scarcely six inches deep by the bay, that I thought it must have seen me, and was crouching still under the bank; but craning my neck, I saw it swimming up to the eel. Then it was standing on its hind-legs on a mossy stone, with a black knot writhing from its mouth, and looking at me. This was the first time I had seen a wild otter so near, other than an otter hunted by hounds. It did not remain staring at me long, but dropped out of sight in the stream, the eel still in its mouth. I followed it, wanting to know if it was afraid; it ran through the rushes and up the slope of the hill, through a hedge, and into a small larch plantation, which I called Goldcrackey Spinney, since gold-crackeys, or golden-crested wrens, nested in the larches every spring. The plantation was overgrown with brambles, and although I peered and poked I did not see the otter again. It must have been used to sleeping there by day in a larger rabbit hole, for it ran to the spinney directly.

THE OLD TROUT

HENRY WILLIAMSON

The best time to see him is in the morning about ten o'clock, any day during a spell of fine weather between April and September. He lies a few yards above the bridge, at the edge of the stream which runs over the gravel and the deeper water of the pool. By stream is meant the swifter defined course of the water moving between the river banks; for if you look at a brook or river which has its sources in moorland – and is therefore bedded with rock or gravel, and subject to spates – you will see that it seldom runs consistently. Trout usually feed in the stream or run, leading into, and out of, the deeper water which is their refuge from danger. There is seldom any food in a pool; so fish seldom feed there.

When first I saw the old trout, he was big-headed, dark and thin. He weighed about a pound. He was old, eight or nine years. A trout is in its prime at three and a half years. He was slow; he could not compete for flies and nymphs with the more lively fish; he was probably an occasional cannibal.

When I put some Lock Leven fish into the river, I was advised to feed them for a while with the food on which they had been reared in the hatchery pits at Dulverton. Released from the confining tanks, the new bluish-green fish leapt and splashed and rolled in the cold water; while the old brown trout waggled his tail and moved into the obscurity of the pool. He was not seen again for several weeks.

Meanwhile the Loch Leven trout lived in the pool, awaiting spoonfuls of food about noon, when usually my accustomed figure appeared above the parapet of the bridge. In the afternoon and evening they took up positions in the run at the bend above, awaiting spinners and sedges which dropped their eggs before sunset. This food changed their yellow-brown spots to red, and their green-blue backs became tinged with gold.

During the first summer the old wild trout became less shy, but he would not take the artificial food. The Loch Leven fish grew quickly, developing thick shoulders and deep flanks. One grew from five ounces to a pound in two months.

When September came, and the sea-trout began to rise up to spawn, the Lock Leven trout went with them. They were away for two months.

The winter was mild, with little rain; and I was able to feed the returned fish about four days a week. Normally a trout feeds hardly at all during the winter; it exists in a state of semi-hibernation; frost numbs it, and food is scarce. Very soon wild brown trout and salmon parr were waiting with Loch Leven trout for the showers of artificial food. While elsewhere in the river the pools held lank and listless trout and discoloured salmon, the Bridge Pool whenever I appeared was aflip and aswirl with keen fish; native brown trout turning greenish-blue and alien Loch Levens looking like fairer brown trout. A trout's colour and shape are determined by its feeding.

The old trout remained aloof, although sometimes he would

cruise among the lively shoal, swish his tail as though excited by his daring, and then drift into deeper water again. Perhaps he had been hooked a few years before, and had not forgotten it. Trout are as timid as rabbits.

Otters regularly travelled up the river during the winter, but the trout remained. I knew when they came, because all otters left the river above the second waterfall and touched at an ant-hill, the grass of which was always killed in a dry winter. When spring came, and the otters hunted salmon in the lower pools, that ant-hill was the greenest thing in the deer park; it was a Golgotha of eels' bones. Now eels are the most destructive things in a trout fishery; they eat much caddis and stone-fly creeper, and they eat the eggs and fry of trout, and the trout themselves if they can get a grip on them.

During May I bought an eel-trap, and having baited it with the head, feet and entrails of a hen, I put it by some alder roots in the bank above the bridge.

The next morning I saw something moving in the cylinder of galvanised wire netting lying on the bed of the river and, running down from the bridge to the bank below, I hauled on the rope. The trap came up dripping with weed. It shook with the flaps of a dark-brown spotted fish within. It was the old brownie. Five other smaller trout were with him. The bait was uneaten.

The head of the trap which had lain upstream was choked with weed, and I realised that the trout had swum up through the narrow one-way funnel not for food, but for shelter. A trout loves a hole where it can hide with sufficient water passing to enable it to breathe.

I lugged the trap to the grass, and opening the door, allowed the fish to slither out. The small trout jumped about on the grass, but the old fellow, who had the head and jaws of a crocodile, began to writhe through the grass towards the river. As he seemed to need no help, I let him continue until his nose stuck in some soft mud made by the feet of cattle. Then, having wetted my hand lest the touch scald him, I eased him into the river. He swam forward, his snout tipped with mud. Having put the other fish back into the water, I ran back to the bridge, to see what the big fish would do.

A spoonful of food, and at once the water was rocking; jaws were snapping, tails swishing on the broken surface. To my surprise the old trout, hitherto so sluggish and suspicious, was quicker than the others. He raised a wave as he came downstream, he made a slashing rise as he leapt to take a piece of floating food before the opening mouth of a Loch Leven fish. I threw in more food. He cut and swirled after it. The mud was still on his snout. He behaved as a dog behaves when released from its mournful wait at the end of a chain; as a boy when released from the class-room of an inefficient master; as an innocent man reprieved from death.

In this sentimentality, is this 'humanising' the emotions of the fish? I saw a fish behaving as I would have behaved had I been the fish. And from that moment the old trout ceased to be shy of my presence on the bridge. He always came down with the others when he saw me, to await the exciting food showers. He had no feeling for me, of course: but the excitation had unsluggished him, he had behaved recklessly on return to the water, taken the food, liked it, and wanted more.

As summer advanced more fish joined that little watery Band of Hope, including salmon parr and one or two small peel (sea-trout), which, escaping the 36 nets working two hours before and two hours after every low tide, ran up from the sea in their silver-spotted dresses during an August freshet.

How well-behaved they were! Each fish in its place, maintaining order of precedence, the old reformed cannibal at their head, where he could get (theoretically) the pick of each cast. Sometimes the cast spoonful fell short and he came down speedily to claim his rights.

He lost his dark colour; his flanks became a light golden hue, the dull red pennant of his adipose fin became a lively vermilion. His big blue-black head changed to brown, and no longer looked too big. He lay beside the fingerling trout, rejuvenated and benevolent. The fishy paradise, or millennium, had arrived.

Herons regularly fish the water, often from one sunrise to another at midsummer. They fly at intervals and in succession up the valley. Each heron has his particular fishing place. Some of these places are common to all. Like the trout taking his stance in the stream where the food is most plentiful, so the heron stands in shallow water on a jut of mossy rock at the tail of an eddy, where the trout await the hatching nymphs.

On many occasions as I went towards the river 50 yards distant from the park gates, the slight metallic sound of the latch being lifted would be heard and a big grey bird arise from beside the Bridge Pool.

While otters in a trout stream are, in my opinion, good for a fishery because of the great number of eels they catch, herons are almost entirely destructive. The heron is a thin, lanky creature, with an enormous appetite; he stands still for long periods awaiting the return of the fingerling trout and the fry, which were scared by his great gliding wings descending and closing. He takes them with a lightning thrust of his sharp yellow beak. I have found sea-trout of 10 lbs and more killed by herons, who cannot possibly eat them, but merely stab them for sport or devilment. Do not deduce from this that I hate herons; I like seeing them in the estuary, where there is enough food for all.

You may imagine my feelings when day after day, at intervals of about an hour or so, heron after heron came up the river and stood motionless in the shallow water at the edge of the pool where the Loch Levens were lying.

All the summer I fed the trout; they came as usual; but I noticed that the smaller wild trout and the salmon parr which had joined them were missing. One morning when I looked over the bridge I saw the old trout moving very slowly to the deeper water where the salmon lay, a strange bluish mark at the back of his head. By the aid of my glass I saw that the back of his head had been pierced in two places, about three-quarters of an inch apart.

The wounds were, I judged, an inch deep. The next morning two herons flew up. I found one of the Loch Leven trout dying in the pool. Two mornings later the pair was there again; a pound-and-a-half fish lay on the sandy scour, with marks as of shears pressed on its head and flanks, where the bird had tried vainly to swallow it.

I kept watch, and learnt that at least nine herons were fishing all day and most of the night along my beat. They would take from it in one day what I might take in one year. 'Old Williamson,' I imagined them saying, 'is all right; he's written most sympathetically about herons. Old Nog, you know, and that melodramatic nonsense. Time he restocked this water again, don't you think?'

The old trout did not feed any more with the other fish. He grew thinner. His wound spread into a black patch towards his tail. Once, when he came directly under the bridge, I saw that he was becoming blind. He was slowly starving to death. He could not take the food I broadcast; the other fish were too quick.

Snails and slugs were collected from the garden, and lobbed over for him. He ate some of the slugs, and seemed a little more lively afterwards. I thought of netting him, but that was illegal; besides, the trout-rearing pond in my garden, where it might be possible to pension him off, had been silted up by a neighbouring farmer's ducks.

One day, however, occurred something which can only be

described as an act of benevolent and inscrutable Providence. As I walked around a tree by the waterfall one of those nine herons fell down dead before me. I skinned the bird; put part of him through the mincing machine; made the mince into little meatballs; tossed them into the water, well above the old trout. He took them slowly at first, and then with more agility. Providence was again kind to us, for the very next day another heron fell down dead before me. The rissoles lasted for four days. And thenceforward the big trout began to get lighter in colour as his eyesight became clearer. In three weeks he was strong and well again.

He remained above the bridge until the spate of February last, after which I saw him no more. Perhaps he went down to the sea and grew into one of those big spotted sea-trout called pugs.

Henry Williamson (1895–1977)

A writer and journalist who was brought up in London, Henry Williamson served in the British Army between 1914 and 1918, and was profoundly affected by the war. His first published work was The Flax of Dream *(1921–28).* Tarka the Otter *won the Hawthornden Prize of 1928. He lived in north Norfolk and north Devon, and completed his 15-part saga,* A Chronicle of Ancient Sunlight *(begun in 1951), with* The Gale of the World *in 1969.*

'The Stream' and 'The Old Trout', from Life in a Devon Village *(Faber & Faber, 1945) and* The Linhay on the Downs *(Alan Sutton, 1984).*

THE BRAAN SALMON

KATHLEEN JAMIE

What you notice when you enter the little chamber is the roaring of the waterfalls. It's much louder inside than out. The chamber – they call it Ossian's Hall – is built on a rocky bluff, which reaches out over the falls. A damp, elegant room, it opens onto a half-moon balcony, and you can stand on the balcony admiring the scene as the spray and updraught dampens your face. Apparently, in its heyday, a couple of hundred years ago, the walls were lined with mirrors to reflect the falls, so the Duke of Atholl and his guests could enjoy the sublime river sound and the peat-tinged, spumy water cascading all about them. A little Romantic eco-art installation.

The Braan, a highland river, is short, fast and rocky. Tall Douglas firs and beeches grow from its banks. Directly below the balcony, the river folds itself down between buttresses of rock. The drop is not great, no more than 20 feet in total – it's hard to judge from above. But today the water was hammering down at a tremendous force. The salmon have to jump against the weight of water. You don't have to wait long, leaning out over the balcony rails, before you see a salmon hurl itself out of the foam, into the useless air, only to drop back. The length of a man's arm, or a woman's arm, they try again, two, three, four at a time, only to be dashed back. For a long moment they hang on the air, like dancers. It was said of Nijinsky that, when he leapt, he seemed to stop in mid-air, and the fish do that: leap, hold themselves in the air, pink bellies and speckled green backs, then fall back to vanish with a twist into the foam as the river crashes over the falls, and the spray dampens your face. From this balcony, this viewpoint, we can be as concerned or as indifferent as gods. Mostly we're concerned.

A photographer arrived with a tripod. We had to bend in toward each other to make out the other's words, but he told me he was teaching a week-long photography course and, sure enough, from among the trees on the river bank a half-dozen photographers with woolly hats and tripods quietly appeared. Below us, the salmon continued to jump and fall. As the photographer twisted the legs of his tripod into place, he said, 'Amazing, isn't it? I wonder how often they can try before they're exhausted. Suppose it's the real survival of the fittest. If they don't make it then ... Ho! Did you see that one?'

'Ho!' is what we say when one of the salmon leaps. Ho! – a coinage somewhere between noble and heroic. I asked the photographer if he specialised in wildlife, and he said something I couldn't make out. Was it 'wildscapes'? Did he tell me that in the winter he went to Finland to do bears?

Birch leaves were twirling down into the water. The rocks in the middle of the river were patted with their gentle shapes. The leaves twirled down, landed on the water, then were swept away merrily over the falls and away. There was a lull, then Ho! – a leaping fish.

Once down the falls the water packs into a narrow linn and

travels at speed until it's released into a wide pool. Spume swirls over the surface. There must be fish in there, backed up, feeling the water, waiting to move up to the front. On my way here, I'd passed a hapless lad with a fishing rod who was being questioned by two gruff men in green Barbour jackets. One had a notebook. The lad stood uncertainly between the bailiffs.

I read somewhere that before the invention of the bicycle, the salmon was the most efficient machine on the planet, power to weight. My bike was leaning against a tree, outside the little chamber. The photographer asked, 'This you going on your regular round? Bit of gut-thrashing on the bike, then replenish the soul here?'

'Something like that.'

Away from the river, a pleasing silence fell. Siskins were working the trees. I cycled upriver a short way, below trees and out over some rough grazing, to the next bridge, Rumbling Bridge, where I leaned the bike on the parapet and looked down at the river. Something about the salmon was bothering me. Wherever I went today, be it cycling or fetching the kids from school, watching the telly, or going to bed, they'd still be there, hurling themselves out of the water into the spray-filled air, empty air. What, I was wondering, were we admiring with all our Ho!-ing? Their apparent heroism? Their endeavour? What we're pleased to call the human spirit. It seemed nature was prepared to wager the whole salmon project on a few individuals who can Ho! and keep on Ho!-ing until somehow they got up over the falls and back to their spawning grounds.

Kathleen Jamie

Kathleen Jamie is an award-winning Scottish author, poet and lecturer in Creative Writing at St Andrews University. Her many writings on nature include The Tree House *(winner of the 2004 Forward prize), and* Findings, *a groundbreaking book based in Scotland that merges the very best of travel and nature writing.*

'*The Braan Salmon*', *from* Findings *(Sort of Books, 2005).*

SHEARWATERS

RONALD LOCKLEY

Each evening, long before sun dropped into the Atlantic Ocean, from March to August, many thousands of shearwaters gathered upon the sea between the islands of Skokholm and Skomer. On fine days it was pure delight for us to sail out to the rafts, trailing a line for mackerel and pollack. The shearwaters might be fishing, too, making their short dives after whitebait which the mackerel were chasing: in the clear water you could see their wings were half-closed – a strong fan or paddle to winnow their way under the water. But most of the time the shearwaters floated, perfectly idle, perfectly silent, waiting for the darkness, a marvellous magic carpet spread over quarter of a square mile of slow-swelling sea. The nearest flocks took wing languidly as the *Storm-Petrel* glided close: ten thousand pied bodies swerved low and tilted over, now white, now ebony in the rosy westward light.

The shearwaters were thickest on land during the blackest, stormiest, spring midnights, roaring home with wailing songs, and spending much time in scuffling outside the burrow, gossiping, disputing, settling their love affairs. Despite the bedlam there were differences in individual calls. I became convinced that the birds recognised each other in the darkness by voice in the first place, and until they made contact physically. How else could they (or for that matter we humans) know each other at a distance in the black void?

It was significant that on moonlit nights fewer shearwaters came home, and always without calling. Were they afraid of the island gulls, which could see and kill them on a bright night, when these predators sleep but lightly? On such nights the homing shearwater could see the burrows of its home colony clearly enough. It would fly silently straight to its hole and disappear immediately; once below it might give voice, in a connubial conversation with its mate, or in disputing territory with an intruder.

But, I was puzzled by the fact that on dark nights the incoming screaming shearwater often got no response from its mate, either because it was not at home, or because when at home its mate did not always reply. Why scream at all? Was it solely from its desire to warn its mate of its arrival and get a welcoming voice in reply; was it just uninhibited *joie de vivre*; or was it also for some other reason?

It was a long time before I realised that one important explanation for the silence on a clear night – and the continuous screaming on dark nights – of the in-flying bird approaching its nesting area, must be associated with the fact that the shearwater can see in the dark no more than we can. I came to believe that the shearwater uses a form of echo-location. Like the near-blind bat uttering its ultrasonic trill, or the oil-bird of Central America and edible-nest swiftlets of Malaysia, which both give forth clicking notes in the utter darkness of their nesting caves, is the shearwater able to judge its distance from objects in the dark by receiving back from the contours of those objects (that is, the land) the echoes of its own screams, echoes whose specific audio-patterns it has learned from previous experience, and those patterns now stored in its memory cells? First of all, perhaps, the loud cries of the incoming bird are reflected back from the main corners of the land, enabling the bird to judge by sound memory its nearness and so prevent collision. Then, circling nearer the home burrows, it picks up the familiar voice echoes of the nesting area, and at last plumps down on the turf.

Waiting beside my back-door colony on many a pitch-dark night, I was amazed at the accuracy with which each of my marked birds screamed its way to alight within a few feet of its burrow, which it could not see. Once on the ground the incoming bird invariably rested a minute or so. After the freedom of flying through the air at 30 to 50 miles an hour it needed to adjust to the solidity of land in the darkness. I could imagine it thinking: 'Well, I'm somewhere near home. Let me see – my bump of location tells me to turn left here, then a little bit up hill by this old rabbit-track – then I'm home. I wish my mate below would sing out.' But, whether there was a mate at home to guide it with invitatory cackles from below ground, or not, the new arrival would waddle solemnly into its burrow, feeling its way on foot with that strong sense of direction, or memory of geographical position, which most creatures seem to have.

Ronald Lockley (1903–2000)

A distinguished field naturalist and one of Britain's foremost authorities on sea birds, Ronald Lockley lived for 13 years on the island of Skokholm, off the Pembrokeshire coast; for the first years entirely on his own. His neighbours were some 10,000 rabbits and 80,000 birds, and his sojourn with them ultimately resulted in his published studies: Shearwaters *and* Puffins, *as well as* The Private Life of the Rabbit. *His work on the island contributed greatly to a better understanding of the migration of Shearwaters in particular, and formed part of the basis for his study:* Animal Navigation.

'Shearwaters', from The Island *(Andre Deutsch, 1969).*

TO THE RIVER

STEVE BACKSHALL

A couple of years back, I broke my back and destroyed my ankle in a rock-climbing accident. By a twist of fate I've since found walking painful and rarely do it for fun, but have managed to fulfil my need for the outdoors with kayaking, much of which has been done on the stretch of the Thames that runs through Oxfordshire, Buckinghamshire and Berkshire – a stretch I have come to see as my own. Through these last few years, the changing Thames has become my friend and saviour; reviving my spirits regardless of season or weather, comforting me with the familiar, thrilling with the spectacular. It's also the place where I can experience total solitude with nature, just ten minutes or so from town.

As the year begins, the river runs full and dark, but as the beech woods echo bleakly and the fields around are set firm against the frosts, my river still bristles with life. Sunrise, before the rest of the world wakes, a thick mist seethes over the surface of the water. It looks like the steaming surface of a giant witch's cauldron, boiling with sinister potions. As my kayak passes, the wake undulates to the reed beds, and the crispy ice audibly creaks and cracks within. Coots and moorhens are startled from their slumber, and scamper out onto the river, tufted ducks cluster together in huge flotillas, their piercing golden eyes regarding me as I pass. And there's more exotic still; after original jailbreaks in West London, ring-necked parakeets push further and further upstream every year, and from the bare branches and watery skies their shrill calls pierce the morning. By now I know the local kingfishers by name. One in particular I name Clive, after a particularly nervy and dopey schoolmate. Every morning as I paddle upstream, Clive is startled from his hunting perch, and dashes ahead of me chitting a warning call, only to pause on another perch no more than 50 metres ahead. A few seconds later I frighten him again and he bounces upstream again, a constant colourful herald until I turn tail and head downstream.

Sometimes I want to take the birds aside and give them a good talking to. You can always tell the immature swans even before noticing their less than perfect plumage, as they try and flee from boats by frantically paddling straight ahead, following the exact same line as the boats are taking. This hectic chase lasts an age until they finally take to panicked flight and head to a totally different part of the river. More experienced adult swans just leisurely swim a few metres sideways, effortlessly avoiding confrontation. Sometimes winter can bring mornings of extraordinary beauty. The bare trees, reeds and fields encrusted in frost, it looks as if the whole world has been sugar-coated. Even better, when the snows turned our countryside into Narnia, the air danced with diamond dust, piercing blue skies and wedding cake trees and hills reflected perfectly in the river. When I heard people on the radio talking about the 'terrible weather', it was all I could do to stop myself phoning in and begging the whole blind population to come and join me on my river. But actually I'd rather put up with the whingeing and keep the river to myself. I paddle on in an eerie silence; wherever the water falls on my paddle or deck it freezes instantly, but even frostbite can't wipe the stupefied grin off my face!

Spring is by far my favourite time on the river. Is there another sight in British wildlife to equal the dances of the Great Crested Grebe, or even the simple symmetry as a cob and pen swan flirt with each other? Suddenly the familiar friends (the cormorant with the grey throat-patch the shape of Africa, who perches on the same dead log seemingly year round) are bolstered by arriving migrants and occasional vagrants (surely the egret I saw here last summer was a little off course?). One avian soap opera plays out in front of me, as one of last year's cygnets is victimised by a rampaging territorial cob. He drives him underwater, rips out his feathers, and would have killed him in front of me. I know I shouldn't intervene, but my soft side takes over, and I drive them apart with my kayak. The youngster is close to death, but still manages enough energy to flap away from me through Marlow churchyard as I try to catch him amongst the gravestones. Eventually he is pinned, and I drive down to Windsor Swan Rescue with him tucked under one arm, shivering with terror. Several months later, he is well fed and recovered and returns to the river, hopefully wiser to the bullies of the banks.

Tumultuous spring rains swell the river, and in some places it bursts banks, spilling over in to the surrounding fields. Suddenly, paddling upriver is not so much fun, but heading for home I feel like a porpoising sea lion, rocketing along with the current. As spring begins in earnest, every time I get the boat out I'm anxious to resolve itching questions: Will the reed buntings and reed warblers return to grace the Phragmites above Marlow this year? Why did those whistling red kites above Temple desert their nest when it was looking so promising? Will those grebes that nested right by Cliveden manage as phenomenal a success as last year in raising their chicks? Riverside flowers bloom, butterflies and bees get busy, mining bees make multiple tunnels on sunny side banks, and night paddles are to the tune of constantly calling tawnies, and even (once) a phantom barn owl in my head-torch beam. And then, as the weather warms, the big spectacles of the river begin, with the coming of the insects.

First notable emergence is the smallest of the caddis flies; they've lived as nymphs underwater protected in casings of silk and twigs or pebbles, but once they metamorphose as winged adults they flutter weakly over the water like lost micro-moths. Remarkably for a species so bound to the water, some clumsily crash onto the surface and, with sodden wings, waste their meagre opportunity to mate. The first dazzling emergences though come later, as the various species of mayflies burst free from their watery kindergarten. On a sunny day in late May or early June, they leap and fall like golden sprites, filamentous tails trailing behind them seeking only a mate from their few airborne hours. Suddenly the air is filled with 'csree csree' calls to arms, and a squadron of impossibly rapid swifts like near silent Spitfires courses across the water snatching the bounty. I say near silent, as apart from the flight calls, you can hear the wind across their wings, almost like the swooping of a sword in a Bruce Lee movie. Even better, for the last few years hobbies have nested somewhere near Hurley weir (I haven't managed to find out where), and they are without equal at hunting on the wing. The sight of them whipping over the water, snatching a flying meal from right over the deck of my kayak in divine dusk light, remains one of my all-time wildlife highlights.

Green woodpeckers are one of the most oft-heard birds, their call sounding somewhat like a goshawk who's trying to call while gargling a mouthful of water. The 'yaffles' though don't seem to like flying across the water; though I hear them every day I can't recall having seen one fly over the river. The mallards are indulging in some of the most brutal sex imaginable right now, drakes pinning their females by the neck, driving them underwater. They'll also viciously rape other males, which is one of the most disturbing sights of the riverbank. Strange that one of our most twee and tame-seeming species has such a dark side.

Summertime, and all of a sudden the rest of the world discovers my river. Fair-weather ramblers throw sticks for lolloping chocolate Labradors, and pleasure boaters in bright-orange life jackets, who can't keep to the speed limits, flood my kayak as I pass. It's back to early-morning paddles when the water is smooth and the floating gin-palace owners are still laid up recovering from Pimm's hangovers. Sometimes I'm lucky enough to catch Clive the kingfisher diving for breakfast, but without a high-speed film camera it's no more than a blur, a splash and a whirr of wings as he zips away with his meal. The big vocalists of the post-dawn singathon are skylarks in the surrounding fields, unbeatable blackbirds, various warblers like chiffchaff, and the yellowhammer. The yellowhammer's hurried and repetitive chant is rarely accompanied by a glimpse of the bird and, incidentally, what ornithologist was it who decided they're singing 'A little bit of bread and no cheese'? And what does that even mean? Sometimes birders can be just plain bonkers!

I don't tend to see much of the herpeto-fauna as I cruise past in my kayak, so the sinuous form of a grass snake sliding across the surface is a real treat, head held up out of the water like a breast-stroking, bathing-capped octogenarian lady at the seaside. He reaches the bank and is gone, but my day has already been made.

The next big bug story is among the dragonfly order. While the fearsome hawkers zip about the heaths and hedgerows in the surrounding countryside, the riversides are home to more decorative, but perhaps less robust fliers. The banded demoiselles are perhaps the most dramatic, looking for all the world as if they've been spray-painted at the Aston Martin factory in metallic racing green. And then there's the azure and the red damselflies, zipping to and fro, many clasped in a copulation wheel as they seek to assure parentage of their offspring. The violent ducks are by now well afloat with their precocial train of fluffy ducklings. It's a sad sight as the summer days lengthen and you see the families dwindle – lost to causes unknown. I can't imagine a full brood ever makes it to maturity, with so many dangers abounding on this busy, wild highway.

Red kites twirl above me every time I go outside these days, but it's still impossible to take them for granted. And any time I think I may be missing their magnificence, I make sure to take my binoculars out with me; it's easy to forget from their familiar silhouette that red kites would rival any raptor in the world for colourfulness of plumage, and perfection of gliding flight. Buzzards, kestrels and sparrowhawks too hunt regularly along this stretch of Thames, the pickings both seen and unseen must be rich indeed.

Autumn brings a little sadness, as some fast friends depart, but has its benefits, too. The changing colours of the trees at the hanging gardens of Cliveden, reflected in still waters, would have to be my most perfect autumn vista in the world (best viewed heading upstream by the way). And as the summer visitors pack their bags, numbers of geese and ducks swell, including exotic harlequin ducks and Egyptian geese. Always overhead the red kites twirl and circle, though they don't seem to bother so much with their thin whistling calls now the business of finding a mate and building a family is done. In pelting autumn rain-storms, the winds and currents make kaleidoscope patterns on the water surface, some parts remaining smooth as if untouched, others milky with bouncing raindrops. I work harder to raise my body temperature, enjoy the solitude the weather affords, pity the rain-battered ducks and look forward to a hot shower and a cuppa on my return home.

Throughout the year, my work as a naturalist presenter takes me around the world, to the most exotic and treasured wildlife hotspots imaginable, but more and more I yearn to return. I mourn the passing of a season when I'm away, or that I might miss the resolution of a little story on my river. Is it that, with my constant travelling, dipping in and out of disparate wild worlds, it's my depth of engagement with this stage and all its characters that makes it so special to me? Or could it be that with increasing years we come to truly value the world outside our window, that maturity teaches us to value history, friends, family, home, the familiar above all else? Perhaps a bit of both. But as I write this now, in the high Himalaya, as far away from England as it's possible to be ... there's a large piece of my heart that longs to be home, on my river.

Steve Backshall
Steve Backshall is a naturalist, writer and wildlife presenter; programmes include Britain's Lost World *and* The Nature of Britain. *He is the author of several books including* Steve Backshall's Deadly 60 *and* Steve Backshall's Wildlife Adventurer's Guide: A Guide to Exploring Wildlife in Britain.

AN APPOINTMENT WITH MRS MAXIMUS

NICK BAKER

I don't know what they're called – those little bobbly bits you grip betwixt your teeth on a snorkel. But, whatever they are referred to doesn't really matter; suffice to say, I bit them clean off! This startled action was promptly followed by a choking fit, partly brought on by the aforementioned and now detached rubber cubes hitting the back of my throat and partly by the realisation of what was swimming towards me, making me bite down with such force in the first place.

The emotions and core reflexes coursing through my body were not what one might expect to experience while taking a dip in Cornwall. I had to keep repeating to myself the mantra: '*This thing eats plankton; it eats plankton, just plankton.*'

This was how the sweetest, most awesome wildlife encounter of my life began, and as much as I loathe making lists and top-ten charts, this one beats them all, without any doubt. It knocks into a cocked hat all the other magical wildlife encounters that my fortunate life as a broadcasting naturalist has given me the opportunity to experience; this one relegates being charged by a Black Rhino, grunted at by a Mountain Gorilla, swimming with Manta Rays and even meeting Sir Dave; all down the list.

And why was this the big moment? Well, I like to think it was a seminal moment, not only meeting a spectacular creature but a truly British one – a Great British moment with a Great British fish in the Great British marine environment. This moment had it all and what made it all the sweeter? The fact that it didn't come easy – a moment made all the more poignant by its reluctance to happen, no matter how much time and effort I seemed to put in. It represents a lesson learned and a teaching that I've used everyday since.

Every naturalist has a bogey beast; that is, an animal whose close proximity to you seems to be inversely proportional to the amount of time, money, energy and resource that you throw at trying to arrange the encounter. I have many such bogey beasts, but one in particular stands out. No matter how much time or dedicated research I put into my personal quest to meet this creature, I just couldn't seem to spin my fortune; lady luck had turned deaf to my silent pleas that metamorphosed into cathartic shouts at the sky, that turned into slightly deranged self-aimed grumblings as I would journey home after yet another failed odyssey.

Being a boy, I've had a rather predictable fascination with the big and impressive, and this combined with a rather unrefined love of sharks, it probably comes as no surprise that I would be drawn to the second-largest fish loafing in the world's oceans. The basking shark was as a consequence high on my life list of things to see.

What made this seem like a relatively easy achievement other than its sheer size, was the fact that you didn't even have to get into it's habitat, displace a bubble or indeed even get a toe wet; basking sharks – I was informed by countless books, experts and societies concerned with the conservation and study of these behemoths – could be seen easily from the high cliffs and promontories of the south-west coast. Well, I live slap-bang in the middle of the said south-western peninsula or 'basking shark central', and all I had to do, it seems, was choose a nice flat, calm, sunny day, take a picnic, pack my binoculars and head for the coast.

This I did, many times. My diaries inform me now that I did this some 38 times over the period of about nine years, to be precise. My shark odysseys started out as a pleasant, solitary summer pursuit; you know the sort of thing; hazy lazy days pootling around the convoluted coasts of Devon and Cornwall, taking in a cream tea here and a quick dip there, between stints of several hours perched atop a rugged headland. When positioned on these panoramic vantage points, I would gaze expectantly at the twinkling sea, looking out for an even bigger flash of coruscated sunlight – this time from the triangular fin of my monster. But nothing flashed back, well at least nothing cartilaginous. I got a couple of dolphin sightings and several porpoise, so I had proved to myself that my technique wasn't too rusty. But where was lady luck? And, more to the point, where were my enigmatic elasmobranchs?

The routine of repeated failure plays heavy on the mind of a naturalist; you start to question your ability to read a situation; confidence sinks, self-doubt rules and then your ego chimes in with unhelpful statements of fact: 'Others are seeing them.' The *Western Morning News* ran a cover story of a shark coming so close to swimmers that they got photographs to prove it. Friends attempting to be helpful tip you off – they've just come back from surfing and saw several – and the local radio 'good news' end-piece tells us of record shoals numbering in the hundreds swimming into the western approaches. Great, I'm a failed fish-twitcher. I can't even find the second-biggest fish in the ocean.

These weekend forays of frustration started turning rapidly

into more organised strategic operations; the fewer sharks I saw, the more heavily I invested. Figuring eventually that I had to succeed, I started involving friends, radios and mobile phones, and the plans became more and more determined.

Various friends were posted on carefully selected promontories, with the instruction that if they even so much got a glimpse of dorsal fin they were to phone me. It happened a couple of times and breaking all rules of the road I would leave my cliff-top car park in a plume of Cornish dust as I raced as fast as my beaten-up Vauxhall and the dithering caravans and campers would allow, towards the hot tip-off, only to find that the fish had vanished from sight. It was only when I was shown some excellent photos of a six-metre shark taken minutes before I arrived and it vanished that I finally could bear it no longer. It seemed I was destined to never meet *Cetorhinus maximus*.

In the meantime, I had to content myself with adrenalin-soaked moments in the company of Mr Maximus' little cousin– the Great White shark.

While bobbing around in a vomit-inducing shark cage with the taste of rotten fish chum seeping in around my regulator, it occurred to me: *Of course*, why not get my career to do all the hard work? I could surely convince the broadcasters to plop me into the water with my wet dream?

On returning home from South Africa, meetings were arranged with the big fish in the broadcasting corporation to see if they could get me an appointment with another kind of big fish. The answer I got was a negative; this was such an unpredictable animal and the English weather was equally unpredictable. It seemed their experience with the basking shark somewhat resembled mine, and they simply weren't prepared to risk it. So it was back to filming things with teeth, exotic colours, wet, watery eyes and fluff.

Eventually I met a gullible TV producer or – depending on how you see it – one with vision and ambition, on whom I worked. I spent quite a bit of time placing the idea that it would be such a scoop for him to pull off such a film, all the time with my own selfish goals in mind.

Eventually I won him over (the failed shark quests had given me a will and a patience that was no match for a first-season producer) and he agreed to get a crew together on standby. As soon as the weather conditions looked favourable, we would go for it.

The call arrived very early one June morning. After a few stand-downs, this day appeared to be the one. Everything hung on this working out – the producer's career expectations and my fish dream. It was one of those English summertime gambles, like planning a BBQ three weeks ahead, or arranging an open-air wedding. Trusting a weather forecast in the British summer should only be done by the robust and desperate, and I guess that says it all – I was definitely the latter.

The sea off the Lizard peninsula was a rare thing that morning. There's a saying that it is like a mill pond when it's calm. It rarely is – usually a light breeze teases the surface and there is a little undulating swell. But this really was like a mill pond – minus the ducks. The glassy calm betrayed every living thing that moved below its surface any deformation, any rise was registered on the flawless satin façade. The watery calm was mirrored by a spotless azure sky. Spotting sharks in these conditions, if they were here, should be a doddle.

We set off, the boat gently tearing the tranquillity; slowly we traced our way around the contorted Cornish coast, its tortured geology, manacles and all. We rounded a headland, and there, less than half an hour after departing, were three of my bogey beasts. Six black-patent triangles of various slants and degrees were randomly taking big sweeping circles, as if they were dancing with each other, but had only just met – never actually touching, obviously following, chasing and associated in some way. They were mesmerising as they twinkled and occasionally flashed as they turned their wetness bouncing that June sun back at us.

The engines were cut and we just drifted and bobbed with them. Getting closer, the scene started to take on that 'other dimension' and the first thing of which I was aware was a sense of power. These were not loosely disassociated objects after all – the yet-to-be-revealed creatures were driving these fins. They were three pairs – each consisted of a large dorsal fin, that classic sharky icon, and a smaller more angled tail fin. It was the latter that was displacing huge quantities of water with each slow, sideways lunge, creating eddies and ripping up the silky surface. It was then that the sheer size of the beast beneath became apparent; the distance between the two fins was only about half the length of the beast – a fact that was driven home when, occasionally, another rounded, mottled object looking a little like a blackened root vegetable broke the surface some way ahead of the dorsal fin. This, I realised, was the tip of the shark's nose.

Looking down through the translucent water, in a moment everything became transpicuous. The picture of what was unfolding in front of us had been building bit by bit, beautiful moment by moment; first fins, then patterns, power and sheer scale, now bulk. Look it up in a book and everyone mentions length; it's as if we are obsessed by big numbers. The length of a mature basking shark is undoubtedly impressive. The biggest of my triad this day was a good-sized animal – not the 'in excess of ten metres' that you might have seen many years ago, before a rapidly ballooning human population plundered and ate without discretion most of what lives in our oceans. Still, my biggest was a respectable eight metres-plus – a lovely leviathan lady. It was the bulk, the girth of her hulk that really blew my mind; nothing quite prepares you for this – a basking shark is big in every dimension!

We sat and watched in awe for over an hour, as the three sharks circled lazily in loose figure-of-eight sweeps of the cove and all around the boat. Eventually the two smaller fish idled off on their own trajectory, and I took the not-difficult decision to hang with the female. After a couple of hours of her mesmerising feeding passes, it was apparent that she wasn't the slightest bit bothered by our close proximity. So, at the risk of messing up the moment completely, we decided to push the boat out (quite literally) and replace it with just me and a snorkel.

Suited in rubber and with appropriate accessories – fins, mask and snorkel – I quietly slipped into the water that, although apparently crystal from the surface, lost a little of its translucency in the lateral plane. I gently finned into what I predicted was the correct position to meet her, as she turned at the end of one of her figure-of-eight feeding loops. There I waited, hanging from the surface, my heart bouncing out of my ribcage, my stomach twisted in anticipation. What was this going to be like? How would I react? How would she react?

I peered into the green and time slowed down, keeping pace with the pulsing planktonic polyps that slowly beat their gelatinous frills and fringes against the glass of my mask. The first I remember was a pale, blurry patch in my peripheral vision, which all too soon manifested itself as the colossal feeding gape of my girl, heading right towards me. It was this split second that will remain with me for ever. It all happened so quickly that I gasped with surprise and bit down on my snorkel. I recovered just in time to see this colossus of a fish, with its refined power and grace, thrust past me in the water.

It's the details that stick with me – odd things like the massive displacement of water, felt rather than seen, and the grey skin, textured with ribs and striations behind the large dumb eye. The colour of plated zinc, but blotched with the pattern of a monochromatic watermelon, there were odd pores and perforation around the snout. Those gills! It's almost as if the shark's head is about to fall off the moment it opens wide; the gills expand as the mouth gapes and instantly the head becomes a basket so big I felt I could easily swim into the pink, cavernous maw and out through any one of the ten slits between it gill-rakers – without touching the sides. As it swam off into the green, I also noticed each gill billowing in the shark-generated current, like a satin curtain on a breeze.

The moment condensed lots of thoughts and perceptions of oceans – British water, in particular – and how little any of us really know about it. The mysterious ways of even the biggest fish remain just that – private and mysterious – and if we are so ignorant of the behemoths, imagine how much less we know about the other more lowly lives that you can find by gazing into the Grecian garden of a common rock pool. There is plenty here to inspire and amaze even the most travel-weary, nearly complacent naturalist. A meeting with Mrs Maximus was a pivotal point in my life. I will never take anything for granted ever again, for our own truly British wildlife can be as exciting and enriching as anything more exotic.

What's more she taught me the most important personal lesson of all. As a naturalist, a bogey beast is not such a bad thing; we all have them and they keep us alive. The many failures, disappointments and blank hours were not a waste of time; they all contributed in a way – only realised after the fact – to the sweetness of that moment when it all comes together. Now it's time to find a Cornish suckerfish.

Nick Baker

Nick Baker is a naturalist, self-confessed wildlife obsessive, TV presenter and author, living in Dartmoor National Park. Presenter of Weird Creatures *and* The Really Wild Show, *he has also written numerous books, including* Nick Baker's Bug Book, Nick Baker's British Wildlife, The New Amateur Naturalist *and* Habitat Explorer *guides to various wildlife in the UK. Nick is also a Vice President of The Wildlife Trusts.*

CHAPTER 4

PAST THE HEDGEROWS

THE HAYFIELDS OF STONEBOROUGH

FRANCIS KILVERT

FRIDAY, 11 AUGUST

A woodpigeon has built her nest in a fir on the lawn, and it is beautiful to hear her soft continual cooing among the branches. After going to the post I strolled down the meadows past Westhay and Lombard's farm to the upper bridge on the Blackwater. The limpid water ran as clear as air in the sunshine over the yellow pebbles and the still smooth pools brimmed cool dark and glassy in the shade.

The lovely lanes beyond were chequered with sunlight and green shade. As I sat upon a fallen tree by the lane side, a gleam of white shirt-sleeves came up the lane between the trees and through the alternate bars of light and shade, and two lusty young men went up to the hay fields of Stoneborough, one with fair hair carrying a scythe over his shoulder. Then came the quick tramp of hoofs and a labourer rode up the steep lane on a dark brown cob. The lane led on to a breezy common, glowing purple with heather. The pimpernel blazed in the grass with wide-open scarlet eyes, and the woods were lighted in their dark green depths by the scarlet bunches of the rowan berries. The scent of hay came mixed with the aromatic odour of the fir trees drawn out by the sun. The wood path was carpeted soft with millions of fir needles and the voices of the gamekeeper's children at play and the barking of a dog came merrily up through the plantations.

In a field among the woods the flax sheaves stood in shocks like wheat, the fine-hung bells on their wiry hair stalks rustling and quaking in the breeze like wag wantons. A mare and foal stood in the shade among the flax sheaves.

In the afternoon I went to pay a farewell visit to the lime avenue. It looked more like a vast church than ever and the strong low sunlight, which came up the green aisle seemed to be pouring through a great distant window. The sunlight streamed between the dark tree trunks, a soft cool breeze rustled the limes overhead and the chequering shadow of the leaves danced and flickered on the rich floor sunny and golden green.

Francis Kilvert (1840–1879)

Francis Kilvert entered Worcester College, Oxford, and was ordained a clergyman in 1864. He first served as his father's assistant in a Wiltshire parish and then as curate of Clyne in Radnorshire. He subsequently became rector of St Harmon's in Radnorshire and finally Bredwardine, in Herefordshire. He died of peritonitis within a month of his marriage in 1879. On his death, Kilvert left 22 volumes of diaries, from which a selection was first published between 1938 and 1940.

'The Hayfields of Stoneborough', from Kilvert's Diary (Jonathan Cape, 1938).

AN ENCOUNTER WITH RURAL WORCESTERSHIRE

CHRIS BEARDSHAW

I grew up in the rolling and rural landscape of Worcestershire with its small field patterns, mixed farming and endless hedgerows, which I remember being festooned with May blossom in spring and dripping with damsons in the autumn.

From an early age I was allowed to roam free through the fields and woods backing onto our family home and thus began my connection with and love of this landscape, which still remain as strong today. The changing seasons and inhabitants are etched into my memory. Wandering through pasture and grassland I would occasionally see a flash of scurrying brown feathers on a low-flying skylark. You hear them before you see them, with the eye having to search to see just a speck high in the sky. For me they have always had an appealing flight pattern, they sing and sing then fold their wings and drop several feet and then sing once more before dropping again almost like descending a set of steps until they are just above the crop level and as low as you can imagine they can fly. Their tone and pattern of song is one that brings a smile to even the most solemn of days and it seems they possess such extraordinary flight and song for a bird that is so modest in its feather pattern.

In the spring I remember walking through the cow pastures, heavy dew on the grass, as I headed down to the deep woodland streams that cut their changing path into the clay, providing a constantly meandering pathway. The woodland vegetation was heaving with sloe and elderberry, both of which were buzzing with pollinating insects, and the stream beds were lined with crack willow. Invariably, the winter storms fractured boughs and trunks, creating impromptu bridges across the stream, and it was climbing through the trees high above the clay stream banks that I was able to watch the water voles at work. Their nervous swimming and desire to hug the bank meant they were only really visible because of the wake they leave in the water. The slightest sound or movement of shadow sent them retreating to the overhanging vegetation or nearby burrow.

If I stuck around in the trees long enough and dusk set in I remember vividly the sweet musky smells of the woodland as I departed and the scent of the soft and warm landscape as I made my way home through the fields. As the cloak of night started to creep in I would invariably be joined by a barn owl quartering the hedgerows and fields – we had one that would fly right along our back hedge absolutely silently and disappear almost ghost-like across the fields.

Chris Beardshaw

Chris Beardshaw is a multi gold-medal-award-winning garden designer and horticulturalist. He runs a private design studio, lectures at postgraduate level and has had several TV series including The Flying Gardener, Hidden Gardens *and* Wild about your Garden. *He is a keen ambassador and campaigner for the horticultural industry and environment. Visit his website at www.chrisbeardshaw.com.*

SUDDEN SNOW

EDWARD THOMAS

The north wind makes walking weather, and the earth is stretched out below us and before us to be conquered. Just a little, perhaps, of the warrior's joy at seeing an enemy's fair land from the hill-top is mingled with the joy in the unfolding landscape. The ploughlands brighten over 20 miles of country, pale and dry, among dark woods and wooded hills; for the wind has crumbled the soil almost white, so that a sudden local sunlight will make one field seem actually of snow. The old road following a terrace of the hillside curves under yews away from the flinty arable and the grey, dry desolation round about the poultry-farmer's iron house, to the side of a rich valley of oak and ash and deepening pastures traversed by water in a glitter. The green fire of the larch woods is yellow at the crest. There and in oak and ash the missel thrush is an embodiment of the north wind, summing it up in the boldness of his form and singing, as the coat of arms sums up a history. Mounted on the plume of the top of the tall fir, and waving with it, he sings of adventure, and puts a spirit into those who pass under and adds a mile to their pace. The gorse is in flower. In the hedges the goose-grass has already set its ladders against the thorns, ladders that will soon have risen to the top of every hedge like scaling ladders of an infinite army. Down from tall yew and ash hang the abandoned ropes of last year's traveller's joy that have leapt that height – who has caught them in the leap? – but the new are on their way, and even the old show what can be done as they sway from the topmost branches.

At sunset an immense and bountiful land lies at our feet and the wine-red sun is pouring out large cups of conquest. The undulating ploughland is warm in the red light, and it is broken up by some squares of old brown stubble and of misty young wheat, and lesser green squares full of bleating and tinkling sheep. Out of these fields the dense beech copses rise sheer. Beyond, in the west, are ridges of many woods in misty conflagration; in the south-west, the line of the Downs under the level white clouds of a spacious and luminous sky. In the south, woods upon the hills are dissolving into a deep-blue smoke, without form except at their upper edges. And in the north and north-west the high lands of Berkshire and Wiltshire are prostrate and violet through 30 miles of witching air. That also is the call to go on and on over St Catherine's Hill and through Winchester until the brain is drowsed with the colours of night and day.

The colour of the dawn is lead and white – white snow falling out of a leaden sky to the white earth. The rose branches bend in sharper and sharper curves to the ground, the loaded yew sprays sweep the snow with white plumes. On the sedges the snow is in fleeces; the light strands of clematis are without motion, and have gathered it in clots. One thrush sings, but cannot long endure the sound of his unchallenged note; the sparrows chirp in the ricks; the blackbird is waiting for the end of that low tingling noise of the snow falling straight in windless air.

At mid-day the snow is finer, and almost rain, and it begins to pour down from its hives among the branches in short showers or in heavy hovering lumps. The leaves of ivy and holly are gradually exposed in all their gloomy polish, and out bursts the purple of the ash buds and the yellow of new foliage. The beech stems seem in their wetness to be made of a dark agate. Out from their tops blows rags of mist, and not far above them clouds like old spiders' webs go rapidly by.

The snow falls again and the voices of the little summer birds are buried in the silence of the flakes that whirl this way and that aimlessly, rising and falling and crossing or darting horizontally, making the trees sway wearily and their light tops toss and their numbers roar continually in the legions of the wind that whine and moan and shriek their hearts out in solitary house roofs and doors and round about. The silence of snow co-exists with this roar. One wren pierces it with a needle of song and is gone. The earth and sky are drowning in night and snow.

SUMMER

EDWARD THOMAS

SUSSEX

Far up on the Downs the air of day and night is flavoured by honeysuckle and new hay. It is good to walk, it is good to lie still; the rain is good and so is the sun; and whether the windy or the quiet air be the better let us leave to a December judgment to decide. One day the rain falls and there is no wind, and all the movement is in the chaos of the dark sky; and thus is made the celestial fairness of an earth that is brighter than the heavens; for the green and lilac of the grasses and the yellow of the goat's-beard flowers glow, and the ripening corn is airy light. But next day the sun is early hot. The wet hay steams and is sweet. The beams pour into a southward coombe of the hills and the dense yew is warm as a fruit-wall, so that the utmost of fragrance is extracted from the marjoram and thyme and fanned by the coming and going of butterflies; and in contrast with this gold and purple heat on flower and wing, through the blue sky and along the hill-top moist clouds are trooping, of the grey colour of melting snow. The great shadows of the clouds brood long over the hay, and in the darker hollows the wind rustles the dripping thickets until mid-day. On another morning after night rain the blue sky is rippled and crimped with high thin white clouds by several opposing breezes. Vast forces seem but now to have ceased their feud. The battle is over, and there are all the signs of it plain to be seen; but they have laid down their arms, and peace is broad and white in the sky, but of many colours on the earth – or there is blue of harebell and purple of rose-bay among the bracken and popping gorse, and heather and foxglove are purple above the sand, and the mint is hoary lilac, the meadow-sweet is foam, there is rose of willow-herb and yellow of flea-bane at the edge of the water, and purple of gentian and cistus yellow on the Downs, and infinite greens in those little dense Edens which nettle and cow-parsnip and bramble and elder make every summer on the banks of the deep lanes. A thousand swifts wheel as if in a fierce wind over the highest places of the hills, over the great sea-ward looking camp and its three graves and antique thorns, down to the chestnuts that stand about the rick-yards in the cornland below.

These are the hours that seem to entice and entrap the airy inhabitants of some land beyond the cloud mountains that rise farther than the farthest of downs. Legend has it that long ago strange children were caught upon the earth, and being asked how they had come there, they said that one day as they were herding their sheep in a far country they chanced on a cave; and within they heard music as of heavenly bells, which lured them on and on through the corridors of that cave until they reached our earth; and here their eyes, used only to a twilight between a sun that had set for ever and a night that had never fallen, were dazed by the August glow, and lying bemused they were caught before they could find the earthly entrance to their cave. Small wonder would this adventure be from a region no matter how blessed, when the earth is wearing the best white wild roses or when August is at its height.

The last hay-wagon has hardly rolled between the elms before the reaper and the reaping-machines begin to work. The oats and wheat are in tents over the land. Then, then it is hard not to walk over the brown in the green of August grass. There is a roving spirit everywhere. The very tents of the corn suggest a bivouac. The white clouds coming up out of the yellow corn and journeying over the blue have set their faces to some goal. The traveller's-joy is tangled over thee hazels and over the faces of the small chalk-pits. The white beam and the poplar and the sycamore fluttering show the silver sides of their leaves and rustle farewells. The perfect road that goes without hedges under elms and through the corn says, 'Leave all and follow.' How the bridges overleap the streams at one leap, or at three, in arches like those of running hounds! The far-scattered, placid sunsets pave the feet of the spirit with many a road to joy; the huge, vacant halls of dawn give a sense of godlike power.

But it is hard to make anything like a truce between these two incompatible desire, the one for going on and on over the earth, the other that would settle for ever, in one place as in a grave and have nothing to do with change. Suppose a man to receive notice of death, it would be hard to decide whether to walk or sail until the end, seeing no man, or none but strangers; or to sit – alone – and by thinking or not thinking to make the change to come as little as is permitted. The two desires will often painfully alternate. Even on these harvest days there is a temptation to take root for ever in some corner of a field or on some hill from which the world and the clouds can be seen at a distance For the wheat is as red as the most red sand, and up above it towers the elms, dark prophets persuading to silence and a stillness like their own. Away on the lesser Downs the fields of pale oats are liquid within their border of dark woods;

they also propose deep draughts of oblivion and rest. Then, again, there is the field – the many fields – where a regiment of shocks of oats are ranked under the white moon between rows of elms on the level Sussex land not far from the sea. The contrast of the airy matter underfoot and the thin moon over head, with the massy dark trees, as it were suspended between; the numbers and the order of the sheaves; their inviolability, though protected but by the gateway through which they are seen – all satisfy the soul as they can never satisfy the frame. Then there are the mists before heat which make us think of autumn or not, according to our tempers. All night the aspens have been shivering and the owls exulting under a clear full moon and above the silver of a great dew. You climb the steep chalk slope, through the privet and dog-wood coppice; among the scattered junipers – in this thick haze as in darkness they group themselves so as to make fantastic likenesses of mounted men, animals, monsters; over the dead earth in the shade of the broad yews, and thence suddenly under lightsome sprays of guelder-rose and their cherry-coloured berries; over the tufted turf; and then through the massed beeches, cold and dark as a church and silent; and so out to the level waste cornland at the top, to the flints and the clay. There a myriad oriflammes of ragwort are borne up on tall stems of equal height, straight and motionless, and near at hand quite clear, but farther away forming a green mist until, farther yet, all but the flowery surface is invisible, and that is but a glow. The stillness of the green and golden multitudes under the grey mist, perfectly still though a wind flutters the high tops of the beech, has an immortal beauty, and that they should ever change does not enter the mind which is thus for the moment lured happily into a strange confidence and ease. But the sun gains power in the south-east. It changes the mist into a fleeting garment, not of cold or of warm grey, but of diaphanous gold. There is a sea-like moan of wind in the half-visible trees, a wavering of the mist to and fro until it is dispersed far and wide as part of the very light, of the blue shade, of the colour of clouds and wood and down. As the mist is unwoven the ghostly moon is disclosed, and a bank of dead white clouds where the Downs should be. Under the very eye of the veiled sun a golden light and warmth begins to nestle among the mounds of foliage at the surface of the low woods. The beeches close by have got a new voice in their crisp, cool leaves, of which every one is doing something – cool, though the air itself is warm. Wood-pigeons coo. The white cloud-bank gives way to an immeasurable half-moon of Downs, some bare, some saddle-backed with woods, and far away and below, out of the ocean of countless trees in the southern veil, a spire. It is a spire which at this hour is doubtless moving a thousand men with a thousand thoughts, and hopes of memories of men and causes, but moves me with the thought alone that just a hundred years ago was buried underneath it a child, a little child whose mother's mother was at the pains to inscribe a tablet saying to all who pass by that he was once 'an amiable and most endearing child'.

And what nights there are on the hills. The ash-sprays break up the low full moon into a flower of many sparks. The Downs are heaved up into the lighted sky – surely they heave in their tranquillity as with a slowly taken breath. The moon is half-way up the sky and exactly over the centre of the long curve of the Downs; just above them lies a long terrace of white cloud, and at their feet gleams a broad pond, the rest of the valley being utterly dark and undistinguishable, save a few scattered lamps and one near meadow that catches the moonlight so as to be transmuted to a lake. But every rainy leaf upon the hill is brighter than any of the few stars above, and from many leaves and blade hang drops as large and bright as the glow-worms in their recesses. Larger by a little, but not brighter, are the threes and fours of lights at windows in the valley. The wind has fallen, but a mile of woods unlading the rain from their leaves make a sound of wind, a noise of rapt content, as if they were telling over again the kisses of the shower. The air itself is heavy as mead with the scent of yew and juniper and thyme.

Edward Thomas (1878–1917)

London-bred, Edward Thomas was a poet, who studied at Lincoln College, Oxford. Thereafter, he made his living as a literary journalist, contributing hundreds of reviews to a number of the leading magazines of his time. He wrote several biographies and volumes of natural history essays, as well as one novel. A lone walker by temperament, his poems and essays convey his intimate relationship with the natural world. He was killed at the battle of Arras in April 1917.

'Sudden Snow' and 'Summer', from South Country *(1909).*

EARLY SPRING

GERARD MANLEY HOPKINS

1866

May 3. Cold. Morning raw and wet, afternoon fine. Walked then with Addis, crossing Bablock Hythe, round by Skinner's Weir through many fields into the Witney road. Sky sleepy blue without liquidity. From Cumnor Hill saw St Philip's and the other spires through blue haze rising pale in pink light. On further side of the Witney road hills, just fleeced with grain or other green growth, by their dips and waves foreshortened here and there and so differenced in brightness and opacity the green on them, with delicate effect. On left, brow of the near hill glistening with very bright newly turned sods and a scarf of vivid green slanting away beyond the skyline, against which the clouds shewed the slightest tinge of rose or purple. Copses in grey-red or grey-yellow – the tinges immediately forerunning the opening of full leaf. Meadows skirting Seven-Bridge road voluptuous green. Some oaks are out in small leaf. Ashes not out, only tufted with their fringy blooms. Hedges springing richly. Elms in small leaf, with more or less opacity. White poplars most beautiful in small grey crisp spray-like leaf. Cowslips capriciously colouring meadows in creamy drifts. Over the green water of the river passing the slums of the town and under its bridges swallows shooting, blue and purple above and shewing their amber-tinged breasts reflected in the water, their flight unsteady with wagging wings and leaning first to one side then the other. Peewits flying. Towards sunset the sky partly swept, as often, with moist white cloud, tailing off across which are morsels of grey-black woolly clouds. Sun seemed to make a bright liquid hole in this, its texture had an upward northerly sweep or drift from the W, marked softly in grey. Dog violets. Eastward after sunset range of clouds rising in bulky heads moulded softly in tufts or bunches of snow – so it looks – and membered somewhat elaborately, rose-coloured. Notice often imperfect fairy rings. Apple and other fruit trees blossomed beautifully ...

May 10. Ascension Day. Fair, with more clouds than sun. Walked alone to Fyfield or rather to a step beyond the great elm (perhaps the greatest I have ever seen) and made a sketch at the turning point. The road went under the elms, their light green darker printed by shadows, chestnut, sweet-smelling firs, etc. Rooks cawing. Beddingfield church with good and curious E. and W. windows, but sadly neglected. Fine elms there with ground-running boughs. In timbered pasture etc. beside road bluebells thick, and tufts of primrose, and campion, the two latter or two former matching gracefully but not so well the three. One effect of sky was a straight line as by a ruler parting white and soft blue, and rolling reefs shaded with pearl grey hanging from this to the earth-line. Children with white rods beating bounds of St Michael's parish.

1871

May 9 ... This day and May 11 the bluebells in the little wood between the College and the highroad and in one of the Hurst

Green cloughs. In the little wood/opposite the light/they stood in blackish spreads of sheddings like the spots of a snake. The heads are then like thongs and solemn in grain and grape-colour. But in the clough/through the light/they came in falls of sky-colour washing the brows and slacks of the ground with vein-blue, thickening at the double, vertical themselves and the young grass and brake fern combed vertical, but the brake struck the upright of all this with light winged transoms. It was a lovely sight. – The bluebells in your hand baffle you with their inscape, made to every sense: if you draw your fingers through them they are lodged and struggle/with a shock of wet heads; the long stalks rub and click and flatten to a fan on one another like your fingers themselves would when you passed the palms hard across one another, making a brittle rub and jostle like the noise of a hurdle strained by leaning against; then there is the faint honey smell and in the mouth the sweet gum when you bite them. But this is easy, it is the eye they baffle. They give on a fancy of pan-pipes and of some wind instrument with stops – a trombone perhaps. The overhung necks – for growing they are little more than a staff with a simple crook but in water, where they stiffen, they take stronger turns, in the head like sheephooks or, when more waved throughout, like the waves riding through a whip that is being smacked – what with these overhung necks and what with the crisped ruffled bells dropping mostly on one side and the gloss these have at their footstalks they have an air of the knights at chess. Then the knot or 'knoop' of buds some shut, some just gaping, which makes the pencil of the whole spike, should be noticed: the inscape of the flower most finely carried out in the siding of the axes, each striking a greater and greater slant, is finished in these clustered buds, which for the most part are not straightened but rise to the end like a tongue and this and their tapering and a little flattening they have make them look like the heads of snakes.

1872

Feb. 23. A lunar halo: I looked at it from the upstairs library window. It was a grave grained sky, the strands rising a little from left to right. The halo was not quite round, for in the first place it was a little pulled and drawn below, by the refraction of the lower air perhaps, but what is more it fell in on the nether left hand side to rhyme the moon itself, which was not quite at full. I could not but strongly feel in my fancy the odd instress of this, the moon leaning on her side, as if fallen back, in the cheerful light floor within the right, after with the magical rightness and success tracing round her the ring the steady copy of her own outline. But this sober grey darkness and pale light was happily broken through by the orange of the pealing of Mitton bells.

Another night from the gallery window I saw a brindled heaven, the moon just marked by a blue spot pushing its way through the darker cloud, underneath and on the skirts of the rack bold long flakes whitened and swaled like feathers, below/the garden with the heads of the trees and shrubs furry grey: I read a broad careless inscape flowing throughout.

At the beginning of March they were felling some of their ashes in our grove.

July 19. The ovary of the blown foxglove surrounded by the green calyx is perhaps that conventional flower in Pointed and other floriated work which I could not before identify. It might also be St John's-wort.

Stepped into a barn of ours, a great shadowy barn, where the hay had been stacked on either side, and looking at the great rudely arched timber frames – principals (?) and tie-beams, which make them look like bold big A's with the cross-bar high up – I thought how sadly beauty of inscape was unknown and buried away from simple people and yet how near at hand it was if they had eyes to see it and it could be called out everywhere again ...

Aug. 10. I was looking at high waves. The breakers always are parallel to the coast and shape themselves to it except where the curve is sharp however the wind blows. They are rolled out by the shallowing shore just as a piece of putty between the palms whatever its shape run into a long roll. The slant ruck or crease one sees in them shows the way of the wind. The regularity of the barrels surprised and charmed the eye; the edge behind the comb or crest was as smooth and bright as glass. It may be noticed to be green behind and silver white in front: the silver marks where the air begins, the pure white is foam, the green/solid water. Then looked at to the right or left they are scrolled over like mouldboards or feathers or jibsails seen by the edge. It is pretty to see the hollow of the barrel disappearing as the white comb on each side runs along the wave gaining ground till the two meet at a pitch and crush and overlap each other.

About all the turns of the scaping from the break and flooding of the waves to its run out again I have not yet satisfied myself. The shores are swimming and the eyes have before them a region of milky surf but it is hard for them to unpack the huddling, and gnarls of the water and law out the shapes and the sequence of the running: I catch however the looped or forked wisp made by every big pebble the backwater runs over – if it were clear and smooth there would be a network from their overlapping, such as can in fact be seen on smooth sand after the tide is out–; then I saw it run browner, the foam dwindling and twitched into long chains of sudes, while the strength of the backdraught shrugged the stones together and clocked them one against another.

Looking from the cliff, I saw well that work of dimpled foam-laps – strings of short loops or halfmoons – which I had studied at Freshwater years ago.

It is pretty to see the dance and swagging of the light green tongues or ripples of waves in a place locked between rocks.

1873

Feb. 24. In the snow flat-topped hillocks and shoulders outlined with wavy edges, ridge below ridge, very like the grains of wood in line and in projection like relief maps. These the wind makes I think and of course drifts, which are in fact snow waves. The sharp nape of a drift is sometimes broken by slant flutes or channels. I think this must be when the wind after shaping the drift first has changed and cast waves in the body of the wave itself. All the world is full of inscape and chance left free to act falls into an order as well as purpose: looking out of my window I caught it in the random clud and broken heaps of snow made by the cast of a broom. The same of the path trenched by footsteps in ankle-deep snow across the fields leading to Hodder wood through which we went to see the river. The sun was bright, the broken brambles and all boughs and banks limed and cloyed with white, the brook down the clough pulling its way by drops and by bubbles in turn under a shell of ice. In March there was much snow.

April 8. The ashtree growing in the corner of the garden was felled. It was lopped first: I heard the sound and looking out and seeing it maimed there came at that moment a great pang and I wished to die and not to see the inscapes of the world destroyed any more.

July 22. Very hot, though the wind, which was south, dappled very sweetly on one's face and when I came out I seemed to put it on like a gown as a man puts on the shadow he walks into and hoods or hats himself with the shelter of a roof, a penthouse, or a copse of trees, I mean it rippled and fluttered like light linen, one could feel the folds and braids of it – and indeed a floating flag is like wind visible and what weeds are in a current; it gives it thew and fires it and bloods in it. – Thunderstorm in the evening, first booming in gong-sounds, as at Aosta, as if high up and so not re-echoed from the hills; the lightning very slender and nimble and, as if playing very near but after supper it was so bright and terrible some people said they had never seen its like. People were killed, but in other parts of the country it was more violent than with us. Flashes lacing two clouds above or the cloud and the earth started upon the eyes in live veins of rincing or riddling liquid white, inched and jagged as if it were the shivering of a bright riband string which had once been kept bound round a blade and danced back into its pleatings. Several strong thrills of light followed the flash but a grey smother of darkness blotted the eyes if they had seen the fork, also dull furry thickened scrapes of it were left in them.

Gerard Manley Hopkins (1844–1889)

Poet and Jesuit priest, Gerard Manley Hopkins was born in Essex, and read classics at Balliol College, Oxford. In 1866, he was received into the Roman Catholic Church by Cardinal Newman, and went on to travel to a number of Jesuit foundations in London, Lancashire and North Wales, holding parishes in Chesterfield, London, Oxford, Liverpool and Glasgow. He taught at Stonyhurst College in Lancashire between 1882 and 1884 and was elected as Professor of Classics at University College, Dublin, where he died of typhoid fever. In his poetry and notebooks, journals and letters alike, he sought a language of inspiration that would capture new experiences in nature.

'Early Spring', from Journal *(1866–1875); (Oxford, 1877).*

THE MAGIC OF HORSES

JULES PRETTY

The chalk downs of southern England are famous for their sweeping hills and grass swards kept flower-rich by sheep and rabbits. They are also stalked by white horses, great beasts created by filling trenches cut in the grassland with blocks of white chalk. There are 24 known white horses in the UK, 13 of which are in Wiltshire. Most date from 1700 to the late 1800s, though the most striking was created by Bronze Age Britons around 3000 years ago. All, though, carry a power and mystery as they prance, canter or race across the landscape. Like the Nazca's geoglyph animals of the high Andes, these are designed to be seen from far away, and each one attracts myths and stories.

The most famous is the oldest of British chalk figures, and this horse races across a steep scarp face near the village of Uffington. It crosses the Ridgeway, an ancient 135-kilometre trade route that winds across hill tops from east of Oxford to Avebury's ring of standing stones. Nearby is a 5000-year-old Neolithic longbarrow, and on the main hilltop are the vast earthworks of the Iron Age

Uffington Castle, expansive and empty now, but indicative of the value the ancients held for this site. You approach the horse across a wide and closely cropped hillside that seems to hover like a space station above the patchwork plains below, once thick forests, and now a spectacular mosaic of fields and farms. A flock of rooks swirls up, a commentary of *kraa* calls to join the evening song of skylarks. Below a train streaks from east to west, and joins other distant echoes of modern life down on the surface of the planet.

Dropping down from the path, you come first upon the horse's five-metre head, and then the whole figure becomes apparent, stretching more than 115 metres to its tail and trailing hind leg. The design looks to be special; it also appears on some Celtic coins, but is not used on other chalk figures. A long thin body with neck and shoulders almost as long; forelegs stretched out in front as if ready to jump an obstacle; hind legs tense and sprung, one in a stylised reverse curve. It gives the impression of being a particular individual horse, like Barry Lopez's stone desert horse, not a generalised one. As you walk around the trenches, it is difficult to make out that is an animal. It appears to have been carved from a distance, as if by a great god in the sky. What is clear, though, is that without regular maintenance, the chalk would quickly disappear under invading grasses. Generation after generation has thought it important enough to look after, but you still wonder, what prompted people to carve a great horse on this hillside 3000 years ago? Why not a cow, or a bear or wolf? And why this horse in particular?

Below me, a pair of swallows dive and twist, and below them in the valley is a conical mound that is supposed to be where George slayed the dragon, and where its blood spilled on the flat top, so preventing any grass from growing. This is other significance in these chalk figures. They attract stories, which become tied to the place. Here the dragon, there the burial site for King Arthur's father. It is said that the Uffington horse will animate and dance on the dragon hill when King Arthur himself awakes. Every 100 years, the horse is supposed to gallop across the sky to the long barrow to be reshod by Wayland, the smithy. The horse, a mare, also comes down at night with her invisible foal to drink in a nearby stream. Standing in the eye of the horse is supposed to bring wishes granted. The horse is important as a landscape icon, but also as a source of stories that make the place somehow more special. How many other places were once full of stories like this, but about which we have collectively forgotten?

The first white horse of the modern era was cut at Westbury around 1700, followed by others at Cherhill in 1780 and Pewsey in 1785. Most of the remainder were cut in the 1800s, though the recent millennium celebrations brought new designs at New Devizes, Heeley and Folkestone between 1999 and 2002. White horses have also been cut in South Africa and New Zealand. Again, all are horses, and the designs are more realistic figures than Uffington's gaunt mare.

A prominent one overlooks the village of Alton Burns from a south-facing slope some six kilometres south of Avebury. Cut in 1812, this horse is again part of an ancient landscape, as on every hill are tumuli, earthwork enclosures, long barrows, kitchen barrows or strip lynchet field marks. This horse carries less of the glamour of Uffington, and is more difficult to approach. Late on a windblown summer evening, I walk from the north, up and over a series of burial mounds, past black cattle chewing curiously on thistles rather than grass, and perched 120 metres above Pewsey Vale look down to see another iconic symbol of today's England. For here is a crop circle in a barley field, a spinning series of geometric shapes again designed to be seen from afar. Two people walk in silence through the flattened corn. And up here is the giant prancing horse, four legs of equal length with a deep body and short stubby tail. As I watch, two weasels streak across the chalk of the body, and disappear in the grass. Apart from the cattle, this hillside appears to be mostly deserted.

Below a field of blackened rape awaits harvest; another of barley is in, and old-style square bales are piled in tottering towers. In another is a crop circle of intricate design. Again, as you approach the horse, it becomes more difficult to recognise. It is made to be magic from the valley floor settlements. At the figure, enclosed each way by 80 metres of rusty barbed wire to keep off the cattle, the grass is longer and unkempt. Here, then, is another animal sign on the land, newer than the Uffington ancient, but again an enduring symbol of our relationships with animals and the land. When we forget who made them, then the myths can begin.

Many mysteries remain in our mostly modernised British landscapes, despite its 24 million hectares containing more than 60 million people. This, it seems to me, is a good thing. Our lives are not so controlled and managed as we might think. Things can happen beyond our understanding. The landscape is ever-changing, and the stories associated with it also change. It exists as one form of reality; it also exists in our imagination.

Horses were easy to domesticate, having no horns or antlers, requiring only a simple grass diet, and not needing to rest after eating, together with having the capability of running at 70 kilometres per hour. The working horse has always attracted stories about magic. Horses were a source of power on farms, and the focus of much folklore, too. Almost all of this revolved around how the horsemen were able to shape their behaviour. Drawing oils were common – these were jading substances or oils used to stop a horse. They were painted on gateposts, and often used while horsemen were in the pub. The toad bone was even more powerful magic. The bones of a frog or toad were thrown into a river at midnight: one of the bones would float upstream, and this was kept as it exerted a magical control over a horse. Sometimes a donkey was put in a field with horses, as this prevented them from trying to escape – they would not leave without the stubborn donkey. A horse hair was sometimes tied around the leg at a joint to cause the horse to limp.

But it is horse-whispering that has recently become famous as a practice. Horsemen always talked to their horses, sometimes putting something in their ear to maintain control. Horse-whisperers are people with the apparent capacity to cure horses of illnesses, yet most do not know how. Some horse owners are convinced that something inexplicable has happened, and the horses become well. Clearly, they might have recovered without the whisperer's help, but individual testimonies on serious injuries cannot easily be dismissed. It is a mystery, and cannot be explained by our current knowledge. One day, that might change. Alternatively, it might turn out to have been just a good story.

One of the rarest animals in the world persists in patches of modern farmed landscapes. It is the Suffolk Punch, the giant horse first bred in the 16th century to work the heavy Suffolk clays of eastern England. Suffolks are tall, often with a white star or blaze on the face, and have long been admired for their calm temperament and ease of care. But in the modern era, such shire horses could not compete with machinery, and from the 1950s were rapidly replaced with tractors and mechanised combines. Farms, of course, became more efficient. More land was cultivated in less time with less labour. But when these horses and their horsemen disappeared from farms, something else was lost, too. For the horsemen had an intimate relationship not just with their horses, but with the whole farm landscape. They were expert botanists, using up to 40 species of wild plants for horse care. Today, having forgotten this knowledge, we call these once useful plants weeds, and the Suffolk only survives through the efforts of dedicated societies and individuals, one or two of whom still farm with shire horses.

From generation to generation, horsemen passed on knowledge about the value of certain plants for treating illness and disease, shining the coat or improving appetite. George Ewart Evans, eloquent observer of English agricultural change, wrote in *The Horse and the Furrow* (1960) of fevers treated with agrimony or with apples sliced and stored until infested with antibiotic-carrying fungi; and of colds and coughs cured with feverfew, belladonna, meadow-rue and horehound. For de-worming, the horsemen used celandine, yellow-flowered indicator of spring, and to encourage appetite, put gentian, elecampane, horehound and felwort into food. They used box to keep down sweat, and burdock, saffron, rosemary, fennel, juniper, tansy and mandrake for coat conditioning. Hazel, holly and willow were fashioned into withies and traces for harnesses. This example shows that there is a simple principle for our modern era of agricultural progress. As food efficiency increases, landscape diversity is lost, and so too goes an intimate knowledge of nature and a duty of care. The Hollesley Bay Open Prison long kept one of the last groups of Suffolk Punches, and these were kept precisely for their therapeutic value. Said John Bromley, the estate manager in the 1970s to Evans, 'We make a big play of the therapeutic value of the heavy horses with the boys … that is why we keep horses. We attach one boy to the horse; and the boy's character changes: he has now got responsibility, direct responsibility … And their attitude changes.' Regrettably, the Prison Service later closed the farm, arguing that cost-cutting was necessary and the horses were only a luxury. We are now lucky that, in 2002, the Suffolk Punch Trust was formed as a charity to save the colony, contribute to prisoner rehabilitation, and develop nature-based education for children.

These growing disconnections must be a concern. Our countrysides have lost many of their animals, including almost all the threatening ones. Now some are increasing in numbers – the deer, otters and wild boar – and beavers are being re-introduced. There is even some discussion about re-introducing wolves. Perhaps these will help to bring back some more mystery to the countryside and its wild places. If we allow it, the land will include us.

Jules Pretty

Jules Pretty is Professor of Environment and Society at the University of Essex. His 16 books include This Luminous Coast *(2010),* The Earth Only Endures *(2007), and* Agri-Culture *(2002). He is a Fellow of the Society of Biology and the Royal Society of Arts, and has served on advisory committees for a number of government departments. He received an OBE in 2006 for services to sustainable agriculture, and an honorary degree from Ohio State University in 2009.*

'*The Magic of Horses', from* The Earth Only Endures *(Earthscan, 2007).*

WELSH FARM

SIR ALFRED RUSSEL WALLACE

The rough pastures on which the cattle get their living and waste their manure a great part of the time consist chiefly of various species of rushes and sedges, a few coarse grasses, and gorse and fern on the drier parts. They are frequently, too, covered with brambles, dwarf willows, and alders.

The 'short-hay meadows', as they are called, are a class of lands entirely unknown in most of England; I shall, therefore, endeavour to describe them.

They consist of large undulating tracts of lands on the lower slopes of the mountains, covered during autumn, winter, and spring with a very short brownish-yellow wet turf. In May, June and July the various plants forming this turf spring up, and at the end of summer are mown, and form 'short-hay'; and well it deserves the name, for it is frequently almost impossible to take it up with a hayfork, in which case it is raked up and gathered by armfuls into the cars. The produce varies from two to six hundredweight per acre; four may be about the average, or five acres of land to produce a ton of hay. During the rest of the year it is almost good for nothing. It is astonishing how such stuff can be worth the labour of mowing and making it into hay. An English farmer would certainly not do it, but the poor Welshman has no choice; he must either cut his short-hay or have no food for his cattle in the winter; so he sets to, and sweeps away with a scythe a breadth that would astonish an English mower.

The soil that produces these meadows is a poor yellow clay resting on the rock; on the surface of the clay is a stratum of peaty vegetable matter, sometimes of considerable thickness though more generally only a few inches, which collects and retains the moisture in a most remarkable manner, so that though the ground should have a very steep slope the water seems to saturate and cling to it like a sponge; so much so that after a considerable period of dry weather, when, from the burnt appearance of the surface, you would imagine it to be perfectly free from moisture, if you venture to kneel or lie down upon it you will almost instantly be wetted to the skin.

The plants that compose these barren slopes are a few grasses, among which are the sweet vernal grass (*Anthoxanthum odoratum*) and the crested hair grass (*Kaleria cristata*), several Cyperaceæ – species of carex or sedge which form a large proportion, and the feathery cotton grass (*Eriophorum vaginatum*). The toad-rush (*Juncus bufonius*) is frequently very plentiful, and many other plants of the same kind. Several rare or interesting British plants are here found often in great profusion. The Lancashire asphodel (*Narthecium ossifragum*) often covers acres with its delicate yellow and red blossoms. The spotted orchis (*O. Maculata*) is almost universally present. The butterwort (*Pinguicula vulgaris*) is also found here, and the beautiful little pimpernel (*Anagallis tenella*). The louseworts (*Pendicularis sylvatica* and *P. palustris*), the melancholy thistle (*Cincus heterophyllus*), and the beautiful blue milkwort (*Polygala vulgaris*), and many others, are generally exceedingly plentiful, and afford much gratification to the botanist and lover of nature.

The number of sheep kept on these farms is about one to each acre of mountain, where they live the greater part of the year, being only brought down to the pastures in the winter, and again turned on the mountain with their lambs in the spring. One hundred acres of pasture and 'short-hay meadow' will support from thirty to forty cattle, ten or a dozen calves and oxen being sold each year.

*   *   *

During the two summers that I and my brother John lived at Neath we spent a good deal of our leisure time wandering about this beautiful district, on my part in search of insects, while my brother always had his eyes open for any uncommon bird or reptile. One day when I was insect hunting on Crymlyn Burrows, a stretch of very interesting sand-hills, rock and bog near the sea, and very rich in curious plants, he came upon several young vipers basking on a rock. They were about eight or nine inches long. As they were quite still, he thought he could catch one by the neck, and endeavoured to do so, but the little creature turned round suddenly, bit his finger and escaped. He immediately sucked out the poison, but his whole hand swelled considerably, and was very painful. Owing, however, to the small size of the animal the swelling soon passed off, and left no bad effects. Another day, towards the autumn, we found the rather uncommon black viper in a wood a few miles from Neath. This he caught with a forked stick, to which he then tied it firmly by the neck, and put it in his coat pocket. Meeting a labourer on the way, he pulled it out of his pocket, wriggling and twisting around the stick and his hand, and asked the man if he knew what it was, holding it towards him. The man's alarm was ludicrous. Of course he declared it to be deadly, and for once was right, and he added that he would not carry such a thing in his pocket for anything we could give him.

Though I have by no means a very wide acquaintance with the mountain districts of Britain, yet I know Wales pretty well; have visited the best parts of the lake district; in Scotland have been to Loch Lomond, Loch Katrine and Loch Tay; have climbed Ben Lawers, and roamed through Glen Clova in search of rare plants; but I cannot call to mind a single valley that in the same extent of country comprises so much beautiful and picturesque scenery, and so many interesting special features, as the Vale of Neath. The town itself is beautifully situated, with fine-wooded and rock-girt Drumau Mountain to the west, while immediately to the east are well-wooded heights crowned by Gnoll House, and to the south-east, three miles away, a rounded hill, up which a chimney has been carried from the Cwm Avon copperworks in the valley beyond, the smoke from which gives the hill much the appearance of an active volcano. To the south-west the view extends down the valley to Swansea Bay, while to the north-east stretches the Vale of Neath itself, nearly straight for twelve miles, the river winding in a level fertile valley about a quarter to half a mile wide, bounded on each side by abrupt hills, whose lower slopes are finely wooded, and backed by mountains from 1500 to 1800 feet high. The view up this valley is delightful, its sides being varied with a few houses peeping out from the woods, abundance of lateral valleys and ravines, with here and there the glint of falling water, while its generally straight direction affords fine perspective effects, sometimes fading in the distance into a warm yellow haze, at others affording a view of the distant mountain ranges beyond ...

Sir Alfred Russel Wallace (1823–1913)
A schoolmaster in Leicester between 1844 and 1846, Alfred Russel

Wallace joined the naturalist Henry Walter Bates on a collecting trip to the Amazon in 1848, returning to England, 1852. He worked in the Malay Archipelago between 1854 and 1862, where he independently discovered the principle of natural selection as key to the understanding of evolution. He sent his views to Charles Darwin and the theory was published in a joint paper in 1858. He returned to England in 1862, and later published The Malay Archipelago *(1869),* Contributions to the Theory of Natural Selection *(1870) and* The Geographical Distribution of Animals *(1876). He was the first Darwin medallist of the Royal Society in 1890.*

'Welsh Farm', *from* The Alfred Russel Wallace Reader *(London, 2002).*

BOLLITREE AND HORNCASTLE

WILLIAM COBBETT

BOLLITREE, WEDNESDAY, 13TH SEPT. [1826]
This morning was most beautiful. There has been rain here
now, and the grass begins (but only begins) to grow. When I got
within 200 yards of Mr Palmers I had the happiness to meet my
son Richard, who said that he had been up an hour. As I came
along I saw one of the prettiest sights in the *flower* way that I
ever saw in my life. It was a little orchard; the grass in it had just
taken a start, and was beautifully fresh; and, very thickly
growing amongst the grass, was the purple-flowered *Colchicum*,
in full bloom. They say, that the leaves of this plant, which come
out in the spring, and die away in the summer, are poisonous to
cattle if they eat much of them in the spring. The flower, if
standing by itself, would be no great beauty; but, contrasted
thus, with the fresh grass, which was a little shorter than itself,
it was very beautiful.

HORNCASTLE, 13TH APRIL, MORNING [1830]

... There is one deficiency, and that, with me, a great one, throughout this country of corn and grass and oxen and sheep, that I have come over, during the last three weeks; namely, the want of *singing birds*. We are now just in that season when they sing most. Here, in all this country, I have seen and heard only about four sky-larks, and not one other singing bird of any description, and, of the small birds that do not sing, I have seen only one *yellow-hammer*, and it was perched on the rail of a pound between Boston and Sibsey. Oh! The thousands of linnets all singing together on one tree, in the sand-hills of Surrey! Oh! The carolling in the coppices and the dingles of Hampshire and Sussex and Kent! At this moment (five o'clock in the morning) the groves at Barn-Elm are echoing with the warbling of thousands upon thousands of birds. The *thrush* begins a little before it is light; next the *blackbird*; next the *larks* begin to rise; all the rest begin the moment the sun gives the signal; and, from the hedges, the bushes, from the middle and the topmost twigs of the trees, comes the singing of endless variety; from the long dead grass comes the sound of the sweet and soft voice of the *white-throat* or *nettle-tom*, while the loud and merry song of the *lark* (songster himself out of sight) seems to descend from the skies. Milton, in his description of paradise, has not omitted the 'song of earliest birds'. However, everything taken together, here, in Lincolnshire, are more good things than man could have had the courage to *ask* of God ...

William Cobbett (1762–1835)

A self-taught essayist, politician and agriculturalist, William Cobbett entered the British Army in 1783, obtained a discharge in 1791, after serving in New Brunswick. He went on to farm in Hampshire between 1804 and 1817 and, after a period in America, returned to a farm in Surrey, becoming MP for Oldham in 1821. Cobbett's Weekly Political

Register *was founded in 1802, and he continued it until his death.* Rural Rides *records his extensive wanderings in the southern shires and his deep affection for the English soil and its population. The natural beauties of the English countryside are the counterpoint to his observations on the people that it supports.*

'*Bollitree and Horncastle*', from Rural Rides *(1830).*

CHAPTER 5

UNDER THE TREES

TREES FROM MY WINDOW

COLIN TUDGE

I live in a city, but surrounded by trees. Our flat is small in a building of absolutely no distinction in the north of Oxford but it has a fabulous view – through what's left of what used to be an orchard before the builders got stuck in; past a fringe of this and that: Scots Pine, Cypress, Horse Chestnut, Common Lime, and miscellaneous willows; over Port Meadow, right now bright with buttercups; then a throng of bushy oaks and Black Poplars, following the Thames; on past some farms, with a serried row of Lombardy Poplars, a touch of Normandy; up a bright green distant hill that sometimes has sheep; and then, splendid along the skyline, Wytham Wood. Without the trees it would be quite different: a housing estate; the canal; the railway; a village; and a plexus of arterial roads (A34, A40, A44). A few hundred yards from here you hear their roar.

The right response to trees is simply to lie back and enjoy them. They do exactly what the myth-makers have been telling us these past few thousand years. They are indeed compounded, as the Old Greeks said, of air, water, earth and fire. They build themselves from carbon, which they get almost entirely from the air as CO_2, and from minerals which they drag from the earth. They need water, of course, because nothing lives without it; and they are powered by the Sun, which is a very peculiar kind of fire, but is fiery nonetheless. They do bind the earth to the sky, as the Vikings said. They do talk to each other as Tolkien's hobbits knew – not in words but in pheromones, so the science now tells us. Science often appears as the killjoy killer of myths – but science is a story, too, and when it is properly construed it enhances the mythology. Its proper role is not to banish mystery but to deepen appreciation, to broaden the emotional response; not simply to evoke awe as we are sometimes told these days, but a proper sense of reverence.

If you read the trees right, wherever you are, they tell the history of the landscape – and hence, by extrapolation, all the people who have ever lived around. The apple trees immediately outside my window (now with Goldfinches and Great Spotted Woodpeckers) are here for the obvious reason that this used to be the orchard of a great house, before the society of great houses collapsed and the economy changed gear and the builders got stuck in. The Scots Pines, good natives (I don't know why the Scots should have claimed them), and the magnificent lime, may well have sprung up spontaneously. The cypresses of course are not native and perhaps were planted, or perhaps were garden escapes, their seeds brought in by some bird. The Collared Doves don't mind if the cypresses are native or not, and nest in them every year, fighting off the ever-circling Jackdaws, like Serengeti lions beating off hyenas, most undovishly and so far successfully. Port Meadow is devoid of trees partly because it is a flood plain (although that wouldn't stop the speculators, if they got half a sniff) but also because it was bequeathed to the locals by King Alfred for feats of ridiculous bravery, to graze their cattle and horses in perpetuity: and so they still do. The cattle and horses love both the floods and the buttercups – splashing around in a wet spring as if on the Camargue. Local people are called 'commoners' and their right to graze depends on rank. I think I am entitled to a goose, although I haven't put it to the test. (There are plenty of Grey Lags and a growing phalanx of Canada Geese already on the meadow, and a great deal more besides in their due season, including hundreds of Teal, Golden Plovers, Lapwings, and what you will.)

As for Wytham – it's one of England's great woods; owned by the University since the 1940s and dedicated to the cause of being a typical, properly managed, semi-natural mixed wood, with oaks and sycamores and yews and hornbeams and many a wonderful beech. Some of it is managed by fisherman-turned-woodsman-cum-farmer David Giles, who trims the big trees where necessary and drags out the timbers with the help of two small but immensely powerful Scandinavian horses, bred for the job and clever as sheepdogs. They do less damage than machines and are infinitely more attractive. Wytham Wood, too, has been home to some of the finest ornithological studies, not least on Great Tits, attracting such luminaries as Niko Tinbergen and David Lack.

All in all, the landscape is probably as good as it can get in a crowded, industrial country like ours. It's not pristine. It's very far removed from what would be here if human beings hadn't been imposing their own stamp for the past 10,000 years – for without people it would surely be wall-to-wall oak, ash and small-leaved lime, and Port Meadow would be a swamp with Red Deer and Aurochs, and so on. But there are still traces of post Ice Age, and the mixture of farming and forestry and houses and gardens, with all their introduced trees and herbs, creates an astonishingly species-rich environment. Here, as everywhere, there are hints of 'green desert' – the invertebrates have largely been zapped by the all-pervasive fingers of agro-chemistry. But overall, it does show that people and other creatures can live together, if only we give a damn.

Does all this sound complacent? Musings of a rich suburbanite? I hope not. Our flat really is modest; the kind that in a country like ours *everyone* could afford, if the housing market wasn't run by bankers for the benefit of bankers. Fifty years ago, before the modern miracle economy, the houses in the village that now cost £400,000 (roughly twice what we paid for this one) were occupied by farm workers.

Everyone who doesn't choose to live on the ocean or in a desert could and should be surrounded by trees. If I was Lord of All – or even just the government – I would be very unobtrusive (believe me) but I would insist that all the world plants trees. You can put the wrong trees in the wrong places but on the whole you really can't have too many. The meanest, ghastliest suburbs – the dustiest, hottest, most hostile quasi-urban environments of the kind that give you an instant headache – are transformed by trees. The most agreeable spot by far in modern Beijing is where the diplomats live – not because the houses are particularly grand but because they are shrouded in trees. I would say to all social reformers, all planners, all who are worried by rising crime and ill-health and general discontent, 'Before you even draw breath – plant trees!' It would pay dividends a hundred times over – including dividends of the crude financial kind, since unhappiness is costly.

Colin Tudge

Colin Tudge is a biologist, writer and broadcaster with a special interest in natural history, evolution and genetics, food and agriculture and philosophy. He has written hundreds of magazine and newspaper articles and was formerly features editor of New Scientist. *His books include* The Variety of Life: A survey and celebration of the all the creatures that have ever lived, Consider the Birds: How They Live and Why They Matter *and the acclaimed* The Secret Life of Trees.

LEAVES

ROGER DEAKIN

21ST NOVEMBER

A sharp, sugaring frost. The mulberry is at its best in November when at last it undresses itself. It does a sort of striptease before my study window, lightly letting go its leaves in a light breeze that seems to touch only this one tree after the stillness of the frosty night. The leaves float down in twos and threes, or just a single leaf at a time.

The glory of the mulberry at this moment of the year is in its pool of frozen leaves: pale yellow softened by pale green and buff (the last from beneath the canopy). The pool is a little sea, choppy with leaves. (Each leaf is a wavelet.)

Mulberry leaves feel tough and gleam like oilskin. They are dull green when they fall from the tree, then turn to chestnut brown as they oxidise. Each leaf is serrated subtly and evenly with little millimetre saw-teeth, and the veins are the tributaries of a river, whose delta leads down to the stem.

Elderberry leaves pale almost to white except for their veins, which blush a deep crimson as though animal or human arteries, filled with coursing blood.

Last year I made a maze in the mulberry leaves to celebrate the birth of a little girl – for her first visit here, a labyrinth.

Why are park-keepers so keen to sweep up leaves? They are the glory of autumn and surely would feed the ground, if left alone to be drawn underground by earthworms and composted?

All the leaves are falling this morning after such a frost. It has loosened them, frozen and cut off the flow of sap, made each stem brittle.

A pair of crows come to the bullace tree on the common before the house and balance on twigs too slender to bear their weight to eat the plums – translucent pearls of pink and yellow, softened and ripened by the frost, their sugars concentrated now. Magpies follow them, then a dozen blackbirds, a pair of song thrushes. A wood pigeon on the hawthorn after haws.

The hazel is dropping its leaves, too, shivering now and then in a breath of slightest breeze. Leaves come to earth like birds to a field for grain, or grubs.

Why don't all the leaves come down at once?

The fun of scuffing leaves as you trudge through them as if through a snowfall, the woodland floor turned to a palette with each tree at the centre of its particular colour (Turner's palette).

As the leaves fall away from them, the naked branches reveal their lichened beauty. The pool of fallen leaves is a mirror, reflecting the tree as it has been: the whole canopy in two dimensions. Only the skeleton of the tree is left to represent the third dimension.

That is what trees give us: the third dimension in our landscape.

Left alone to cloak the woodland floor, leaves accumulate layer by layer over the years into a deep crust of leaf mould. Walking or clambering, through an old beech or chestnut woods in France or Poland, I have sometimes fallen through the leaf crust and dropped many feet into a soft drift of leaves. These leaf drifts often fill hollows or old quarrying sites for limestone or chalk.

I go for an early swim and notice the fine old ash pollards on the road back to Thrandeston, and on Thrandeston Green. They need cutting too, but who will do it? I must make a map of Mellis pollards. All need attention to survive. And why not start new pollards, too, as I have with my pollard windows?

18TH NOVEMBER

I set out up Clay Street in Thornham Magna this afternoon, in quest of a little medieval meadow full of ancient pollard oaks. It was, I have been told in strictest confidence by a local tree-detective, a pheasant park in miniature, a tiny wood pasture, and so it proved.

Clay Street is a narrow no-through road branching away from the Thornham Horseshoes between old hedges of ash, maple and blackthorn with an old pollard oak every 15 or 20 yards, and patches of the shocking pink fruits of the spindle tree.

Every now and again I passed a pink thatched cottage, with a modest garden, two or three apple trees, and a makeshift garage and a range of tin sheds slanting towards oblivion. Nearly all of them had the builders in. A white van, a cement mixer, a pile of Durox building blocks and the beginnings of an extension or porch were the only evidence of activity. Not a sign of anyone actually at work, not even Radio Norfolk to break the silence.

At the corner of two fields and the road, a digger had been excavating a pond. There are so often ponds at the intersections of fields here in Suffolk, and it was good to see how sensitively the big machine had been eased in amongst the trees that fringed the pond; how it had deftly scraped out only the leaf silt, leaving the hard clay-bottom intact.

A multiple covey, or an extended covey, of dozens of partridges whirred up like an aeroplane the other side of the hedge and dived straight ahead, flying two feet off the ground. They landed, stood about long enough to realise I was still gaining on them and broke into their comical run, eventually taking off with their usual reluctance.

The country began to roll a bit just here, and the dark cushions of ancient maple and sloe hedgerows snaked and curved away downhill, following the classic undulations that signal old field boundaries. I had turned off Clay Street into a green land signposted 'The Six-Mile Loop', passed another shadowed pond winking out from a canopy of trees and turned left along a banked field boundary. The line of massive pollard hedgerow oaks, and sheer bulk of bank and width of ditch, suggested that this may once have been the boundary of the medieval park at Thornham. The trees were hollow and black with ivy. Out of the shaggy log of one of them flew a little owl.

Rabbits had made their burrows amongst the huge roots in the sandy, dry earth inside the hollows, and a beefsteak fungus jutted out of the trunk.

I entered a wood of overgrown ash and old hazel coppice bursting densely from old stools and followed the rides on a course that curled back towards the road behind the cottage and gardens that occasionally fringed it.

I ducked through the hazels into a clearing and saw the first of the old coppice oaks. It was a giant, superbly misshapen, its trunk a cluster of carbuncles and its branches withering and bursting forth at the same time. It was alive and dead, young and old, all at one. There were 14 trees grouped about no more than an acre and a half of tangled blackberry and nettle jungle. Two or three oaks had collapsed, splitting themselves apart under the weight of their own crowns and falling outwards in several directions. Another had simply died on its feet, standing straight up like a ghost, but more petrified than rotten, riddled with beetle burrows and woodpecker drills.

Seized by a nerdish urge to measure and to count, I spread out my arms and flung myself flat against the trunks of these oaks, hugging them close to my bosom and stretching out my fingertips as far as they would go, then worked around the tree back to the point where I had begun. Each tree was just over three arm spans in girth five feet off the ground. My arm span is a fraction under six feet, so the trees are 18 feet in girth, or 215 inches. Applying the unreliable method of a half-inch to every year for a tree in a wood (or an inch a year for free-standing trees) they would be at least 430 years old. That would place them around 1570. Oliver Rackham says he knows of pollarded oaks in Epping Forest of only 50 inches in gift that are known to be at least 350 years old. The trunks of pollards grow more slowly because the tree is concentrating on growing its topmost boughs: doing what it is meant to do. The trunk is simply the body of a roman candle, shooting out leafy fireworks every spring and summer.

Beyond these oaks, the kitchen lights of one of the thatched estate cottages winked out as dusk began to fall. The cottage had a lawn and an apple tree still festooned with pale yellow fruit, unharvested, and more windfalls all over the lawn beneath. This was a sight you would never have seen in the past, any more than pollard oaks left uncut; such things were the staples of the lives of working people.

This place, with its oaks, is still known as 'the meadow' and would have been a miniature wood pasture, with sheep or a cow or two grazing beneath the oaks, and perhaps some pigs let in to eat the acorns.

I searched for acorns to plant and propagate descendants of these trees but found none. They must all have been gathered already by squirrels and mice.

Walking back down Clay Street, I chased the same whirring partridges and passed more bright pink spindle trees.

Great ropes of ivy, six inches thick, clambered up the wayside oaks, and they seemed none the worse for it. On some trees the ivy had been sawn through to kill it, though it sometimes managed to mend itself and grow back together.

I passed barns converted to houses with the regulation full-length glazing, floor-to-eaves, affording too public a cross-section of life inside, as though the inhabitants were living on the set of a rural *Big Brother* show. The barns are always weather-boarded and creosoted a uniform black, and they always have crisp shingle drives and open-fronted pseudo-cowsheds as garages. Water butts are in vogue too, and the barn I passed on Clay Street contained a long-legged Persian cat, too domesticated to be allowed out of doors.

Most of the barns used to be prime habitats for bats until converted. A recent survey amongst the barn conversions of Hertfordshire shows that, in spite of the fitting of the regulation bat lofts, access holes and the rest of it, as required by the planners, bats have disappeared from 75 per cent of them.

The gamekeeper, patrolling the stubble fields round the woods and copses in his Toyota pick-up – sinister, impersonal, detached, alienated from nature.

Roger Deakin (1943–2006)
Roger Deakin was perhaps one of the UK's best-loved environmentalists, writers and documentary-makers. Founder of Common Ground, he produced several acclaimed publications including Waterlog, Wildwood *and* Notes from Walnut Tree Farm, *a collection of writing taken from his personal notebooks and largely focusing on the wildlife and ecology of the area around his farmhouse in Suffolk.*
'Leaves', from Notes from Walnut Tree Farm *(Hamish Hamilton, 2008).*

THE PINE WOOD

RICHARD JEFFERIES

There was a humming in the tops of the young pines as if a swarm of bees were busy at the green cones. They were not visible through the thick needles, and on listening longer it seemed as if the sound was not exactly the note of a bee – a slightly different pitch, and the hum was different, while bees have a habit of working close together. Where there is one bee there are usually five or six, and the hum is that of a group; here there only appeared one or two insects to a pine. Nor was the buzz like that of the humble-bee, for every now and then one came along low down, flying between the stems, and his note was much deeper. By-and-by, crossing to the edge of the plantation, where the boughs could be examined, being within reach, I found it was wasps. A yellow wasp wandered over the blue-green needles till he found a pair with a drop of liquid like dew between them. There he fastened himself and sucked at it; you could see the drop gradually drying up till it was gone. The largest of these drops was generally between two needles – those of the Scotch fir or pine grow in pairs – but there were smaller drops on the outside of other needles. In search for this exuding turpentine the wasps filled the whole plantation with the sound of their wings. There must have been many thousands of them. They caused no inconvenience to any one walking in the copse, because they were high overhead.

Watching these wasps, I found two cocoons of pale yellow silk on a branch of larch, and by them a green spider. He was quite green – two shades, lightest on the back, but little lighter than the green larch bough. An ant had climbed up a pine and over to the extreme end of a bough; she seemed slow and stupefied in her motions, as if she had drunken of the turpentine and had lost her intelligence. The soft cones of the larch could be easily cut down the centre with a penknife, showing the structure of the cone and the seeds inside each scale. It is for these seeds that birds frequent the fir copses, shearing off the scales with their beaks. One larch cone had still the tuft at the top – a pineapple in miniature. The loudest sound in the wood was the humming in the trees; there was no wind, no sunshine; a summer day, still and shadowy, under large clouds high up. To this low humming the sense of hearing soon became accustomed, and it served but to render the silence deeper. In time, as I sat waiting and listening, there came the merest thin upstroke of sound, slight in structure, the echo of the strong spring singing. This was the summer repetition, dying away. A willow-wren still remembered his love, and whispered about it to the silent fir tops, as in after days we turn over the pages of letters, withered as leaves, and sigh. So gentle, so low, so tender a song the willow-wren sang that it could scarce be known as the voice of a bird, but was like that of some yet more delicate creature with the heart of a woman.

A butterfly with folded wings clung to a stalk of grass; upon the under side of his wing thus exposed there were buff spots, and dark dots and streaks drawn on the finest ground of pearl-grey, through which there came a hint of blue; there was a blue, too, shut up between the wings, visible at the edges. The spots, and dots, and streaks were not exactly the same on each wing; at first sight they appeared similar, but, on comparing one with the other, differences could be traced. The pattern was not mechanical; it was hand-painted by Nature, and the painter's eye and fingers varied in their work.

How fond Nature is of spot-markings! – the wings of butterflies, the feathers of birds, the surface of eggs, the leaves and petals of plants are constantly spotted; so, too, fish – as trout. From the wing of the butterfly I looked involuntarily at the foxglove I had just gathered; inside, the bells were thickly spotted – dots and dustings that might have been transferred to a butterfly's wing. The potted meadow-orchid; the brown dots on the cowslips; brown, black, greenish, reddish dots and spots and dustings on the eggs of the finches, the whitethroats, and so many others – some of the spots seem as if they had been splashed on and had run into short streaks, some mottled, some gathered together at the end; all spots, dots, dustings of minute specks, mottling and irregular markings. The histories, the stories, the library of knowledge contained in those signs! It was thought a wonderful thing when at last the strange inscriptions of Assyria were read, made of nail-headed characters whose sound was lost; it was thought a triumph when the yet older hieroglyphics of Egypt were compelled to give up their messages, and the world hoped that we should know the secrets of life. That hope was disappointed; there was nothing in the records but superstition and useless ritual. But here we go back to the beginning; the antiquity of Egypt is nothing to the age of these signs – they date from unfathomable time. In them the sun has written his commands, and the wind inscribed deep thought. They were before superstition began; they were composed in the old, old world, when the Immortals walked on earth. They have been handed down thousands upon thousands of years to tell us that to-day we are still in the presence of the heavenly visitants, if only we will give up the soul to these pure influences. The language in which they are written has no alphabet, and cannot be reduced to order. It can only be understood by the heart and spirit. Look down into this foxglove bell and you will know that; look long and lovingly at this blue butterfly's underwing, and a feeling will rise to your consciousness.

Some time passed, but the butterfly did not move; a touch presently disturbed him, and flutter, flutter went his blue wings, only for a few seconds, to another grass-stalk, and so on from grass-stalk to grass-stalk as compelled, a yard flight at most. There was no sunshine, and under the clouds he had no animation. A swallow went by singing in the air, and as he flew his forked tail was shut, and but one streak of feathers drawn past. Though but young trees, there was a coating of fallen needles under the firs an inch thick, and beneath it the dry earth touched warm. A fern here and there came up through it, the palest of pale green, quite a different colour to the same species growing in the hedges away from the copse. A yellow fungus, streaked with scarlet as if blood had soaked into it, stood at the foot of a tree occasionally. Black fungi, dry, shrivelled, and dead, lay fallen about, detached from the places where they had grown, and crumbling if handled. Still more silent after sunset, the wood was utterly quiet; the swallows no longer passed twittering, the willow-wren was gone, there was no hum or rustle; the wood was as silent as a shadow.

But before the darkness a song and an answer arose in a tree, one bird singing a few notes and another replying side by side. Two goldfinches sat on the cross of a larch-fir and sang, looking towards the west, where the light lingered. High up, the larch-fir boughs with the top shoot form a cross; on this one goldfinch sat, the other was immediately beneath. At even the birds often turn to the west as they sing.

Next morning the August sun shone, and the wood was all a-hum with insects. The wasps were working at the pine boughs high overhead; the bees by dozens were crowding to the bramble flowers; swarming on them, they seemed so delighted; humble-bees went wandering among the ferns in the copse and in the ditches – they sometimes alight on fern – and calling at every purple heath-blossom, at the purple knap-weeds, purple thistles, and broad handfuls of yellow-weed flowers. Wasp-like flies barred with yellow suspended themselves in the air between the pine-trunks like hawks hovering, and suddenly shot themselves a yard forward or to one side, as if the rapid vibration of their wings while hovering had accumulated force which drove them as if discharged from a cross-bow. The sun had set all things in motion.

There was a hum under the oak by the hedge, a hum in the pine wood, a humming among the heat and the dry grass which heat had browned. The air was alive and merry with sound, so that the day seemed quite different and twice as pleasant. Three blue butterflies fluttered in one flowery corner, the warmth gave them vigour; two had a silvery edging to their wings, one was brown and blue. The nuts reddening at the tips appeared ripening like apples in the sunshine. This corner is a favourite with wild bees and butterflies; if the sun shines they are sure to be found there at the heath-bloom and tall yellow-weed, and among the dry seeding bennets or grass-stalks. All things, even butterflies, are local in their habits. Far up on the hillside, the blue-green of the pines beneath shone in the sun – a burnished colour; the high hillside is covered with heath and heather. Where there are open places a small species of gorse, scarcely six inches high, is in bloom, the yellow blossom on the extremity of the stalk.

Some of these gorse plants seemed to have a different flower growing at the side of the stem, instead of at the extremity. These florets were cream-coloured, so that it looked like a new species of gorse. On gathering it to examine the thick-set florets, it was found that a slender runner or creeper had been torn up with it. Like a thread the creeper had wound itself round and round the furze, buried in and hidden by the prickles, and it was this creeper that bore the white or cream florets. It was tied round as tightly as thread could be, so that the florets seemed to start from the stem, deceiving the eye at first. In some places this parasite plant had grown up the heath and strangled it, so that the tips turned brown and died. The runners extended in every direction across the ground, like those of strawberries. One creeper had climbed up a bennet, or seeding grass-stalk, binding the stalk and a blade of the grass together, and flowering there. On the ground there were patches of grey lichen; many of the pillar-like stems were crowned with a red top. Under a small boulder stone there was an ants' nest. These boulders, or, as they are called locally, 'bowlers', were scattered about the heath. Many of stones were spotted with dark dots of lichen, not unlike a toad.

Thoughtlessly turning over a boulder about nine inches square, lo! There was subject enough for thinking underneath it – a subject that has been thought about many thousand years; for this piece of rock had formed the roof of an ants' nest. The stone had sunk three inches deep into the dry soil of sand and peaty mould, and in the floor of the hole the ants had worked out their excavations, which resembled an outline map. The largest excavation was like England; at the top, or north, they had left a narrow bridge, an eighth of an inch wide, under which to pass into Scotland, and from Scotland again another narrow arch led to the Orkney Islands; these last, however, were dug in the perpendicular side of the hole. In the corners of these excavations tunnels ran deeper into the ground, and the ants immediately began hurrying their treasures, the eggs, down into these cellars. At one angle a tunnel went beneath the heath into further excavations beneath a second boulder stone. Without, a fern grew, and the dead dry steams of heather crossed each other.

This discovery led to the turning over of another boulder stone not far off, and under it there appeared a much more extensive and complete series of galleries, bridges, cellars and tunnels. In these the whole life-history of the ant was exposed at a single glance, as if one had taken off the roofs of a city. One cell contained a dust-like deposit, another a collection resembling the dust, but now elongated and a little greenish; a third treasury, much larger, was piled up with yellowish grains about the size of wheat, each with a black dot on the top, and looking like minute hop-pockets. Besides these, there was a pure white substance in a corridor, which the irritated ants seemed particularly anxious to remove out of sight, and quickly carried away. Among the ants rushing about there were several with wings; one took flight; one was seized by a wingless ant and dragged down into a cellar, as if to prevent its taking wing. A helpless green fly was in the midst, and round the outside galleries there crept a creature like a spider, seeming to try to hide itself. If the nest had been formed under glass, it could not have been more open to view. The stone was carefully replaced.

Richard Jefferies (1848–1887)

A naturalist and novelist, Richard Jefferies was the son of a Wiltshire farmer. He contributed to local papers before moving to London, where he wrote for the Pall Mall Gazette, *which first published his* The Gamekeeper at Home *(1877) and* Wildlife in a Southern County *(1879). He subsequently returned to the country. Edward Thomas called* The Gamekeeper at Home, *'The first thoroughly rustic book in English, by a countryman and about the country, with no alien savours whatever.' 'The Pine Wood' from* The Open Air *(London, 1885).*

CHAPTER 6

IN THE WILD

VERY CLOSE ENCOUNTERS WITH BRITISH WILDLIFE

BILL ODDIE

I'll never forget the first time I handled a bird.

It was in 1955, in mid-August, and I was 14. The event took place near the seashore, in the sand dunes, alongside the estuary of a small river, on the Northumberland coast. I was part of a group that had driven down that morning from Monk's House Bird Observatory, a few miles to the north. Six of us had crammed into a Morris Minor estate, with real wood trimmings inside and out.

Squeezing six adults into a Morris Minor would probably have set a record, but five of us were not yet fully grown. Including me, we were five schoolboys on an 'educational' adventure holiday. The only grown up – the driver, of course – was the almost legendary Dr Eric Ennion: a pioneering naturalist, exquisitely distinctive artist, truly inspiring person, and a very nice man. Dr Ennion was *more* than fully grown. In fact, he was larger than life in many totally agreeable respects – including physically. Imagine an extra-large Mr Pickwick, with wellies and binoculars. However, I can't imagine Mr Pickwick organising an expedition to go wader trapping, which is what we were doing. Mind you, it is more than likely that country folk in Dickensian days did go in for trapping small birds, and it is equally likely that the methods and equipment they used were much the same as the ones that we were using in 1955. Of course our respective motives were different – we were serving science. They were serving dinner.

Nowadays, nearly all bird trapping by ornithologists is done with 'mist nets'. These are like giant hair nets, stretched between poles – effectively an invisible wall that turns into a hammock when a bird flies into it. However, back in 1955, mist nets were still at the testing stage. As it happens, a couple of years later, the first consignments from Japan were delivered to Monk's House, whose ringers prided themselves on leading the way in new trapping techniques. But the techniques we were using that day were not new – and nor were the traps.

One of them was a 'spring net', which looked like something that might have been used by a medieval torturer. When laid open, it resembled a large metal hoop with string mesh stretched across it. When closed – or set – it folded back into a semi-circle. It worked on the mouse-trap principle – the bird was supposed to wander along and trip the trap, thus releasing a strong spring that snapped the net open at a quite alarming speed, catching the bird underneath it. That was the theory, anyhow.

The reality was slightly different. There are a couple of major flaws with spring nets. One was that it's pretty much impossible to put out bait for waders. The equivalent of a mouse's irresistible chunk of cheese would, for a wader, be a beakful of minuscule mud-worms. Not only are these very hard to collect, but it's even harder to persuade them to sit still and wait to be eaten. You have to hope the bird will simply stumble into the trap – by accident, as it were. This brings me to the second flaw.

The word 'accident' is not entirely absent from the annals of spring-netting. Frankly, they were quite dangerous – both to the people setting them, who risked having a finger snapped off, and to the birds who could lose something even more vital, like their life. I never witnessed it myself, but I do know that the very occasional bird wasn't so much trapped as beheaded. Fortunately, the one major consolation about spring nets was that they hardly ever caught anything.

To be honest, the same could be said for 'clap nets', but I much preferred them. They were fairer to the birds, and more fun for the ringers. A clap net was also comprised of netting on a frame but, in this case, the frame was rectangular and not so heavy. It was placed out on the mud, with one side weighted down with stones and seaweed. A long light rope operated a sort of simple pulley arrangement attached to another side of the net. Once laid in position out on the mud, the final touch was to disguise the trap's presence with more bits of seaweed and small shells.

It was a contraption that is as hard to explain as it was to set up. Eventually though, the ringer or the ringer's assistant – for example, me – retired to the cover of the dunes, keeping hold of the end of the pull rope. There, he or she waited – often all day, and probably nodding off now and then, although hopefully waking up before the rising tide swamped the trap and the waves carried it out to sea. The one cardinal rule was 'never let go of the rope'. As long as you managed this feat, clap netting was – if nothing else – rather relaxing.

What's more, it could also be rather thrilling. It ran a gamut of emotions that reminds me of the kids on the wrapper of a 'Five Boys' chocolate bar. You won't remember these delightful bars unless you are of a certain – considerable – age, but believe me, back in the 1950s, the Five Boys were iconic. Their photos on the wrapper depicted five facial expressions conveying five emotional responses to the possibility of obtaining and eating the chocolate within.

So, applying the same principle to clap netting: there is *anticipation*, as a wader probes and potters across the mud towards the trap zone; *procrastination*, as you try to judge the right moment to pull the rope; *frustration*, when you yank too early, and the net simply flips a shower of seaweed and sand over the startled bird (which instantly flees over the horizon in search of somewhere more peaceful to feed); and, finally, there is *elation*, when you realise that you've timed it right. That doesn't even take into account the *satisfaction* experienced when you scamper down to the trap, lift the mesh a smidgeon, and find the bird has indeed been securely caught. *That's* the equivalent of unwrapping the chocolate. The equivalent of taking a bite is when the bird is safely and firmly in your grip.

On that day in 1955, those emotions were indeed experienced by five boys – including me. We were, of course, supervised by Dr Ennion. The good doctor wasn't built for speed, but I was. Consequently he was on pulling duty and I was the runner. For a tantalising ten minutes we watched a bird tiptoeing towards the camouflaged trap. Then, suddenly, the flip of a wrist, the whip of the rope, the splat of the netting, and a cry of: 'Bill! Quick as you can!' I belted across the mudflats and dropped to my knees to check that the mesh had held firm and that the bird was calm.

Almost speechless with excitement, but anxious to make sure the doctor realised I knew my birds, I yelled out: 'Ringed Plover. Juvenile. Or maybe an adult going into winter plumage. No, mid-August, too early for that, isn't it?'

Dr Ennion arrived at my side, knelt down, and expertly and tenderly extracted the plump little bird, confirming my identification as he did so.

'Ringed Plover. Juvenile. Born only a month or two ago. OK, let's ring this little chap. Bill, would you fold up the trap please? The tide's coming in fast.'

The doctor must have sensed my anxiety. 'Don't worry,' he assured me, 'we'll wait for you in the dunes.'

And ten minutes later, it happened. In mid-August, in the Northumbrian dunes, I handled my first bird. Strictly speaking, it was, I suspect, illegal. Ringing was and still is governed by stringent controls. A licence is only granted after a period of training and experience, which I certainly didn't have at that point. I also dare say there was an over-18 rule – so, no doubt, I was underage. But, Dr Ennion was a dispenser of magic moments, and magicians make their own rules.

With a deftness approaching sleight of hand, he passed the bird from the cradle of his fingers into mine. No nervousness, no panic – from me, or the Ringed Plover. The bird was perfectly calm. It blinked a couple of times, looked at me with its shiny button eyes and then glanced at the doctor, as if for assurance that it was in safe hands. Then – reassuringly for us all – it began to fall asleep. It felt fluffy in my fingers – warm, soft, fragile, and very tiny. And, yet, at the same time, it felt strong and confident – almost tough. As I struggled to put my feelings into words, the doctor provided them for me.

'What you are holding in your hands is a little miracle. It can do all sorts of things we can't. It can put up with all kinds of weather. It can fly. And it can travel hundreds or even thousands of miles, without a map, sometimes at night, not even with its parents. This Ringed Plover may stay here this winter, or it may fly down to Africa and come back in a couple of years' time. There's so much we still don't know about birds and migration. That's why we put rings on them. When we get back to the Observatory I'll show you a map of ringing recoveries ...' he said.

I could sense the magic moment melting into an educational monologue. This was fine, because we'd come to Monk's House to learn – but not just now. I was totally entranced by the 'little miracle' in my hands. What word would express what I was feeling? Was it 'fun'? Well, yes. 'Excitement'? Sure. But, more than that, to hold a miracle in the palm of your hands, that was a *privilege*. That's exactly what it was, is, and always will be.

After more visits to Monk's House, I qualified as a ringer and held a licence for many years. I became a whiz with my mist nets and every bird I caught I subjected to a thorough 'processing', to use the rather prosaic 'ringer's jargon'. I became expert at ageing, sexing and weighing the birds, measuring their mandibles, tarsi and primary projections, perusing them for abrasions and emarginations, and calculating their wing formulae. It would have been all too easy to regard my findings as merely notes and numbers in a data bank, but it has never happened. I can honestly say that every single time I get to handle a bird – whatever the species – there is always a moment when I pause, look into its eyes and say, 'This is a privilege. Thank you.'

I'd like to think the birds respond with a 'You're welcome', too. Yes, I do talk to the birds – out loud – and I often pretend they answer. In fact, we sometimes have quite long conversations. When I let them go, I always wish them 'good luck, – which, in their world, they certainly need.

Over the years, I have learned several things about birds in the hand. They are always a lot smaller than you expect. A Heron seems hardly bigger than a chicken, and even the largest of owls turns out to be little more than a living feather duster, insulating a skinny stick of a skeleton. Birds really are that small. Goldcrests, for example, are hardly bigger than a bee and have to be handled every bit as gingerly – though, of course, they won't sting, and they probably won't even bite or scratch. That's another thing I have learned: the majority of birds do not struggle if they are handled expertly. Many just settle down cosily, like my Ringed Plover. Some nod off, while others can be lulled into a trance-like torpor, simply by turning your hand so that they are lying on their backs. In this state, and as if hypnotised, they often don't even notice if you open your fingers. Only when they are turned back over do they realise they are free to go.

I have to concede that Dr Ennion broke me in very gently. There is hardly a more placid species than a Ringed Plover, which tend to be as docile as a dove. However, on my next Monk's House trip the following spring, the doctor supervised my initiation into the less gentle side of bird catching when he took us to the Farne Islands. Here, we were literally 'bloodied' by what many people regard as the cutest and most comical bird of them all: Puffins. Well, let me tell you, they may waddle and grunt in an amusing manner, but when they lacerate your wrists with their needle-sharp little claws, it is not so funny. Indeed, when it comes to 'presenting' them in the hand, I would vote Puffins as the most belligerent little blighters in the bird world.

Hang on, though – what do I mean by 'presenting' them? Surely that's not a ringer's expression, is it? It sounds more like television jargon – and, quite so. For the past decade or two I have been a wildlife 'presenter' on the telly and, on many occasions, this has involved 'presenting' a wild creature to the camera. This doesn't mean pointing it out from a safe distance, but getting hold of it firmly enough for the camera can get a real close-up. This requires manoeuvring the creature into the position that you, the director or the cameraman want it to be in. It goes without saying this may well differ from the position that *it* wants to be in. At such times, the creature is likely to express its disapproval or discomfort in the only way it knows how: by inflicting pain onto whoever is handling it. In this case, that 'whoever' is me.

*   *   *

I'm sure that all wildlife presenters have been asked whether they have been attacked by anything, and the answer will most certainly be 'yes'. This, of course, leads to a second question: 'What's the worst thing that's ever bitten, pecked or stung you?' The answer to this one will vary according to the budget and location of the TV series. The intrepid traveller-type presenter may have suffered anything from being gnawed by a crocodile, to being charged by a rhino, anywhere from Africa to Asia, or Brazil to Borneo. However, all of my rather-too-close encounters have been British. This is not so much a reflection of my less-than-lavish budget, as it is my love for British wildlife. Even when it hurts!

Apart from Puffins, birds have generally been as gentle with me as I have with them. I have, however, learned that when handling a Heron one eye must be kept on its beak. Otherwise, one eye is all you'll end up with. The rule with birds of prey is much the same as it is with Puffins – it's not the beak that will have you, but the claws. Falconers wear those whacking great leather gloves for a reason – as I realised after I'd had a Sparrowhawk's talons sunk into my bare arm for ten minutes. The irony is that I'm sure it wasn't trying to hurt me; it just didn't want to fall off, and look silly on telly.

Luckily, I have yet to be badly stung on air – or anywhere else – despite allowing several hornets to promenade round my hands. They look big and scary, but they are much less aggressive than wasps. This lot just tickled. I have been bitten – no, eaten alive – by midges in Scotland in summer, but I wasn't trying to present them to camera. Anyway, midges don't really sting. But some plants do. I was filming at a rabbit warren, in Norfolk's Breckland – looking at the camera rather than where I was going – when I stepped into a hole, tripped and fell headlong, and spread- eagled, into a bed of nettles. It was absolute agony – for days.

I have, of course, been nipped, too – and by many a small crab, a few middle-sized ones, and one big one that really didn't want to let go. This guy came very close to breaking my skin (and I came very close to breaking its shell!). However, the only crustacean to actually draw blood was a Signal Crayfish, an alien species that is causing big problems in British rivers. I admit I was holding it up to camera and threatening to have it cooked, which is maybe what provoked it to snap its pincers onto my thumb like a pair of secateurs. Hey, there's a thought; maybe all those unwelcome crayfish could be put to work in the garden doing a bit of pruning.

This may sound silly, but once upon a time people did use nippy creatures for practical purposes; for example, the Wart-biter Cricket. Honestly. What's more, I can believe that it worked, judging from the wound I received from the jaws of a Great Bush Cricket; it would surely have severed a bunion. Great Bush Cricket? Bunion Buster Cricket, more like. Or how about Callous Crusher Cricket? I came up with quite few alternative names for the Great Bush Cricket before we finally managed to prise it off my arm, where it left a pair of punctures of which any vampire would've been proud.

However, if it's my blood you're after, then bring on the small mammals. Most of them are not only small, but also shy, elusive and nocturnal. In many cases, the only way of getting a decent close-up of a small mammal is to catch it and hold it up to the camera. The trapping part is safe enough. You simply put out lots of small tin boxes with a hinged door at one end, which will click shut if any little creature wanders inside. The animal may have a hour or so in the dark waiting for the 'trapper' to come back, but they won't be scared. They live in dark holes and tunnels anyway, and they'll have a generous supply of fruit and nuts, which is what lured them there in the first place. At the crack of dawn, along comes 'the trapper' – a qualified mammal handler who will have little problem gently shaking out whatever has been caught in the metal box, straight into a nice, cosy little cloth bag.

What happens next may be a bit undignified, but it's all in the aid of science. The vole, mouse or shrew is transferred into a little, transparent plastic pouch, in order to be hung onto a miniature scale and weighed. This may be followed by the minor embarrassment of having its genitals examined, and maybe a few measurements taken. A small dab of coloured paint may be applied to its nether regions or – on rare occasions – it may receive a tiny injection of anaesthetic and have an even tinier transmitter slipped into the scruff of its neck. All of this rigmarole is undertaken as quickly and as deftly as possible by qualified experts, and the animals are certainly not harmed, distressed, frightened or angry. I do suspect, however, that some of them may become a teeny bit cheesed off. They would like to be returned to the wild now, please.

I was handed the short straw, of course – or, rather, the short-tempered mammal. I reckon he was thinking: 'OK, trap me, bag me, weigh me, measure me, dab me, drug me and rummage down below if your must; but, I warn you, if you try to hold me up to the camera for a close-up …' I still bear the tooth marks.

If you are wondering which small British mammal has the sharpest incisors, I can tell you that a Water Vole could gnaw through your wrist as quickly as a Beaver fells a tree, and its gnashers can penetrate all except the thickest of leather gauntlets. If you are about to handle a Water Vole, I would recommend the type of gloves worn by a Hell's Angel or a wicket-keeper. The gardening gloves supplied by the BBC simply proved that you can be bitten *through* material, and experience some pretty extreme pain!

For a small mammal, a Water Vole is a quite big. So, what about the really small ones, like Shrews? I had a unique opportunity to compare three species after one particularly productive trap round – the main purpose of which was to catch Harvest Mice. These very small mammals were appropriately docile in the hand.

Shrews are equally tiny, but docile they are not! The Pygmy Shrew
– smaller even than the Harvest Mouse – gave me a pygmy nip,
and the Common Shrew's bite was nothing out of the ordinary. So
I was a little complacent when I attempted to grab hold of the
Water Shrew. All shrews are hyperactive, but the Water Shrew was
alarmingly manic. While the other two species had sat demurely in
their plastic pouches waiting until presenter-biting time, the
Water Shrew had been frantically exercising its teeth by nibbling
several holes through its bag, and was in the very act of wriggling
to freedom when I grabbed it.

At this point it bit me. 'Point' is the operative word here, as its
front teeth were as sharp as red-hot needles and every bit as
painful. With every lunge, another spot of blood appeared on
my skin, until I let the tiny terror make a leap for freedom. What
did I feel as he scampered back to the marsh? Well, a fair amount
of agony – yes – but mainly admiration. What a fabulous feisty
little demon.

A memorable small-mammal attack, but not the worst. For
sheer surprise, gore and horror, I don't think I will ever beat my
close encounter with an Orkney Vole. I say 'surprise' because
Orkney Voles have a reputation for being non-aggressive. I had
read this in a reputable book about mammals, and our researchers
had confirmed it. And just to make the chance of an unpleasant
incident seem even less likely, the particular animal I was due to
handle was one that was already in the care of an Orkney islander.
I was assured that this individual was particularly docile. It
certainly looked as harmless as a hamster, curled up cosily in the
corner of the fish tank in which it had been transported. The water
– and the fish – had been replaced with straw, lettuce leaves, bits
of bark, and other things small mammals like. Unfortunately,
there was so much stuff in there that the cameraman couldn't even
find the vole in his viewfinder, let alone get decent close-ups.

'Oh, just pick him up,' said the islander. 'He's never bitten anyone in his life.'

Well, he soon had! I don't know if he severed an artery or a vein or something, but within seconds my arm was literally gushing blood. When I tried to prise open his jaws, he clamped them round my finger. More blood spurted. The Orkney man attempted to rescue me – or his vole? – and more blood spattered across his Orkney knit sweater. The sound recorder exhorted me to hurl the vole over the nearby cliff. I retorted that I could never do such a thing; however, regardless of my good intentions, it simply wouldn't let go! I finally managed to shake it off my lacerated hand and back into its fish tank, where it immediately retired to a corner and began licking blood off its fur. Even for a vole, it was a pretty spooky image. There was blood dripping down the glass sides of the tank, there was blood on my binoculars, and both of my arms were streaked and blotched with blood.

For a moment, there was a strange silence, rather like at the end of a battle. Then somebody asked if I was OK.

'Yeah, yeah,' I replied. 'It probably looked at lot worse than it was.'

'Well, it looked pretty awful,' said the cameraman.

'Anyway,' I continued, ever the professional, 'it'll make great television!'

'It won't,' contradicted the cameraman. 'I stopped filming. I can't stand the sight of blood!'

Last I heard, he'd got a job on CBeebies.

Of course, I bear no grudge against Orkney – or any other – voles, nor against shrews, or any other small or large mammals. Over the years, I have handled a considerable selection of British wildlife and, hopefully, will continue to do so. It has always been and always will be a *privilege*.

Bill Oddie

Bill Oddie is an ornithologist, conservationist and a presenter of TV wildlife programmes, including Britain Goes Wild. *He is the author of several books, including* One Flew into the Cuckoo's Nest – My Autobiography *and* Gripping Yarns: Tales of Birds and Birding, *and is a Vice President of The Wildlife Trusts.*

FLIGHT

NAN SHEPHERD

The first time I found summer on the plateau – for although my earliest expeditions were all made in June or July, I experienced cloud, mist, howling wind, hailstones, rain and even a blizzard – the first time the sun blazed and the air was balmy, we were standing on the edge of an outward-facing precipice, when I was startled by a whizzing sound behind me. Something dark swished past the side of my head at a speed that made me giddy. Hardly had I got back my balance when it came again, whistling through the windless air, which eddied around me with the motion. This time my eyes were ready, and I realised that a swift was sweeping in mighty curves over the edge of the plateau, plunging down the face of the rock and rising again like a jet of water. No one had told me I should find swifts on the mountain. Eagles and ptarmigan, yes: but that first sight of the mad, joyous abandon of the swift over and over the very edge of the precipice shocked me with the thrill of elation. All that volley of speed, those convolutions of delight, to catch a few flies! The discrepancy between purpose and performance made me laugh aloud – a laugh that gave the same feeling of release as though I had been dancing for a long time.

It seems odd that merely to watch the motion of flight should give the body not only vicarious exhilaration but release. So urgent is the rhythm that invades the blood. This power of flight to take us into itself through the eye as though we had actually shared in the motion, I have never felt so strongly as when watching swifts on the mountaintop. Their headlong rush, each curve of which is at the same time a miracle of grace, the swishing sound of their cleavage of the air and the occasional high-pitched cry that is hardly like the note of an earthly bird, seem to make visible and audible some essence of the free, wild spirit of the mountain.

The flight of the eagle, if less immediately exciting than that of the swift, is more profoundly satisfying. The great spiral of his ascent, rising coil over coil in slow symmetry, has in its movement all the amplitude of space. And when he has soared to the top of his bent, there comes the level of flight as far as the eye can follow – straight, clean and as effortless as breathing. The wings hardly move, now and then perhaps a lazy flap as though a cyclist, free-wheeling on a gentle slope, turned the crank a time or two. The bird seems to float, but to float with a direct and undeviating force. It is only when one remarks that he is floating up-wind that the magnitude of that force becomes apparent. I stood once about the 2500-feet level – in January when the world was quite white – and watched an eagle well below me following up the river valley in search of food. He flew right into the wind. The wings were slightly tilted, but so far as I could judge from above he held them steady. And he came on with a purposeful urgency behind which must have been the very terror of strength.

*   *   *

It is tantalising to see something unusual, but not its ending. One January afternoon, in a frozen silent world, I saw two stags with antlers interlaced dragging each other backwards and forwards across the ringing frozen floor of a hollow. Their dark forms stood out against the snow. I watched till dusk came on and I could barely see but could still near the noise of the scuffle. It is the only time I have seen this phenomenon of interlocked antlers, and as I have always been told that stags so caught cannot extricate themselves and fight on till one or both die, I wanted badly to see what happened. I went back next day but found no stags, dead or alive. The crofter-ghillie in whose house I was staying said that they probably saved themselves by the breaking of an antler.

The roaring of the stags set me another problem to which I have not found a definitive answer. On one of those potent days of mid-October, golden as whisky, I was wandering on the slopes of Ben Avon above Loch Builg. Suddenly I was startled by a musical call that resounded across the hill, and was answered by a like call from another direction. Yodelling, I thought. There was such gaiety in the sound that I looked eagerly about, thinking: these are students, they are hailing one another from sheer exuberance of spirit. But I saw no one. The yodelling went on. The yodelling went on all day, clear, bell-like and musical; and it was not long till I realised that there was no other human being on the mountain and that the stags were the yodellers. The clear bell notes were new to me. I had heard stags roar often enough, in deep raucous tones. Bellowing. The dictionary would have me believe that belling is merely a variant of bellowing. For me belling will always mean the music of that golden day. All the time I listened, there was not a single harsh note.

But why? That is what I don't understand. Why sometimes

raucous and sometimes like a bell? Hillmen whom I have asked give different suggestions. That the bell notes are from young stags and the raucous from old. But against that, one gamekeeper sets the tale of a gruff-voiced bellower that the shooting-party to a man declared would be an old beast and turned out when they got him to be comparatively young. That the note changes to express different needs. But that theory does not seem to be borne out by the way in which two stags kept up an antiphon one day in my hearing, the raucous answering the bell across a ravine with absolute consistency. That stags are like human beings and some have tenor voices, some bass. Then were they all tenor stags on that morning when the hill broke into a cantata? All young? Or all tenor? Or all in love with the morning?

Normally deer are silent creatures, but when alarmed they bark like an angry dog. I have heard the warning bark far off on a distant slope and only then been aware of the presence of a herd. Then they are off, flowing up the hill and over the horizon. Their patterns against the sky are endless – a frieze of doe and fawn and doe and fawn. Or a tossing forest of massed antlers. Or with long necks to the ground, feeding, like hens pecking. Those mobile necks are a thought uncanny at times. I have seen five necks rise like swaying snakes, a small snake-like head on each, the bodies hidden. Find hinds. And I have seen a hind turn her head to look at me, twisting her neck around until the face seemed to hang suspended in air alongside the rump and some atavistic fear awoke in me. Bird, animal and reptile – there is something of them all in the deer. Its flight is fluid as a bird's. Especially the roes, the very young ones, dappled, with limbs like the stalks of flowers, move over the heather with an incredible lightness. They seem to float; yet their motion is in a way more wonderful even than flight, for each of these gleaming hooves does touch the ground. The lovely pattern of the limbs is fixed to the earth and cannot be detached from it.

Indeed there are times when the earth seems to re-absorb this creature of air and light. Roes melt into the wood – I have stared a long time into birches where I knew a doe was standing and saw her only when at last she flicked an ear. In December on an open heath I have found myself close upon a feeding red roe so like her background that I had thought the white scut another patch of snow. She becomes aware of me, her ears lift, her head goes sharply up, the neck elongated. I stand very still, the head drops, she becomes again part of the earth. Further up on the slopes one can watch a fawn learning his hillcraft from his mother, pausing in exactly her attitude, turning a wary head as she turns hers.

But find a fawn alone in a hidden hollow, he will not endure with his mother's patience. It is not easy to make a doe move before you do, but when the fawn, after his first startled jump to the far side of the hollow, stands to gaze at you on the other side, if you keep perfectly still he grows restive, moves his head now side on to you, now front, an ear twitches, a nostril, finally he turns and walks away, like a reluctant but inquisitive child, pausing at every third step to look back.

I have never had the incredible fortune, as a young doctor I know once had, of seeing a hind give birth; but I have found very young fawns, left by their mothers beside a stone on heather. Once I had gone off the track to visit a small tarn. Something impelled me to walk round the back of the tarn, scrambling between the rock and the water, and then to continue downwards over a heathery slope that is not very often crossed. From the corner of my eye I noticed two or three hinds making off; and a moment later I came on a tiny fawn lying crouched into the heather near a stone. It lay in an oddly rigid way, the limbs contorted in unnatural positions. Could it be dead? I bent over it – very gently touched it. It was warm. The contorted limbs were fluid as water in my hands. The little creature gave no sign of life. The neck was stretched, stiff and ungainly, the head almost hidden; the eyes stared, undeviating. Only the flanks pulsated. Nothing moved but the pulsing flanks. There was no voluntary movement whatsoever, no smallest twitch or flicker. I had never before seen a fawn shamming dead, as young birds do.

A young squirrel, caught upon his own occasions, will behave like the young fawn you have surprised walking out alone: both are a little reckless about humanity. I have come upon a small squirrel the size of a well-grown mouse, on the ground under fir trees, scampering from cone to cone, picking up each in turn, scrutinising, sampling, tossing it away, with a sort of wilful petulance in his movements such as I have seen in small children who have too many toys. He becomes aware of me, pauses, eyes me, eyes his cone. Cupidity and caution struggle within him, I am quite still, caution loses, he goes on with his game among the goodies. When he stops to crunch, I move forward. At last I move so near that he is suddenly alarmed. He makes for a huge old pine tree whose bark hangs in scales so thick and solid that his small limbs can hardly compass them. He can't get up; and now, like his red-gold parents, he wallops his thin long ribbon-like tail, not yet grown bushy, in a small futile way, and scrabbles against the mountainous humps of bark. At last he is up, he runs out on a side branch and jeers down at me in triumph.

Other young things – leverets in the form wrapped in silky hair – fox cubs playing in the sun in a distant fold of the hill – the fox himself with his fat red brush – the red-brown squirrel in the woods below, whacking his tail against the tree-trunk and chattering through closed lips (I think) against the intruder – gold-brown lizards and the gold-brown floss of cocoons in the heather – small golden bees and small blue butterflies – green dragon flies and emerald beetles – moths like oiled paper and moths like burnt paper – water-beetles skimming the highest tarns – small mice so rarely seen but leaving a thousand tracks upon the snow – ant-heaps of birch-twigs or pine-needles (*preens*, in the northern word) flickering with activity when the sun shines – midges, mosquitoes, flies by the hundred thousand, adders and a rare strange slowworm – small frogs jumping like tiddly-winks – rich brown hairy caterpillars by the handful and fat green ones with blobs of amethyst, a perfect camouflage on heather – life in so many guises.

It is not just now sheep country. The sheep were cleared to make room for deer, today in one district the deer are giving place to Highland cattle, those placid and abstemious beasts to whom thin fare is a necessity and whose shaggy winter mats protect them from the bitter winds. They look ferocious and are very gentle – in this resembling some of the blackface ewes, hags as ugly as sin that are found in every mountain flock, grim old malignants whose cankered horns above a black physiognomy must, I feel sure, be the origin of the Scots conception of the Devil.

Nan Shepherd (1893–1981)

A novelist and lecturer, Nan Shepherd was born in Deeside. She graduated from Aberdeen University and lectured in English at what is now Aberdeen College of Education. An enthusiastic gardener and hill-walker, she was a keen member of the Deeside Field Club and made many visits to the Cairngorms. Though widely travelled in Europe and South Africa, she remained devoted to the house in which she grew up and spent most of her adult life, three miles from Aberdeen. The Living Mountain *was published in 1996 as part of* The Grampian Quartet. *'Flight', from* The Living Mountain *(Canongate Books, 2008).*

THE AUTUMN STALK

SIR JOHN LISTER-KAYE

OCTOBER 12TH

I am out to see a stag I have been listening to all night. He came close to the house, perhaps only 250 yards away, in the steep field that backs on to the loch woods. His hinds and their calves have been down to the rich grazing under cover of darkness. Although he is not eating at all – and won't again until the rut is over – he will have followed them down through the woods, constantly roaring and circling, checking them out for the next hind to come into season. In the field he would have held them there on the rutting stand of his own choosing, guarding them against any other stag that might arrive to fancy his chances. I know that at dawn they will drift uphill again, leaving the field over the fence, often with the give-away ping of the top wire plucked like a guitar string by a lazy cloven hoof. Once back in the woods they will melt away like shadows, their departure revealed only by the gradual softening of their stag's bellowing.

I lie in bed until I know they are well inside the woods. Stalking them in the dark is well-nigh impossible, our crimped vision only adding to the technical difficulties of stalking wild animals as keenly tuned as deer. Standing at the open window I take a bearing on direction, where I think they are. I wait for the roars, coming now at 10- or 15-minute intervals, until they seem to have stopped in one place. That's where I think they will settle for the day, lying up in the rust-tinged bracken, the stag only perfunctorily roaring unless he is challenged. The dawn is gathering. It is time to move.

It has rained in the night, but the sky is clear now and I can still see the stars, although pockets of mist loiter in the field hollows so that I can barely see the forest edge. First I must check the wind. A faint breeze is drifting up the glen from the south-east. Stringy wisps of cloud pass across a silver segment of moon sinking towards the western rim of the hills above the loch. I watch to make sure breeze and clouds are passing in the same direction. An eddying wind can be treacherous. It's OK, both are flowing in unison, the clouds and the handful of grass seeds I throw up matching the chill on my cheek. I cross the fence into the field – must be careful not to ping the wires.

Powering up the open pasture is quick and easy. I stop to recover my breath, calm myself down before I enter the woods; the rank odour of deer is all round me. It is raw and elemental, not the heavily overburdened stench of a cowshed or a pigsty, but warmer, closer to that of a potting shed with a hint of dog kennel. It's musky and earthy together, and reminds me of a brown bear I once met in a Finnish forest.

By the time I reach the forest, it is daylight – still dim and the mist has slid away down the slope to collect over the river far below like a new lake, but daylight all the same, sufficient to see the leaf litter under my feet and to avoid that other great giveaway: snapping sticks. Deer don't snap sticks. Wild animals place their feet with precision and care; only humans blunder along. I test the wind again. I'm still well placed; the breeze is crossing my face, barely detectable, taking the dreaded man smell away from the deer. Slowly and carefully I move off along the fence until I find the place where the deer have crossed. Here their slotted imprints are clearly visible, deep where they leapt over the fence, lighter where they delicately landed and moved off through the trees. I follow. My stag is plain to see. His size and weight are writ large on the forest floor, a trail so fresh that it seems to call out to me.

Woodland stalking is an exercise in wildness that stretches and teases every sense; it stirs every slumbering primeval instinct and tests patience and physical control to screaming pitch. Sometimes dropping onto knees in wet grass or boggy patches, or, when the wind shifts or an unexpected and unwanted roe deer comes tripping through, capable of spoiling everything, having to sit through a totally motionless half-hour unable to scratch your nose and forced to ignore the midges grazing the rims of your ears, while the water oozing from sphagnum moss wicks slowly up and into your clothes wherever they touch the ground.

This morning the gods are kind to me: no roe deer to give the game away, no woodcock bursting from beneath my feet, no eddying breezes, no discomfort at all. My stag is up there, only half a mile away now, still roaring sporadically, still in the same place, still undisturbed. I press slowly on, stealthily, thinking carefully about the placing of each foot: heel gently down; ease forward; take weight on that foot; scour ground; take weight on crummack in right hand; ease forward again; heel, sole, toe; test before taking whole weight in case something hidden beneath the leaf litter might snap or creak.

I have to wrest my mind back to the task in hand every time it wanders off, moving from tree to tree like a guerrilla resistance fighter, watching, listening, feeling my way through the forest as if my life depends on it. Deer footprints are all around me. They haven't travelled in single file – far from it – they have spread out across the slope, and every now and again the stag has broken into a run along the contours as if to herd his hinds back together again. After a few more minutes the first rays of the sun top the hill to the east and tiger-stripe the needly litter around me. Now I can identify the woodland plants under my feet: clumps of hard fern, bracken in frost-touched patches, a penny bun fungus, the *Boletus* cep that is so good to eat and nearly distracts me. I *must* concentrate. The birch leaves flare from amber to grapefruit gold.

Why am I doing this? Why, when I have seen red deer so many thousands of times, and when I can drive a few miles up the glen and see deer by the dozen through my telescope or binoculars in open hill country, do I want to stalk a stag on my own patch? What, I ask myself, is it all about, this obsession with wildness, this gut need to be a part of wild nature and to join it at its own level to no obvious end? I suspect that many naturalists may seek to study their interest as closely and unobtrusively as they can; film-makers and wildlife photographers like to pit their wits against their quarry and will demonstrate quite extraordinary patience and suffer agonising discomfort sometimes for weeks on end to get that special sequence of shots. But I can boast none of those material goals. My needs are much closer to the hunter ancient and modern, the deer-stalker whose triumph is fresh meat to carry home rejoicing at the end of the day, although I carry no gun and no longer have any desire to kill. I suspect that in the name of sport or deer control, deep down the modern hunter is responding to the ancient imperatives of all predatory species: the need to kill for survival.

Sir John Lister-Kaye

Sir John Lister-Kaye is one of Scotland's best-known naturalists and conservationists, living at Aigas, near Beauly, where he is director of the internationally acclaimed Aigas Field Centre. In a 30-year career he was the first Chairman of Scottish Natural Heritage for the Highlands & Islands, President of the Scottish Wildlife Trust and Chairman of the government's Environmental Training Organisation. He is a Vice President of RSPB, a Times *columnist and the author of nine books on nature and wildlife including the best-selling* Song of the Rolling Earth, *its sequel* Nature's Child *and* At The Water's Edge.

'The Autumn Stalk' from At The Water's Edge: A Personal Quest for Wildlife *(Canongate Books, 2010).*

CHAPTER 7

FROM MY WINDOW

FROM WILD HARES AND HUMMINGBIRDS: THE NATURAL HISTORY OF AN ENGLISH VILLAGE

STEPHEN MOSS

JANUARY

Overnight, an unexpected, silent visitor has come to the village. Powering southwards down England, across the Cotswold and Mendip Hills, it reached here in the early hours. As dawn breaks, we open our curtains to a landscape transformed into a sea of white. Our village, the county, and the whole country, have come to a standstill, in the worst winter weather for 30 years.

The village children cannot believe their luck. A cheery local radio announcer confirms what they all hope to hear: school has been cancelled. And every child, in every home, has undergone a miraculous transformation. Clothes have been pulled on, breakfasts eaten up, and coats and boots donned with joyful enthusiasm. They can hardly wait to get out of the door – not for their lessons, but to play with an unfamiliar and exciting substance: snow.

With the snow still falling, all is silent. Apart from the occasional sparrow's chirp from the snow-covered hedgerow along the lane, I hear nothing. The birds are far too busy to think of anything other than finding something to eat. If they fail to do so, they will die – and soon. Cold weather does not kill birds, but snow does: for it covers up their food. So the arrival of this white blanket from the north is very bad news indeed.

Which is why, since first light, the bird-feeders outside my kitchen window have been chock-full of birds. As well as the usual great tits and goldfinches there are greenfinches, chaffinches – even a robin, grimly clinging on to the side of the feeder as it pecks at the life-giving seeds within.

Out in the fields, where the wind blows the falling snow almost horizontally across the flat land, nothing stirs. All wild creatures have sought shelter. Even the sheep have forsaken their usual feeding places, and are huddled together in a corner of the apple orchard; where the dirty yellow of their wool presents a stark contrast with the white surroundings.

FEBRUARY

In the neighbouring village of Blackford, half a mile to the east of the parish boundary, the rooks are already checking out their nests in the churchyard.

Rooks love churchyards – for one simple reason. In the past, these holy places would have been one of the few places these glossy blue-black birds would have been safe from the shotgun. Loathed by farmers for their habit of flocking together to feed on grain, and their alleged attacks on newborn lambs, rooks have nevertheless prospered since Neolithic man first tilled the soil and cast his precious seeds onto the ground. For they are the quintessential bird of open grassland; a bird that must have been much scarcer when most of lowland Britain was mainly covered with trees.

Across the road from the churchyard, by the old school, stands a children's playground. On a cold and windy day in February, at four o'clock in the afternoon, there is now enough light for boys and girls from the nearby middle school to come to play for 20 minutes or so before they catch the bus home. For them, and indeed for any casual visitor, it would be easy to miss one of the first true signs of spring, right here by the slide and swings.

A lone hazel tree, in the hedgerow separating the playground from the next field, is covered in bunches of long, greenish-yellow catkins. They hang in groups of three or four, each catkin about as long as my thumb, and superficially resembling a rather thin caterpillar in shape.

Hazel catkins are, along with newborn lambs, one of the main events of early spring – an association which, along with their drooping appearance, has given them the country name of 'lamb's tails'.

Although we call them catkins, they are in fact flowers – but flowers that don't have to wait until spring to bloom. Because their pollen is carried by the wind, rather than by insects, it suits them to appear when there are no leaves on the trees to block the pollen's spread. Hence their emergence at this early stage of the year, often when there is still snow on the ground.

But these long, showy objects only tell half the story. For they are all male; the female flowers are so small and unobtrusive it is easy to miss them. I look closer, and can just make out a tiny red tuft sprouting out of a swollen bud; the female flower.

Once pollination has occurred, and the female flower has been fertilised, she will begin to grow into a cluster of nuts. These will slowly grow and ripen until the early autumn, when they will fall to the ground below, and provide much-needed food for woodpeckers, voles and wood mice.

APRIL

Some time around the middle of April, earlier in some years than others, a ridge of high pressure builds out in the Atlantic Ocean, blocking the usual procession of depressions that sweep up the Bristol Channel and over our heads.

Clear skies bring chilly nights and the risk of frost for the village gardeners. But once the sun is up, the days become warm and pleasant; and each evening, drinkers sit outside the White Horse Inn to enjoy a pint, and the unexpected feeling of sunshine on their faces.

High above them, in the clear blue sky, millions of tiny insects buzz unseen, like plankton floating in the vast expanse of the ocean. And into this sea of blue sails a creature: dark blue-black above, snow-white below, uncannily reminiscent of a killer whale in appearance.

Like the killer whale it is an extraordinary traveller; capable of covering thousands of miles on its global journeys. Unlike the killer whale, it weighs less than an ounce, making its voyaging and navigational abilities even more impressive. It is a house martin, whose slender, streamlined body cuts through the cool air, its beak hoovering up the tiny insects it uses to fuel its passage.

I'd like to tell you where it has come from, but the truth is we have very little idea where house martins spend their time when they are away from us, apart from knowing that it is somewhere south of the Equator. Of more than 300,000 house martins ringed in Britain in the past hundred years or so, only a single one has ever been 'recovered' – trapped again or found dead – on its wintering grounds.

The maths is sobering: 20 million European breeding pairs and their young – upwards of 100 million birds in all – simply disappear. Some have speculated that they live high above the densest jungles, feeding on insects dislodged by heat or forest fires; others that they fly low over the open savannah. But whatever the truth, the paradox remains: how can a bird so familiar that we name it after our homes (and the French after their windows – *hirondelle de fenêtre*) vanish so effectively for half its lifespan?

Shakespeare not only knew the house martin, but used it in one of the most memorable of his speeches, uttered by the doomed Banquo as he arrives at the castle where he will meet his terrible fate. But for the moment, at least, all is fine with the world:

> This guest of summer,
> The temple-haunting martlet, does approve,
> By his loved mansionry, that the heaven's breath
> Smells wooingly here: no jutty, frieze,
> Buttress, nor coign of vantage, but this bird
> Hath made his pendent bed and procreant cradle:
> Where they most breed and haunt, I have observed,
> The air is delicate.

Sadly the air is no longer so delicate for the house martin, whose fortunes are now on a downward path. In my own lifetime I have seen this familiar summer visitor disappear from many of its former homes; perhaps as a result of hostile householders who don't want to be woken at dawn by the cries of hungry chicks. Personally I can't imagine a better way to start a summer's day.

JULY

Of all the myriad insects that buzz and flutter along the lanes, one of my favourites is the gatekeeper butterfly. Sometimes known as the hedge brown, this attractive little creature is a smaller and more elegant version of the meadow brown – our most widespread, and arguably our plainest, butterfly.

The name gatekeeper refers to its habit of loitering alongside footpaths along the edges of fields, often close to stiles or gates.

For the butterfly, this is the perfect place to live; with plenty of brambles, on whose small white and yellow flowers the adults feed; and patches of cock's foot, fescues and other grasses, where they can lay their tiny, ivory-coloured eggs.

Meadow browns emerge here in the middle of June, a month or so before the gatekeepers, by which time they are looking pretty battered, especially if it has been a wet summer. I am always struck by the brightness of the first gatekeeper I see: like the dust-jacket of a brand-new book, the browns and oranges seem to glow in the summer sunshine.

Like the meadow brown, the gatekeeper has two prominent 'eyes', one on each forewing, to confuse predators. On seeing the 'eye' a hungry bird may be fooled into pecking at the butterfly's wingtip rather than its body, which is why in late summer I often see meadow browns and gatekeepers with part of their wing missing.

The gatekeeper is only on the wing for a few weeks, from the middle of July to late August. On a sunny day in late July I have seen the adults emerging *en masse*, with dozens of them thronging the rhynes along Perry Road, before fluttering away to feed in fields and gardens throughout the parish.

SEPTEMBER

The nights are lengthening and the days are getting cooler – and the butterflies in our garden are having their final fling before autumn. With fallen fruits littering the lawn, a troupe of red admirals has arrived to make the most of this bumper harvest. The other morning, as I was hanging out the washing, at least half a dozen of these gaudy insects, just hatched and box-fresh in appearance, were feasting on a glut of apples, pears and plums.

Drinking this half-rotted fruit has an unexpected side-effect: the butterflies become intoxicated – effectively drunk – by the products of fermentation. This has an unexpected bonus for me, as I can get so close I need to take out my reading-glasses to focus on them. Only then can I truly appreciate their stunning colours, a delicate and perfectly symmetrical pattern of black and orange-red, set off by the snow-white patches towards the tips of the wings.

Can there be a more beautiful British butterfly? I'm hard pushed to think of one, and wonder if this were a rarity, like the swallowtail or one of the fritillaries, people might rate it more highly than they do. As it is, we usually notice the first one of the year, and then dismiss them – 'it's only another red admiral' – instead of stopping to admire their gorgeous patterns and colours.

Like the painted ladies that visit us in huge numbers from time to time, red admirals are migrants, coming to our shores from continental Europe each spring. Once here they spread throughout Britain, all the way to Shetland. After laying their eggs on the upper surface of stinging nettles, these migrants die, so the ones I see in my garden in the autumn are the newly hatched offspring of these long-distance travellers.

In a month or so, as the cold weather really takes hold, these red admirals will move off to find one of the final flowers of the year, ivy blossom. Most will then die, but in the past few years some red admirals have begun to overwinter in southern England, hibernating in garden sheds and outhouses before emerging on sunny days in the New Year. I remind myself to make a note to take a look for these hibernating beauties come November.

Stephen Moss
Stephen Moss is a naturalist, author, and broadcaster, based at the BBC Natural History Unit in Bristol. His latest book is The Bumper Book of Nature *(Square Peg). He lives on the Somerset Levels.*
From Wild Hares and Hummingbirds: The Natural History of an English Village *(Square Peg, 2011).*

FROM *NATURAL HISTORY LETTERS*

JOHN CLARE

MARCH 25TH 1825

I took a walk to-day to botanise & found that the spring had taken
up her dwelling in good earnest she has covered the woods with
the white anemone which the children call Lady smocks & the
harebells are just venturing to unfold their blue drooping bells the
green is coverd with daiseys & the little Celandine the hedge
bottoms are crowded with the green leaves of the arum were the
boy is peeping for pootys with eager anticipations & delight – the
swallows are cloathed in their golden palms were the bees are
singing a busy welcome to spring they seem uncommonly fond of
these flowers & gather round them in swarms – I have often
wondered how these little travellers found their way home agen
from the woods & solitudes were they journey for wax & honey I
have seen them to-day at least three miles from any village in
Langley wood working at the palms & some of them with their
little thighs so loaded with the yellow dust as to seem almost
unable to flye it is curious to see how they collect their load they

266

keep wiping their legs over their faces to gather the dust that settles there after creeping the flowers till they have got a sufficient load & then flye homewards to their hives – I have heard that a man curious to know how far his bees travelld in a summers day got up early one morning & stood by one of the hives to powder them as they came out with a fine flower to know them agen & in the course of an hour afterwards he observed some of them at the extremity of the Lordship & having to go to the market that day he passed by a turnip field in full flower about 5 miles from home & to his supprise he found some of his own in their white powdered coats busily humming at their labour with the rest – the Ivy berrys too are quite ripe & the wood pigeons are busily flusking among the Ivied dotterels on the skirts of the common they are very fond of them & a little nameless bird with a black head & olive green back & wings – not known – it seems to peck the Ivy berries for its food & I have remarked that it comes as soon as they are ripe to the Ivy trees & disappears from them when they are gone – I fancy it is one of the tribe of the Titmice & I have often found a nest clinging by the side of the trees among the Ivy which I think belongs to it I know nothing further of its Life & habits – I think I had the good luck to-day to hear the bird which you so spoke of last March as singing early in spring & which you so appropriately named the mock nightingale for some of its notes are exactly similar I heard it singing in 'Open Wood' & was startled at first to think it was the nightingale & tryd to creep into the thicket to see if I coud discover what bird it was but it seemed to be very shoy & got farther from me as I approachd till I give up the pursuit – I askd some woodmen who were planting underwood at the time wether they knew the bird & its song seemed to be very familiar to them they said it always came with the first fine days of spring & assured me it was the wood chat but they could not agree with each others opinion for another believd

it to be the large black cap or black headed Titmouse so I could
get nothing for fact but I shall keep a sharp lookout when I hear
it again – you have often wished for a blue Anemonie the
Anemonie pulsatilla of botanists & I can now send you some for
I have found some in flower to-day which is very early but it is a
very early spring the heathen mythology is fond of indulging in
the metamorphing of the memory of lovers and heroes into the
births of flowers & I coud almost fancy that this blue Anemonie
sprang from the blood or dust of the romans for it haunts the
roman bank in this neighbourhood & is found no were else it
grows on the roman bank agen Swordy well & did grow in great
plenty but the plough that destroyer of wild flowers has rooted it
out of its long inherited dwelling it grows also on the roman bank
agen Burghley Park in Barnack Lordship it is a very fine flower &
is easily cultivated by transporting some of its own soil with it a
heathy sandy soil seems to suit it best – you enquired last summer
wether we had any plants indigenous to our neighbourhood I
think we have some but I dont know much of the new christning
system of modern botany that has such a host of alphabetical
arrangements as would fill a book to describe the Flora of a
Village like the types of Chinese characters that fill a printing
house to print one book with – we have a very fine fern of the
maiden hair kin that grows large with a leaf very like the hemlock
but of a much paler green & another very small one that grows on
the old stools of swallows in damp hollows in the woods & by the
sides of brooks & rivers we have also the thorn pointed fern of
Linnaeus that grows on one spot in the dyke by Harrisons Closes
near a roman station & the harts tongue that grows on the brinks
of the badger holes in Open wood in fact we have a many ferns
there is a beautiful one which a friend of mine calls the 'Lady Fern'
growing among the boggy spots on Whittlesea Mere & a dwarf
willow grows there about a foot high which it never exceeds it is

also a place very common for the cranberry that trails by the brink of the mere there are several water weeds too with very beautiful or peculiar flowers that have not yet been honoured with christenings from modern botany – we have a great variety of Orchises among them the Bee orchis & Spider orchis are reckoned the finest both of them may be found in an old deserted quarry calld Ashton stone pits – but perhaps they are more common on Whittering Heath were grows the 'Cross leaved heath' & a fine tall yellow flower of the Mullein species which the villagers call Goldilocks these are all the rare flowers that I am acquainted with & botanists will come miles to gather them which makes me fancy they are not common elsewhere I will send you some dryd specimens in their successions of flowering this season – have you never heard that croaking jarring noise in the woods at this early season I heard it to-day & went into the woods to examine what thing it was that caused the sound & I discoverd that it was the common green woodpecker busily employd at boring his holes which he effected by twisting his bill round in the way that a carpenter twists his wimble with this difference that when he has got it to a certain extent he turns it back & pecks awhile & then twists agen his beak seems to serve all the purposes of a nail paper gough & wimble effectually what endless new lessons may we learn from nature.

FEB 7 [1825]

You ask me wether I have resumed my botanising & naturalising excutions & you will laugh at my commencement for I have been seriously & busily employed this last three weeks hunting Pooty shells & if you are not above them I must get you to assist me in the arrangement or classification of them I have been making some drawing of them but they are so miserable that I must send the shells with them.

There is a pleasing association attachd to these things they rmind me & I think every one of happy hours who has not been a gatherer of them in his schoolboy days – how anxious I usd to creep among the black thorn thickets & down the hedge sides on my hands & knees seeking them as soon as the sun lookd warm on the hedges & banks & wakend the daisey to open its golden eye & the arum to throw up its fine green leaves I cannot forget such times as these we usd to gather them to string on threat as birds eggs are strung & sometimes to play with them at what we calld 'cock fighting' by pressing the knibbs hard against each other till one broke – I think there is one shell peculiar to our neighbourhood & almost to one spot in it is a large one of a yellow green colour with a black rim around the base there is another yellow one very common which we calld when boys 'painted Ladys' but the one I imagine as scarce is very different from this – they are found in low places by brooks sides the snail is of a blackish yellow & appears to feed on a species of brooklime – there is another not very common I have stiled it the yellow one banded the others are common the red one banded the red self & the red many banded & small many banded with a mottld sort calld badgers by schoolboys – there is many others but they all seem variations of the same kinds the large mozzld garden snail is well known but I found many of them in a spot where it woud puzzle reason to know how they got there.

... The instinct of the snail is very remarkable & worth notice tho such things are lookd over with a careless eye – it has such a knowledge of its own speed that it can get home to a moment to be safe from the sun as a moment too late woud be its death – as soon as the sun has lost its power to hurt in the evening it leaves its hiding place in search of food which it is generally aware were to find if it is a good way off it makes no stoppages in the road but appears to be in great haste & when it has divided its time to the utmost by travelling to such a length as will occupy all the rest of its spare time to return its instinct will suddenly stop & feed on what it finds there & if it finds nothing it will go no further but return homewards & feed on what it chances to meet with & if after it gets home the sun should chance to be under a cloud it will potter about its door way to seek food but it goes no further & is ready to hide when the sun looks out – when they find any food which suits them they will feed on it till it lasts & travel to this same spot as accurately as if they knew geography or was guided by a mariners compass – the power of instinct in the most trifling insect is very remarkable & displays the omnipotence of its maker in an illustrious manner nature is a fine preacher & her sermons are always worth attention.

John Clare (1793–1864)

The son of a Northamptonshire labourer, John Clare was a well-known poet. Serving as a herd boy and under-gardener, he went on to publish his first poetry in 1820. Clare failed as a farmer and lived in desperate poverty, until he was finally committed to an asylum in 1837. Clare never learned to spell or punctuate, but wrote prolifically; most of it unpublished in his lifetime. Between 1824 and1825, he drafted a number of letters to his publisher for a projected Natural History of Helpstone *(qv Gilbert White). These letters provide further evidence of his powers of observation of the natural world and his extraordinarily sensitive intimacy with it.*

'Spring', from Natural History Letters *(1825).*

THE TURNING EARTH: SEVEN DAYS IN SEPTEMBER

RUTH PADEL

SATURDAY

You really feel the earth turn in September. Each early morning is darker. From the kitchen I see three starlings on the bird feeder outside and a dawn glow through the geisha fans of their wings when they try to eat while fluttering, like hummingbirds. They may have flown in from Eastern Europe or may be resident; some starlings migrate, some don't. Huge flocks of them, twisting like smoke in a cyclone, arrive for winter on the east coast of England. In autumn 1997, 400,000 were counted passing over Norfolk, 87,000 on one day – one innocent October 16th – alone. They join resident starlings across the country and in spring go back to Eastern Europe.

I let the dog out and the starlings fly up to the plum tree. The dog doesn't see them. She is 15, half blind, surprised by dew sinking into blond fur round her toes. She belongs to my daughter and was a puppy when we came here. All her life, everyone has thought she was a puppy. Now she has been diagnosed with senile dementia, an item only discovered in dogs in the 1990s. The vet says she's not in pain or distressed; we'll know when the time is right. Beside a silver-droppletted cobweb she stares into the lightening air for a moment of long, existential questioning, then walks through wet grass sniffing.

She used to be such an enjoyer. Now sniffing, eating and cuddling are the only pleasures, though she still frisks with puppy gaiety when she greets a friend. She goes on walks reluctantly and scampers only when we turn for home. Dogs have firm ideas about home. Few Canids migrate.

Overhead come calls, the haunting ancient sound of geese on a journey. Sonic hand-holding: *I'm here, are you?* The dog used to quiver with excitement when she heard. Now she can't hear them at all.

I watch alone the asymmetrical V, sliding across white, white sky, like the long black tick to a maths problem. Geese migrate in family units, parents guiding young and taking it in turns to lead.

My daughter is home for good at last, after one gap year teaching in Paraguay and then four years of college. In the same five years I've been finding out about migration. I've learned there is no universally accepted definition of animal migration because it is so various – so many bodies moving across the globe in so many different ways, for many reasons but only one cause: the spinning of the earth. Those geese are here because where they are is changing. Because the earth tilts; because temperatures drop. Their food in Scandinavia where they bred is going to vanish any minute under ice and snow.

The evolutionary point of migration is to survive.

SUNDAY

Two bright green parakeets streak above the trees, shrieking. There is a flock of these glamorous invaders on the common. Steve, who is servicing the boiler, stands still and watches them with me. We are used to modest greens, the Great Tit's shoulders, the olive and ochre of a Greenfinch. Suddenly in front of us is a tropical palette, a new note.

Something has been digging holes in the shady flowerbed where a peach tree once grew. Maybe there are colonies of grubs down there in rotting roots. Whatever-it-is has tunnelled right through the lawn as if it was a fraying rug. I put stones in the hole, rake earth over and pat back the tossed-out tufts of grass.

My daughter, speckled as though someone had upended a salt-cellar of autumn light over her blonde hair, stands on a step-ladder picking small dark plums. Once handled, they change colour for ever, the indigo sheen disappears, you see the violet beneath. The dog lies by one of the silvery aluminium struts, happy to have her home, not knowing that she is not really home for good at all. She is starting an internship tomorrow and growing up is a path that leads away.

The plums are damsons, unusually thick on the bough. The tree is blue with them; they have dragged the branches low over the grass. Also over our neighbour's grass, we must pick those, too. Our neighbour is ninety and looks after the dog when we're away – as we looked after her Golden Retriever, before it died.

This is home. A loved neighbour. Memories. An ageing dog. Sunlight on a small garden where my daughter grew up. She folds up the ladder and takes it next door and I look at buckets of damask plums, introduced to Britain by the Romans, who found them where they were first cultivated. A hundred years before they conquered Britain, they took over Syria. The damson comes from the ancient city of Damascus.

What does 'native' mean for British trees? Even our 33 so-called native trees are post-glacial migrants. The DNA of Britain's most ancient oak trees says they came from the Iberian peninsula. What is native, really, when the royal oak, emblem of England, is a Spanish immigrant?

MONDAY

I am looking at our only sunny bed. A bush I planted here ten years ago has grown larger than I expected. It never has flowers and is sitting there like a giant sea anemone, taking up all the space. The late afternoon air smells of smoke and cut grass. Under September sun, our house and tiny garden, the blackbirds sewing the back gardens together with alarm calls across wood fences, seem normal. They are not. Listening to my daughter talking about asylum-seekers, I realise how abnormal any home is, especially one with a garden and a fence.

I think of the Ampullae of Lorenzini, rows of gel-filled pores dotting the underside of a shark's top lip, which detect electromagnetic fields. They orientate the shark so it can respond to paths of magnetism on the sea bed. Maybe that is what anyone navigating migration should do. Detect and follow invisible paths on an ocean floor. Maybe I should take the images of migration separately like cells in a honeycomb. Animal and human. Causes and preparing. The journey and the aftermath. Let them speak to each other, work together like the gel-filled pores on a migrating shark's upper lip.

TUESDAY

Off Gravesend, divers from Marine Life Rescue have seen a whale in the Thames. Three years ago, a young female Bottlenose Whale, who should have been cavorting in Scottish waters, was seen in central London. The media watched her swim the Thames towards Battersea where she was stranded and finally died, just as rescuers were transporting her towards deeper water. The divers believe this new one a minke. There are lots around Mull. Minke whales are very inquisitive, but to stray off a migration route into a river system is a very unwise move.

WEDNESDAY

I have seen what is digging up the bed. The fox is brown all over, no white on her, and sauntered onto the lawn when I was at the window, as if she owned it. She went straight to that bed, sniffed like someone browsing a supermarket, peed on the earth like a cat and then started digging. Not with paws but with her nose, tossing the earth ahead of her as if using a spade.

The colonisers. I met three foxes engaged in a pressing argument in the road last night. The dog must know all about this. Why didn't she tell me?

THURSDAY

They have found that whale dead in the Thames, near Dartford. A young male, about two. His stomach was empty; he probably starved to death. He was a humpback. Humpback whales are sometimes seen off West Scotland but it's amazing to have one in the Thames. In September he should have been making his way slowly from the arctic to the tropics. Like all young males he was exploring and it went wrong.

Young humpbacks are born in tropical waters and swim with their mothers to the North Pole (or, for the other population, South Pole) to feed on summer plankton. Then they go back. Because seasons are reversed either side of the equator, the northern and southern humpbacks probably never meet. Northern ones travel towards their breeding ground in tropical waters, as the southern ones are swimming towards their own Pole to feed. At 16,000 miles a year, humpbacks are the farthest migrating mammals, but often accompanied by the ultimate stay-at-home. A barnacle, once past the free-floating larva stage, cements its forehead to the place where it stays the rest of its life. But suppose it commits its tiny self to a migrant whale?

FRIDAY

A robin is watching me weed. I stop at the monster bush, which is taking too much space. Why don't we have flowers in our only sunny bed? I feel guilty; it has done well for itself here, but you have to let things go.

It turns out to have two surprisingly long root-arms clutching into earth. I dig up half the bed to get out the second and then it snaps. I replant it further away, dig the other root a long trench and stand back. The robin hops down to investigate.

Robins seem ordinary in a garden but there is a mystery to them, which lies at the heart of all migration. They can choose. Or it looks like choosing. Like starlings and goldfinches, they are partial migrants. In winter some leave for Spain while others arrive from north and east Europe.

John Masters's novel *The Lotus and the Wind* is about the 'Great Game', the 19th-century Anglo-Russian spy-war over Afghanistan, and also about the sex war. It divides stay-at-home personalities from gypsy wanderers by gender. Men need freedom, like the wind. Women, like the lotus, need to be rooted.

My daughter wouldn't agree. After this internship she is going to work in human rights in Colombia. That, she says, is where she wants to live.

Robins, however, would agree about a sexual divide, but for them it is the other way round. Also for chaffinches, whose scientific name is *Fringilla coelebs* from *coelebs*, 'bachelor', because in winter, in north Europe, you normally only see males. It is mainly the females who migrate while the males stay – to be an emblem of Christmas for us, but really to hang onto their feeding territory till spring.

Partial migration may have been a between-stage in the evolution of migration. Some individuals began, then some did some didn't, then everyone was doing it and those who didn't died. Migrating became an Evolutionarily Stable Strategy, an 'ESS': a way of doing things that sees off any other strategy that comes along. ESS is a key concept in Game Theory and the robins' great game is partial migration, genetically controlled by parental bet-hedging.

But when things get tough, how does anyone, robin or human, 'decide' to stay or to go? Among partial migrants, older birds often don't. You have to be fit. So how does a robin decide?

Deciding for robins, I realise, standing there thinking about Colombia, is really a shorthand for saying, 'This is what the bird has been programmed to do by natural selection.' But what about people? Is there an innate personality divide that lets some people uproot easily, not others?

Before we lived here, we had a flat. The German woman upstairs told me that in the 1930s, when she was 16, she asked her Jewish parents if they should leave Germany. No, they said. No. It will be all right. She was on the last train out and spent the war in Delhi as a nurse. Her family all died.

Getting away may save you. But for birds and people alike migrating is a high-risk strategy and a high-cost solution.

The journey is always dangerous.

Ruth Padel

Ruth Padel is a prize-winning poet, Fellow of Royal Society of Literature and Zoological Society of London. Darwin: A Life in Poems *is a verse biography of her great-great-grandfather Charles Darwin,* Tigers in Red Weather *describes tiger conservation throughout Asia and her first novel,* Where the Serpent Lives, *was praised for 'a sense of the wordless world of animals watching humans'. (TLS). 'Only Emily Brontë has*

embraced Padel's radical and sympathetic inclusiveness of creaturely life'
(The Guardian).
From The Turning Earth: Seven Days in September (Not yet published).

CHAPTER 8

NATURE TRAILS

MILKWORT ON THE GOWER PENINSULA, WALES

ANDREW LACK

Plants have interested me from an early age. Their obvious and much celebrated beauty is just the start. There is a great variety of British plants, and looking for them, seeing how one can be identified from another, and finding where they grow and why they grow there, is a source of endless fascination. And there are other things too; even as a child, I became caught up in their names – white campion and corn spurrey, mugwort and Venus's looking-glass – the latter now, sadly, a rather rare cornfield weed.

This developed into an abiding passion that has taken me to many parts of these islands – from Highland Scotland and the chalk downs of southern England to the sand dunes of the west – to search out some of our loveliest and rarest plants. The exhilaration at finding a rarity is always present. But rarity is not all, and sometimes it is the common plants that can show us something we have not previously considered. This was brought home to me on one particular occasion, nearly 30 years ago, while walking on the sand dunes of the Gower peninsula.

It was early June, and definitely 'flaming June' that day, with glorious warm sunshine after a dewy start, and everything fresh and growing vigorously. I was lucky enough to be able to get out on a weekday and could go down onto the sand dunes below Nicholaston village. As I emerged from a patch of dense sycamores, the dunes stretched out in front of me, surrounded on both sides by the limestone cliffs of Gower, and there was not a soul about. The dunes were shimmering in the heat. In the more sheltered spots they were covered with two plants flowering so vigorously one could almost sense that they were competing to attract visiting insects. Intensely prickly burnet rose, knee-high and covered with its satiny white flowers, was interspersed and set off by the deep magenta of the bloody cranesbill. There were other plants, naturally, but the dunes were ablaze with these two as I walked slowly down towards the sea. I was familiar with both plants from other places, but I had never seen them in such abundance and proximity to each other.

As I walked further, these were gradually displaced by the more subdued marram grass and smaller plants, until I came to the stream – or 'pill' in this part of the world – that divides Nicholaston dunes from those of Oxwich. I paddled across this, and found myself in a place that was quite unlike what I had left. The dunes, superficially, looked similar in shape and were immediately adjacent, but the vegetation was different – no burnet rose or bloody cranesbill at all, but much creeping willow, dewberries, orchids in the slacks, large patches of rest-harrow, a plant so covered with sticky glands that it gave the whole system a most distinctive smell, and many smaller plants. In particular, there was another plant familiar to me from other places – the milkwort.

This milkwort is a fairly modest, but attractive, plant, with a short frilly petal and two large sepals giving it an unusual shape. One of its features is that it varies in flower colour in most places.

In fact, it varies more and more consistently in flower colour than any other plant in the British flora. It is usually illustrated blue in floras, and that is the most common colour, but it has reddish-purple and pink forms of varying intensity and a white form. It is a fairly common plant of chalk and limestone grassland across the country. Its close relatives – the heath and chalk milkwort – have a similar range of colour forms, although in many places they are only blue.

This milkwort that I was now walking past was all one colour, a vivid reddish purple. It lined the dune slack in a narrow band just above where the slack might have standing water in winter. It is unusual to have a single colour and I was beginning to wonder why that might be. To continue my walk I had to cross over a high dune and into another slack. There were milkworts there, too, but paler, rather more pinkish in colour, and again in some abundance. Walking further on, and into the largest central slack of the dune system, I was taken up with some other plants when I noticed the milkwort again, but this time they were all white-flowered. What on earth was happening? How could they change from one form to the other? And where were the boundaries?

I walked back over the dune and into the first slack to see whether I had missed any other colour – all red-purple. So I took a different route round that particular dune back into the central slack. Some of this was quite thick with creeping willow and some grasses, and the milkwort was not there, but towards the sides I found it again, and only white. Then, however, a walk to the other side, and … purple. I had to crisscross the slack, and I was constantly finding white on one side and purple on the other. Eventually I found a spot where the purple and white forms almost met – they were only about two metres apart. There was an invisible line that clearly the plants knew about and I could only wonder at. Why was it there? The white plants were mostly rather smaller than the purple ones, and grew almost flat on the ground, whereas the purples were slightly more upright. And the vegetation seemed thicker where the whites were growing, although there was so much variation, it seemed that it could not possibly explain why the boundary was exactly there.

I continued – most puzzled as to the reasons for this distribution – when the story was complicated further. Going away from the sea and towards the back of the dune system I found myself among purely blue plants. Not a big clump and a rather pale blue, but quite different again, and again a single colour in the one area. This was clearly going to take more exploration, and I had better be armed with a map and pencil.

A few days later, I mapped out the dune system. The pink form was clearly distinct from the others, so I was mapping, in effect, four different colour forms. The white was the most widespread, but there were several places with pink or purple forms, and two separated clumps of pale blue, both quite small. The pink and purple forms almost met at one spot, like the purple and white forms. All the colour forms had clearly demarcated areas. It was as if there was an agreement to parcel out the dune slacks between them.

Over the next few years, I followed the fate of individual plants, and discovered that what I was seeing was far from static. We tend to think that plants are long-term fixtures in the landscape, even if we know that things must change. What I found was that even the longest-lived of milkworts at Oxwich only reached the great age of five years old, and most of those that reached their first summer only flowered once. I also saw the colour distribution change.

After two years, and to my surprise, I found five plants with blue flowers right by the purple/white boundary and a further six by the purple/pink boundary. These were big plants, too, and a rich, deep blue unlike the rather pallid blue plants I had mapped earlier. It seemed that they must be hybrids – crosses between purple and white and purple and pink. How that produced blue I could not fathom, but it had to be so. I had already detected, using the laboratory technique of electrophoresis, that different forms of certain enzymes were associated with the different flower colours. All I needed to do was to test these blue plants. Sure enough, each blue plant on the purple/white boundary had the enzyme forms from both purple and white plants; and those on the purple/pink boundary had both of those two forms. This confirmed their hybrid status.

The map I had drawn was clearly a snapshot. Plants move, but the part that does so is often hard to observe. Milkworts produce two seeds per flower, and they are large considering the size of the flower – about 2.5 x1mm. They are simply dropped onto the ground immediately beneath the flowers. They have a small fat-rich attachment that is attractive to ants. I could watch the ants collecting them and taking them into their nests. Some of those seeds I found later – discarded outside and with the fat body chewed off – though some seeds probably remained in the ant nest. It means that the seeds are generally not dispersed far, but can be taken to good places for germination.

And then I discovered a bit more about the dune system itself. It turned out that Oxwich dunes had been used as a training ground for armoured vehicles during the Second World War, and an aerial photograph from 1946 showed a lot of bare sand with only pockets of vegetation. The pieces of the puzzle were slotting into place.

I can imagine that one or a few plants, or even seeds, were left in scattered places. Milkworts can self-fertilise, and different colour forms were left in different parts. The milkworts must have colonised from a few starting points. Since then, these plants had been marching across the dunes. It was a slow march, just a metre or two a year for the most part. A phalanx of purples set out from one spot or perhaps more than one; an alternative phalanx of whites from another; pale blues and pinks from further favoured spots. It had taken nearly 40 years for them to meet. And when they met? Clearly, they followed the 1960s slogan to 'Make love not war'! They hybridised, and produced vigorous rich blue progeny.

The disruption to Oxwich dunes by the war might also explain the very first observation I made – the fact that the two dune systems differed so markedly. The tanks never crossed Nicholaston Pill. Perhaps in the 1930s Oxwich, too, had burnet rose and bloody cranesbill, the plants that had greeted me with such splendour on that first June day.

What did become clear is that the variety that we can see has been influenced by so many different factors. There is a constant state of flux. Plants come and go, some quickly, some slowly, but ever changing in response to the natural cycles and variations around them and, frequently, with our actions superimposed. Even something as disruptive as a military training ground can, after some years, give rise to an unexpected and colourful scene of plant colonisation.

I never fully worked out how a reddish-purple crossed with a white could produce a blue, but I suspect that the whites, effectively an unpigmented flower, have a block in the synthesis of any pigment – but do contain the potential. That potential could be realised in the hybrid as the purple parent could provide the link.

A few years later I moved away from the area, but visiting Oxwich again in the 1990s the vegetation had thickened dramatically, and the milkworts had mostly gone. Where they were growing, the colours had mixed more. Oxwich, deservedly, is now a National Nature Reserve and it is unlikely, and undesirable, that such disruption will ever happen again. But if it had not happened in the 1940s I would never have found the situation I encountered that day, and perhaps never have learned about these delightful plants.

Andrew Lack

Andrew Lack is a Senior Lecturer at Oxford Brookes University and an Ecology, Science and Society, and Conservation Biology Researcher. He is the author of The Natural History of Pollination *and* Redbreast: The Robin in Life and Literature – *updated from the classic* The Life of the Robin *by his father, David Lack.*

LIKENESSES

SAMUEL TAYLOR COLERIDGE

OCTOBER 19TH 1801

On the Greta, over the bridge by Mr Edmundson's father-in-law, the ashes – their leaves of that light yellow which autumn gives them – cast a reflection on the river like a painter's sunshine.

The first sight of green fields with the numberless nodding gold cups, and the winding river with alders on its banks, affected me, coming out of a city confinement, with the sweetness and power of a sudden strain of music.

In natural objects we feel ourselves, or think of ourselves, only by *likenesses*; among men, too often by *differences*. Hence the soothing, love-kindling effect of rural nature – the bad passions of human societies. And why is difference linked with hatred?

SUNDAY DECEMBER 19

Remember the pear-trees in the lovely vale of Teme. Every season Nature converts me from some unloving heresy, and will make a Catholic of me at last.

Repose after agitation is like the pool under a waterfall, which the waterfall has made.

COUNTRY AND TOWN

The rocks and stones put on a vital resemblance, and life itself seemed, thereby, to forgo its restlessness, to anticipate in its own nature an infinite repose, and to become, as it were, compatible with immovability.

THE POET AND THE SPIDER

On St Herbert's Island, I saw a large spider with most beautiful legs, floating in the air on his back by a single thread which he was spinning out, and still, as he spun, heaving on the air, as if the air beneath was a pavement elastic to his strokes. From the top of a very high tree he had spun his line; at length reached the bottom, tied his thread round a piece of grass, and re-ascended to spin another – a net to hang, as a fisherman's sea-net hangs, in the sun and wind to dry.

BRIGHT OCTOBER FRIDAY MORNING

A drizzling rain. Heavy masses of shapeless vapour upon the mountains (O the perpetual forms of Borlight – on the lakeward ridge of that huge armchair of Lodore fell a gleam of softest light, that brought out the rich hues of the late autumn. The woody Castle Crag between me and Lodore is a rich flower-garden of colours – the brightest yellows with the deepest crimsons and the infinite shades of brown and green, the *infinite* diversity of which blends the whole, so that the brighter colours seem to be colours upon a ground, not coloured things. Little wool-packs of white bright vapour rest on different summits and declivities. The vale is narrowed by the mist and cloud, yet through the wall of mist you can see into a bower of sunny light, in Borrowdale; the birds are singing in tender rain, as if it were the rain of April, and the decaying foliage were flowers and blossoms. The pillar of smoke from the chimney rises up in the mist, and is just distinguishable from it, and the mountain forms in the gorge of Borrowdale, consubstantiates with the mist and cloud, even as the pillar'd smoke – a shade deeper and a determinate form.

Samuel Taylor Coleridge (1772–1834)

Samuel Taylor Coleridge was one of the most important of the Romantic poets, a philosopher and a scholar of Jesus College, Cambridge. He published his first volume of poems in 1796, and in 1797 he visited William Wordsworth and collaborated with him on Lyrical Ballads *(1798). Coleridge settled in Keswick in 1800 and, after various enterprises and travels, became dependent on Wordsworth at Grasmere in 1809. The countryside of the English Lakes fired his imagination and his sensitive and subtle response to natural phenomena is clear in the* Notebooks, *which his grandson edited under the title* Anima Poetae *in 1895. Above all, Coleridge understood man's need to participate in the cosmic harmony of the universe – and that through such participation he would uncover his sense of oneness leading to spiritual well-being. 'Likenesses', from* Anima Poetae *(1895).*

THE END OF AN EXCURSION

SIR JOSEPH BANKS

Went this morn to see the Views from Walkden Lodge* & Sr Abraham Eltons Summerhouse; found them very Beautifull; as many very different & very fine in a Small Compass of Riding as I Ever Saw, I mean in the Course of the Road from the Summer house through Walkden town to the Lodge. The top of the hill on which the Summer house stands is markd with Lines of a very singular nature: the Ruins of [them] Crossing Each other, which are now all but Level with the Ground; of different figures, some squares or Polygons containing from half an acre to three or four & sometimes much more; some circular, some of which are very small. What they can have been I do not at all Conjecture, but about a mile from them in the way to Bristol is a very fine Encampment with a double Vallum, probably Roman**.

*Walton Lodge. Sir Abraham Elton of Clevedon Court was Master of the Merchant Venturers.

**Cadbury Camp.

*** Alexander Catcot, Vicar of the Temple Church in Bristol.

This morn discoverd by accident an immense quantity of Bulbs probably of *Scilla autumnalis* growing on the very Brink of the precipice of St Vincents Rock nearest the Lime-kiln on the sides of Zigzag walk; also abundance of *Ophrys apifera* now in full Perfection. Went at noon to see Mr Catcot's*** fossils at Bristol; spent two hours with him in Looking over them perfectly agreeably. His Collection, tho small, is Certainly the most amusing, possibly the Best, as it is also the most instructing I have ever seen. His Specimens, particularly of Extraneous, are all so Compleetly good that you have not a moments doubt of their having Existed in a recent state. The most Capital are Many of the Bones of an Elephant found bedded in Ocre on the Mendip hills, which are very little changed, & a s[k]eleton of some large animal – Possibly *Lemur macauco* – almost intire, the bones placed in their proper order, which was found in the same place.

Got up this Morn Early to go in search of the *Veronica Hybrida*? Which I heard from Mr Catcot shewed me a very good specimen of *Lycoperdon Fornicatum* which was found on the other side of the water Last autumn. It was cut into no more than four Laciniæ but from its whole appearance I could not but Conjecture that it is no more than *L: Stellatum* with its Volva adhering to it which is very seldom found as it is very Liable to be broke from it, the volva being fixd in the ground. I should in this Place also remember that I myself found one of the *L: Stellatum* the other day Lying Loose upon the Ground on the Green hill Just beyond St Vincents Rock.

After breakfast set out for Mr Innis's Garden at Redland, which I had heard a great Character of; found it very trifling, scarce one good Plant in the whole Collection. Mr Innis* Values himself chiefly upon officinal Plants, consequently is well stored with nettles, docks &c: yet were not able to puzle out the name of *Lysimachia nummularia*,

*John Innys of Redland Court.

at Least so the Gardener told me who askd me the name and desird me to set it down on paper which I did. From hence set out for London & in my way to Bath was agreeably surprizd by finding *ornithogalum Pyrenaicum* in tolerable plenty on the Right hand side about a Quarter of a mile before I came to Kensham on the beginning of the descent.

Set out for London, observed between Silbury & Marlborough the stones called Grey weathers which in one particular Valley are scattered about in great numbers on the Surface of the ground. The people in that neighbourhood were breaking great numbers of them either to mend the roads or build houses, which gave me an opportunity of Examining them & bringing away some pieces which I found to be of a very hard & fine graind Sand Stone. Whether it is found in beds in any part of this Countrey I will not venture to say, but Remember that some time ago in seeing Gen Conways place near Henly I saw a large heap of such Stones, some of them of an immence size, & on asking where they were got from was told that they were found scatterd all over that Countrey Laying in the Stratum over the Chalk at Different Depths, & that those I Saw had been got together at a large Expence for some work to be done in the Generals Grounds, I think a bridge.

Sir Joseph Banks (1743–1820)

President of the Royal Society between 1778 and 1820, Sir Joseph Banks studied at Christ Church, Oxford, showing passion for natural history. Made a fellow of the Royal Society in 1766, he travelled in Newfoundland, Canada, and joined Captain Cook's Endeavour expedition round the world between 1768 and 1771, collecting natural history specimens. His collections and his library are housed in the British Museum.

'The End of an Excursion', from The Journal of Sir Joseph Banks *(Private printing, 1989).*

GORDALE SCAR

THOMAS GRAY

Oct. 13 to visit *Gordale-Scar*. Wind N.E. Day gloomy & cold. It lay but 6 m. from Settle, but that way was directly over a Fell & it might rain, so I went round in a chaise the only way one could get near it in a carriage, which made it full 13 m. & half of it such a road! But I got safe over it, so there's an end, & came to *Malham* (pronounce *Maum*) a village in the bosom of the mountains seated in a wild & dreary valley. From thence I was to walk a mile over a very rough ground, a torrent rattling along on the left hand. On the cliffs above hung a few goats: one of them danced & scratched an ear with its hind-foot in a place where I would not have stood stock-still.

for all beneath the moon.

As I advanced the crags seem'd to close in, but discover'd a narrow entrance turning to the left between them. I followed my guide a few paces, & lo, the hills open'd again into no large space, & then all farther way is bar'd by a stream, that at the height of about 50 feet gushes from a hole in the rock, & spreading in large sheets over its broken front dashes from steep to steep, & then rattles away in a torrent down the valley. The rock on the left rises perpendicular with stubbed yew-trees & shrubs, staring from its side to the height of at least 300 feet. But these are not the thing! it is that to the right, under which you stand to see the fall, that forms the principal horror of the place. From its very base it begins to slope forwards over you in one black & solid mass without any crevice in its surface, & overshadows half the area below with its dreadful canopy. When I stood at (I believe) full 4 yards distance from its foot, the drops which perpetually distill from its brow, fell on my head, & in one part of the top more exposed to the weather there are loose stones that hang in the air, & threaten visibly some idle spectator with instant destruction. It is safer to shelter yourself close to its bottom, & trust the mercy of the enormous mass, which nothing but an earthquake can stir. The gloomy uncomfortable day well suited the savage aspect of the place, & made it still more formidable. I stay'd there (not without shuddering) a quarter of an hour, & thought my trouble richly paid, for the impression will last for life ...

Thomas Gray (1716–1771)

Thomas Gray was a well-known British poet who was appointed Professor of history and modern languages at the University of Cambridge in 1768. He was an avid traveller, touring in England, Scotland and Europe, and his letters are among the best of this period. He included a great number of topographical observations on his travels, and during the last decade of his life, he devoted himself to the study of natural history, keeping detailed annual calendars and dates of first arrivals of blossom and fruit, as well as migrant birds.
'Gordale Scar', from Journal of a Tour through the English Lakes (1774).

THE MOUNTAIN
IN SNOW

FRANCIS KILVERT

TUESDAY, 14 MARCH [1871]

The afternoon had been stormy but it cleared towards sunset.

Gradually the heavy rain clouds rolled across the valley to the foot of the opposite mountains and began climbing up their sides wreathing in rolling masses of vapour. One solitary cloud still hung over the brilliant sunlit town, and that whole cloud was a rainbow. Gradually it lost its bright prismatic hues and moved away up the Cusop Dingle in the shape of a pillar and of the colour of golden dark smoke. The Black Mountains were invisible, being wrapped in clouds, and I saw one very white brilliant dazzling cloud where the mountains ought to have been. This cloud grew more white and dazzling every moment, till a clearer burst of sunlight scattered the mists and revealed the truth. This brilliant white cloud that I had been looking and wondering at was the mountain in snow. The last cloud and mist rolled away over the mountaintops and the mountains stood up in the clear blue heaven, a long rampart line of dazzling glittering snow so as no fuller on earth can white them. I stood rooted to the ground, struck with amazement and overwhelmed at the extraordinary splendour of this marvellous spectacle. I never saw anything equal to it I think, even among the high Alps. One's first involuntary thought in the presence of these magnificent sights is to lift up the heart to God and humbly thank Him for having made the earth so beautiful. An intense glare of primrose light streamed from the west deepening into rose and crimson. There was not a flake of snow anywhere but on the mountains and they stood up, the great white range rising high into the blue sky, while all the rest of the world at their feet lay ruddy rosy brown. The sudden contrast was tremendous, electrifying. I could have cried with the excitement of the overwhelming spectacle.

I wanted someone to admire the sight with me. A man came whistling along the road riding upon a cart horse. I would have stopped him and drawn his attention to the mountains but I thought he would probably consider me mad. He did not seem to be the least struck by or to be taking the smallest notice of the great sight. But it seemed to me as if one might never see such a sight again. The great white range which had at first gleamed with an intense brilliant yellow light gradually deepened with the sky to the indescribable red tinge that snowfields assume in sunset light, and then the grey cold tint crept up the great slopes quenching the rosy warmth which lingered still a few minutes on the summits. Soon all was cold and grey and all that was left of the brilliant gleaming range was the dim ghostly phantom of the mountain rampart scarce distinguishable from the greying sky.

Francis Kilvert (1840–1879)

Francis Kilvert entered Worcester College, Oxford, and was ordained a clergyman in 1864. He first served as his father's assistant in a Wiltshire parish and then as curate of Clyne in Radnorshire. He subsequently became rector of St Harmon's in Radnorshire and finally Bredwardine, in Herefordshire. He died of peritonitis within a month of his marriage in 1879. On his death, Kilvert left 22 volumes of diaries, from which a selection was first published between 1938 and 1940.

'The Mountain in Snow', from Kilvert's Diary *(Jonathan Cape, 1938).*

THE LAKE SHORE AT GOWBARROW PARK

DOROTHY WORDSWORTH

APRIL 15TH, THURSDAY.

It was a threatening, misty morning, but mild. We set off after dinner from Eusemere. Mrs Clarkson went a short way with us, but turned back. The wind was furious, and we thought we must have returned. We first rested in the large boat-house, then under a furze bush opposite Mr Clarkson's. Saw the plough going in the field. The wind seized our breath. The Lake was rough. There was a boat by itself floating in the middle of the bay below Water Millock. We rested again in the Water Millock Lane. The hawthorns are black and green, the birches here and there greenish, but there is yet more of purple to be seen on the twigs. We got over into a field to avoid some cows – people working. A few primroses by the roadside – woodsorrel flower, the anemone, scentless violets, strawberries, and that starry, yellow flower which Mrs C. Calls pile wort. When we were in the woods beyond Gowbarrow Park we saw a few daffodils close to the water-side. We fancied that the lake had floated the seeds ashore, and that the little colony had so sprung up. But as we went along there were more and yet more; and at last, under the boughs of the trees, we saw that there was a long belt of them along the shore, about the breadth of a country turnpike road. I never saw daffodils so beautiful.

They grew among the mossy stones about and about them; some rested their heads upon these stones as on a pillow for weariness; and the rest tossed and reeled and danced, and seemed as if they verily laughed with the wind, that blew upon them over the lake; they looked so gay, ever glancing, ever changing. This wind blew directly over the lake to them. There was here and there a little knot, and a few stragglers a few yards higher up; but they were so few as not to disturb the simplicity, unity, and life of that one busy highway.

We rested again and again. The bays were stormy, and we heard the waves at different distances, and in the middle of the water, like the sea. Rain came on – we were wet when we reached Luff's, but we called in. Luckily all was cheerless and gloomy, so we faced the storm – we *must* have been wet if we had waited – put on dry clothes at Dobson's. I was very kindly treated by a young woman, the landlady looked sour, but it is her way. She gave us a goodish supper, excellent ham and potatoes. We paid 7/- when we came away. William was sitting by a bright fire when I came downstairs. He soon made his way to the library, piled up in a corner of the window. He brought out a volume of Enfield's *Speaker*, another miscellany, and an odd volume of Congreve's plays. We had a glass of warm rum and water. We enjoyed ourselves, and wished for Mary. It rained and blew, when we went to bed. N.B. Deer in Gowbarrow Park like skeletons.

Dorothy Wordsworth (1771–1855)
Companion to her poet brother William, with whom she settled at Grasmere, Cumbria, in 1799, Dorothy Wordsworth was not just

housekeeper and family mentor, but the inspiration for some of William's most important poetry. Her Journals *record her deep affinity for nature and are a record of her delight in the experiences that she shared with her brother. William said that his sister gave him 'eyes', and he understood her rapturous and often immediate response to natural beauty.*

'The Lake Shore at Gowbarrow Park', *from* Journals of Dorothy Wordsworth *(1897).*

LIFE OF THE STREAM

COLIN ELFORD

The frost had done its work overnight, coating the countryside in billions of sparkling jewels, each encrusted in its own tomb of ice. Under foot russet muddied leaves form a crispy carpet, and complains noisily when trodden on. Stacked in layers by the winter winds, they are joined, moulded together by the thinnest film of frosted ice, once a seam of moisture from a passing cloud of fine drizzle.

On this frozen path a pair of enraged territorial cock blackbird's rise from the ground facing each other, only the width of a feather apart. They rise to the height of a small child then fall back to earth as spiteful as a pair of bantam cocks. Blind with battle they are far too busy to notice a stranger in their territory.

Bobbing, a balancing pied wagtail looks down on the foray below, while swinging back and forth on the electric wires a flick, flick of black and white. The commotion also disturbs a nomadic fieldfare perched on a cattle fence; this flash of blue brightens the scene as this winter visitor, cuckoo-shaped in silhouette, sweeps away low over the frosted field.

Silent, blue haze and shadow paints the valley bottom. Across the valley on the distant bank rabbits both buck and doe frolic in courtship in the enclosed glades between the clusters of gorse. On the ground around my feet woolly tufts of blueish grey hair as soft to the touch as a baby lay scattered, torn from the coat of a rival Coney. Before mounting the stile I stop and rub the overnight stubble on my chin, suddenly awakened and tickled by the sharp north-easterly. The arrival in the sky of the hazy weak winter sun offers no warmth; the gold leaf it spreads on the opposite bank barely casts light onto the tussocky grass. The long shadows it styles, conjures an image similar to that of melting snow. This arid desert like grass wears its dry garb, sapped of colour and beaten by the winter. Its lack of vigour is in complete contrast to an adjacent field, triangular in shape, whose short rich green grass is being grazed by hungry bi-coloured cattle.

From this vantage point it feels as though you could reach out and stroke the top layer of cloud, which looks as close to any arctic snow scene you could imagine. The sun slips slowly behind one of these; false dream-like pressure ridges of virgin snow and is gone.

On the track across the field you have to take care where and how you walk. Grey rocks with even greyer lichens attached erupt from the soil, these ankle high gravestones are happy to trip any unobservant walker. Terraces of pasture and down, moulded like waves, roll down as gentle ridges, to the valley floor. In a narrow thicket a squabble erupts, breaking the stillness of morning in the scrubland home of a tiding of dominating magpies. They clamour about and surround a lone buzzard resting too close to their future territories, pecking at the hunched victim, shrieking abuse. The buzzard outnumbered but determined to stay put, clumsily raises at full stretch a barred wing at its attackers in protest at being disturbed. Overhead, a gang of excited rooks add to the noise in long drawn out raspy calls, each tone unique, identifying the caller. They drop as a group to investigate the noisy argument raging in-between the bare branches. Over the magpie's position they make an unmajestic swoop, but instead of joining in the disturbance they lift, rising fast and high as one body, thinking better of the situation once the buzzard was noticed, leaving the sky quieter than when they had arrived. In time the magpies are joined by several of the local bird population all raising their annoyance at this large outsider. Undeterred, and as still as a rock the buzzard remained. I left the neighbours arguing and picked my way down the slope toward the valley bottom. To my right, running from just beneath the ridge of the slope, a strip of over grazed rush and heavily trampled ground, cattle prints have trapped pools of still water. This water sodden ground, pot marked with ringed tracks carve a soft inscription on the hillside, a chain of raised tufts attracting whatever form of light available. This part of the hillside shimmers as I walk past, glistening and glinting, sending out shafts of flickering light as the beam of a lighthouse. In the damp ground in the valley I manage to spook a snipe that explodes from a frozen hoof indent into the sky, it calls while twisting and jinking into the grey, vanishing in all but sound.

Various shrubs and thorn make up lines and clumps of scrub travelling the length of the valley toward the sea. The lower levels of hedgerow vegetation on this raw February morning look bare and woody, the only green and sign of life, the ivy, well out of reach above the browse line of both cattle and deer.

Rolling and laying the grass down in the direction of flow, a young stream heads down through the valley. The start, a mere crease in the grass, but the slow momentum builds along the route of its journey. Barely ankle deep the water travels under a stock fence, flowing silkily over submerged pastoral grasses, and then cascading over an occasional raised hoof print as splendid to view in effort as any large waterfall. Side channels form miniature still lakes searching for any light; when found, they reflect this gift back as the glare of a mirror.

Such pools of brightness if rippled by the wind, dance, sparkling as though shattered into hundreds of pieces. This very young trickle of water finds ways of gently skirting around and sliding under obstacles. Further along it reaches a narrow cut formed and shaped from past movements over its stony bottom. The water here is as clear as any chalk stream; it runs smoothly sending out a soothing sound to the ear. It's a place to rest, encouraging you to listen, and reflect. Babbling and talking, the stream ascends into a channel running alongside some thorny vegetation, here the soft, jingling cow bell music changes in tone. The water passes unseen through this hedge, hidden behind a thorn shield of wild rose and bramble. Dry barbs as sharp as talons, guard and keep prying eyes out. Once hidden, the stream song changes, it could be the kinks and curves or maybe an incline, but it changes occasionally, giving out a long winded groan as an injured animal. I pause, listening to each changing sound, the odd unusual crackle and strange guttural groan. Peering into the gloom of the hedge I can just make out a small sand bar and shelves, containing washed up debris, a mix of dried bramble sticks and leaves. On leaving the hedge it reappears into the overcast light of the day, the stream has gained more strength. Earlier, it flowed around small boulders of rock, now it delights in scaling and gliding over the peaks. The music it produces is louder and constant. The voice of the stream differing on what ever it encounters, whether mineral or matter. Crowfoot plants, anchor on the edges of the sand bars, while further down rotting leaf litter brought down on the current collect, clinging together for a foothold. Now the thrust of the stream has more purpose tackling small cascades in its stride, while releasing excitable frothy bubbles in mass, at every opportunity. At times the water lets out a shriek, the energy rippling the surface in pulsing rings and sounding like a fast running tap.

Chest feathers and two primaries of a blackbird, its life cut short by a hungry raptor sway on the edge of the stream. A single feather clings to a dry strand of last seasons goose grass, half in, half out of the water caught in between two worlds. Orange berries, drowned haws are swept along on the sandy bed of the stream rolled along over the stones, until they are caught by waving arms of under water vegetation. No longer quiet the stream exerts its new found strength passing deep holes with ease, diving over and under stones, massing around a large stubborn rock, stirring the waves and rippling the surface as salmon fighting their way up stream. At times it bubbles with sheer enjoyment, laughing at the maelstrom it produces, glorying in the whirlpools and the fish scale ripples it sends spiralling across its surface. A fallen fence stake across its path has slowed the pace, this part barrier has created an island of dirty froth, and sections of this island peel off as bubbles into this revolving rhythm of water, each floating toward one another clinging together like shipwrecked sailors, growing larger as a cell. Together, they circle, caught in this endless whirlpool; one by one the outside smaller ones explode regenerating the ever growing centre bubble with every sacrifice. This selfless ceremony continues until the last remaining sphere resembles a clear dome, the perfect fish eye before it too pops and the process of birth starts all over again.

Once past the fence stake the stream finds its own course, crossing crevices, spreading over shallows, widening and narrowing as the land permits. As the valley levels out the song of the stream quietens and once again the song of an excited chaffinch can be heard looking forward to spring over the noise of the water. Odd single trees stand along the streams path, one a russet hawthorn ancient and scarred, listens to the water coursing past her roots as a robin sings and a cock chaffinch pinks from her bare branches. On her limbs, swelling buds wait for the first signs of spring, a new season. Near the tree the edges of the stream have been disturbed by thirsty cattle crushing the sides leaving them badly trodden and misshaped. Each half moon track between the cattle cropped rushes slows down the progress of the stream, diverting the flow, and sending seeping fingers into dead end channels. Within a centre channel a blood red dock stem softened by the water has caught a batch of quivering lacelike bubbles, more delicate than the finest crystal chandelier.

Other than the chirring of a greenfinch in the distant scrub there is no sound, the stream is silent running. The only movement of life is the occasional horse tail swishes breaking the surface in vibrating ripples, resembling sound waves as the stream glides under a raft of small sticks temporarily lodged into the side of the bank. Past the single plank that makes for a bridge, the ground softens and the stream barely audible, slinks away into a moist furrow seeping into the ground to some unknown underground pathway as though it wants to leave unnoticed. Slipping away like an old relative, not wanting to be a hindrance. As it leaks away under my feet I thought of its journey, and how much it had in common with a human life, to start as a very young trickle, quiet and reserved, to become an adolescent growing in size, noise and confidence, learning to run and jump, skipping over obstacles, finding endless strength and vigour. As the stream widened it used wisdom, experience, avoiding the pitfalls, for exploring the wrong path could lead to it becoming ensnared and stagnant. As the stream neared its task, it slowed, quiet and ready to return to its waiting mother through secret ancestral cracks in some cave wall, to be reborn again.

Colin Elford

Colin Elford has had a lifelong interest in animals. He has worked in Forestry and wildlife conservation and control for 35 years, now working for the Forestry Commission as a wildlife ranger. Colin's first book Practical Woodland Stalking, *printed in 1988 was a common sense stalking guide for the novice. To date he has written 'A Year in the Woods,' a true account of a rangers work seen through the eyes of a person who has a passion for forests and wild places.*

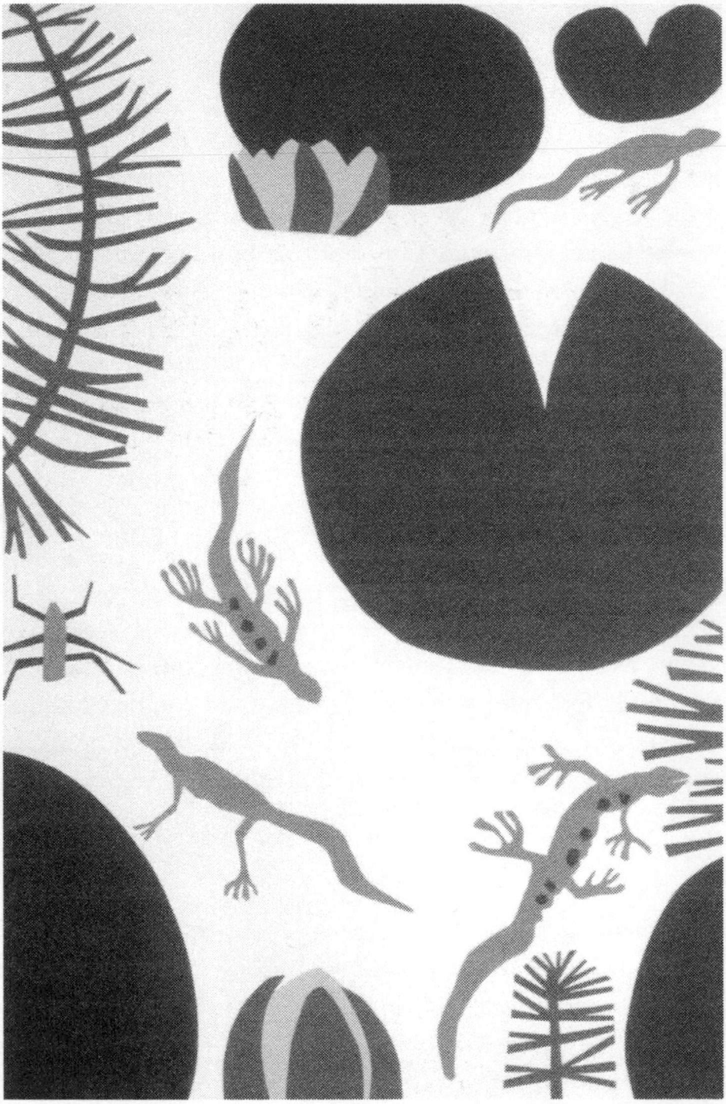

CHAPTER 9

WORDS AND NATURE

THE GANNET

JOHN WOOLNER

'Where did you get these?' She asked sternly, giving me that disapproving stare only my staunchly religious mother could give.

How was I to explain the frilly black knickers she'd found in the back pocket of my shorts; the shorts I'd thrown in the wash basket without a second thought? She held the damning evidence in the tips of her thumb and forefinger on an outstretched arm, a foot or so away from my face. I'd wanted to tell her about them, but this was our first encounter since my father and I had returned. I began to colour.

'You're only thirteen!' she cried, fixing me with accusatory eyes.

'Mum, it's not what you think.'

Underwear had been far from my mind as we'd slid the canoe into the unruffled inky-black water of the Exe at dawn that day, paddling softly into wisps of milky mist that hovered above the surface of the river, shattering the reflected full moon into shimmering ripples.

'You're very quiet,' my father said. He'd heard nothing but my excitement for days. Coming from the urban surroundings of London, and never having been in a Canadian canoe before, this was an adventure worthy of Huckleberry Finn.

'I'm just thinking.' I replied. But the truth was – though I never said it for fear of him ridiculing me – that everything was so still, so perfectly calm, that speaking felt somehow wrong, almost irreverent. Dew hung from intricate webs that adorned trees and shrubs on the banks; light frost bedecked clinker fishing boats, sparkling in the moonlight; and several swans appeared, gliding by nonchalantly before disappearing into the mist and half-light. Only the steady rhythmic splash of the paddles and an alarmed moorhen that cried and then scurried across the water into tall reed beds broke the silence.

After fifteen minutes of steady paddling we left in our wake the small harbour area, ancient church, 17th Century Dutch gabled houses, grazing marshes, and reed beds of Topsham.

'Will you look at that,' my father said, his face animated. I hadn't seen him so relaxed or enthused for years. In fact I'd hardly seen him at all; he was always so busy with work.

We were at the mouth of the meandering Clyst where it meets the Exe. The estuary and vista had opened up dramatically before us, the river channel snaking its way between vast mounds of shimmering and bubbling black mud. The moon was sinking into the soft blue-grey hues of the Haldon hills; while to the east, the mid-March sun – seemingly with some effort – climbed above Woodbury Common, shining through stalwart beech trees that lined the iron-age hill fort of Woodbury Castle.

The silence had given way to a chorus of different cries: lapwings, sandpipers, redshanks, snipe, curlews, teal, and wigeon. They poked and prodded the mud, pulling out worms and shellfish. Several silhouetted cormorants stretched their wings lazily, warming and drying themselves in the morning sun. Two elegant snow-white egrets and a grey heron stood stock still and expectant at the water's edge. Seemingly unaware of us, its small beady eye focussed on the water, the heron's head suddenly flinched, and with the speed of a whipping lasso its beak stabbed the water, pulling out a silvery flash of wriggling fish, swallowing it in one gulp.

It was the grey mullet that most excited me. As we paddled around the bends of the low tide channel, we saw vast shoals of them. Their mouths were open as they fed on the surface of the water, their dorsal and caudal fins fluttering. Startled by the approaching canoe, a whole shoal would suddenly dive below out of sight, only to reappear like silvery-grey ghosts close by. A seal, its head breaking the surface of the river, snorted loudly, and then vanished as quickly as it had appeared, only to break the surface again repeatedly, its dark eyes observing us with the utmost curiosity.

As we rounded a huge arc in the channel, the fishing village and harbour of Lympstone appeared, nestling between prehistoric red sandstone cliffs, the furthest edge of Devon's Jurassic coastline. The snug fishing cottages, Italianate red brick clock tower, fishing vessels, and washing strewn on lines across the beach, appeared ethereal and dreamlike, as if floating on a sea of white mist. And from this mist, like wind-driven flurries of black snow, sprang darting flocks of crying godwits and dunlin.

Half an hour later the mist had lifted and the twisting channel had opened into a wide expanse of iridescent estuary water, the mud banks replaced by sand banks dotted with screeching herring gulls, and deep blue cockle beds on which fed bright-billed oystercatchers. We could smell sea air, and towards the mouth of the estuary glimpse the shimmering thin line of yellow-white sand at Dawlish-Warren – now a Devon Wildlife Trust Reserve – with its habitats of dunes, grassland, ponds, salt marsh and mudflats. There were piercing guttural cries as a V-shaped flock of black headed Brent Geese, making their long journey north, flew in a formation above us. Soon after we passed more geese feeding on eel grass.

Reaching the river mouth, some fifty miles or so from its source on Exmoor, we found ourselves being pulled out to sea by powerful currents, the water forced into a narrow channel by the elongated sand spit of the Warren. My dad had said we were to paddle along the East Devon coast line, below the lofty Triassic cliffs. I was getting anxious about the choppy water ahead when I saw it: a strange shape, moving at the edge of the warren some distance away. At first it appeared like a ball, but then it leapt, stumbled, and leapt again, struggling to maintain any consistent pose. 'What the hell's that dad?' I cried.

'Let's go see,' he replied, looking bemused.

With that we turned the canoe and began to paddle furiously.

'Put some effort in!' my father shouted, laughing, as the current turned the boat towards the side I was paddling, facing us downstream again.

'I am!' I protested. I'm sure now, looking back all those years that he hadn't meant it as a barbed comment. But then his comments were often disparaging. I never seemed to get anything quite right. I began to paddle as if there was a tribe of bloodthirsty cannibals on our tail.

Going against the current required huge effort, but eventually, by paddling at an angle, we were able to reach slack water at the edge of the warren, pulling the canoe up on to the beach. The strange shape however, had seen us approaching, for it waddled up towards the dunes, fell flat, picked itself up, changed direction, ran frantically, and dived into the sea. It was tossed about like some flotsam or jetsam, until the next crashing frothy wave threw it up the beach, depositing it on the glistening sand. I followed my father as he bounded across the sand.

'It's a gannet!' he called out to me, still breathless from the run as I caught up with him. 'What's a gannet doing here?'

Lying prostrate on the sand, seemingly defeated, was a huge white bird. It was at least a metre long, with a pointed tail, black wing tips, long neck and beak, and yellow feathered head. Its chest was rising and falling, as if gasping for life.

'How did it manage to get its wings trapped in a pair of knickers?' I asked.

'I can only think they were floating at sea and it got caught up in them when it dived for fish,' said my father, kneeling down in the sand. He gingerly put out his hands in an attempt to free it from the underwear, but the bird twitched anxiously. 'It's okay, it's okay,' he said quietly, with a tenderness that surprised me.

The gannet was having none of it. It struggled to its feet again, lunged at my father with its long pointed beak and started waddling towards the sea, its webbed feet on the wet sand making a sucking flapping sound. It repeatedly tried to unfold its wings in its desperation to fly; momentarily stretching the frilly knickers. But it fell again and was thrown off its feet by the next wave. And as the wave retracted, it got to its feet again and ran towards the dunes at surprising speed. That's when my father ran and threw himself forwards as if he was doing a rugby tackle. He wrestled with the gannet, his powerful arms struggling to get those knickers off as it stabbed at him, making powerful lunges at his body and neck, wriggling to get free with all the energy it had left.

'I've got it!' howled my father, the bird's long neck and beak held in his folded arms. 'Get the knickers off!' But I couldn't. I stood by feeling helpless, ineffectual, the gannet stabbing my father's chest and then lying overpowered, crushed, and hopeless, looking at me intensely with its dark rimmed, light blue eye, making mournful cries. It was as if we were somehow strangely connected, that majestic bird representing the rich abundance of wildlife in the estuary, the daily rhythm of the tides, everything I'd seen and heard, trapped in some synthetic, man-made product. 'Help,' the bird seemed to be asking in its plaintive cry, 'I'm dying.'

'Don't just stand there. Get the knickers off.' I began to tug at the frilly knickers, and then more carefully stretched them over the wing bones of the huge wings, careful not to break any feathers, the gannet struggling beneath me. 'They're off dad,' I said, jumping up, triumphantly holding the frilly black knickers in my hand.

Quite suddenly he let the gannet go. Freed from the underwear, it ran frenetically towards the sea. With a slow, heavy beating of its large wings, looking back just once, it rose erratically above the crashing waves.

'We did it!' my father said, his arm around my shoulder. 'We did it dad!' I said, looking up at his face, his eyes sparkling and alive as he took in the ascending gannet. I don't think I ever told him how much that arm around my shoulder and the 'we did it' meant to me. Father and son, we stood and watched as the gannet steadily climbed, flying gracefully now, smaller and smaller into cloudless blue sky, reducing gradually to a white speck. And then, it was gone.

'So,' said my mother, 'where did you get them?'

'I got them off a bird mum!'

John Woolner is the winner of The Wildlife Trusts' writing competition for unpublished authors. The competition was held in early 2010, in partnership with Elliott & Thompson, Foyles and Completelynovel.com. He lives in Devon. This is his first published work.

ENDINGS

ROBERT MACFARLANE

While he was writing *Tarka The Otter*, Henry Williamson went feral. Daily, for months, he walked out alone into the great wedge of moor that is held between the rivers Taw and Torridge, where they tumble, divergent, off the north-west slope of Dartmoor. During those seasons of river haunting, Williamson lived through the moor's different weathers. Big scapular-shaped rain clouds, light trimming the wet rocks, coffee-coloured spate-water. At other times, sunlight, softness, wild swans beating through blue sky. Sometimes he slept out overnight, in the lee of a bank or in a stand of trees. He would wake starred with frost, or hung with dew.

In the course of that strange and restless time, Williamson became, by his own reckoning, an otter-man. He rarely saw other people. Those he did, he sought to avoid. His affinity was with the moor's creatures, and with its earth and water. His ferality was, in part, an escape: the Great War had left Williamson deeply damaged, and the moor offered space and solace. But he was also in pursuit of a literary ideal. Williamson wanted to write about the

Devon landscape he had come to love; to press the wildness of the river and the moor into words. And for that, the long months of fieldwork were necessary.

Williamson's research was obsessive-compulsive – writing as method acting. He returned repeatedly to the scenes of Tarka's story as it developed. He crawled on hands and knees, squinting out sightlines, peering at close-up textures, working out what an otter's-eye view of West Gully or Dark Hams Wood or Horsey Marsh would be. So it is that the landscape in *Tarka* is always seen from a few inches' height: water bubbles 'as large as apples', the spines of 'blackened thistles', reeds in ice like wire in clear flex. The prose of the book has little interest in panoramas – in the sweeps and long horizons that are given to eyes carried at five feet.

Tarka is a short book that took a long time to write. Williamson revised the eleventh chapter, set in the remote moorland fen of Cranmere, more than 30 times – going back to the fen between each version – before he was satisfied. The book as a whole was re-written 17 times. 'Each word,' he said afterwards, 'was chipped from the breastbone.'

The best writing about nature – deserts, skies, forests, mountains, tundra, glaciers, prairies, forests, moors and their non-human inhabitants – has come from an intensity of commitment similar to Williamson's. J. A. Baker's *The Peregrine* is the result of ten years spent in the winter woods and fields of Essex. Barry Lopez's *Arctic Dreams*, of five years' travel in polar Canada and Alaska. Antoine Saint-Exupery's *Wind, Sand and Stars*, of a career spent flying over desert and sea. Willa Cather's *O Pioneers!*, of a childhood in Nebraska. For landscape cannot, on the whole, be mocked up; cannot be dreamed into descriptive being. Light, water, angles, textures of air, water and stone, the curves and straights of horizon and slope: these are the basic components of natural places, and they combine in ways too subtle and particular to be invented.

This – the dedication it demands – is one of the difficulties of writing about a natural place. Another, contrasting difficulty is that landscapes have had too much written about them in the past. For centuries, they have provoked in their viewers an urge to communicate their magnificence. The result is that landscapes have become coated with thick layers of dead language. Wreck-divers use the word 'crud', a dialect form of 'curd', to describe the submarine minerals that clot around any long-sunken metal object, and which have to be laboriously chipped and leached away before that object can be exposed to sight again. It is – as Williamson knew – effortful work to get back through the verbal crud: to divulge nature to what he once called 'authentic sunlight'.

The finest writing about nature is almost always modest, exact and attentive. It is precise without ever being curt. It understands that lyricism is a function of detail, and not of abstraction. And it is ethically alert. One thinks of Emily Dickinson's miniaturist genius, and the deceptively small poems she wrote about sunrises, flies, flowers, and light falling through space. Dickinson's tiny poems have vast interiors. Reading a poem by her is like ducking into a bungalow, to find oneself within a cathedral.

Or one turns to Lopez, a writer seriously under-known in this country. Lopez writes about the Canadian Arctic: about snowfields that stretch levelly for thousands of miles, and about tundra that has been flattened by the to and fro of ice-masses, and planed by fierce winds. Yet, even in these most lateral of terrains, Lopez consistently plumbs a meaning and a human interest. His prose resembles the film of mercury on the back of a mirror, which allows a flat thing to contain ever-receding depth.

Why should the ability to write well about nature and landscape matter? Surely, it might be objected, there are more interesting and important things to be written about? Or, with the world proceeding so adamantly towards a final wrecking of the environment, discriminating between types of nature writing might seem like choosing between deckchair patterns on the *Titanic*.

The novelist and philosopher Iris Murdoch can, unexpectedly, be of help here. Murdoch's ethical vision was based upon a concept that she, after Simone Weil, called 'attention'. 'Attention,' Murdoch proposed, is an especially vigilant kind of 'looking'. When we exercise a care of attention towards a person, we note their gestures, their tones of voice, their facial expressions, their turns of phrase and thought. In this way, by interpreting these signs, we proceed an important distance towards understanding the hopes, wishes and needs of that person.

This 'attention', Murdoch noted, is the most basic and indispensable form of moral work. It is 'effortful', but its rewards are immense. For this attention, she memorably wrote, 'teaches us how real things can be looked at and loved without being seized and used, without being appropriated into the greedy organism of the self'. Murdoch's ideal of 'attention', of a compelling particularity of vision, pertains to landscapes and creatures as well as to people. It is harder to dispose of anything, or to act selfishly towards it, once one has paid attention to its details. This is an environmentalist's truth, as well as a humanist's.

The best nature writers have been attentive, in the sense that Murdoch and Weil meant that word, to the terrains through which they have moved. Their imaginations have responded with gripping exactitude to certain forms of matter (ice, rock, light, sand, moorland, water, air), to certain arrangements of space (altitude, edges, valleys, ridges, plains, horizons, slopes), and to certain creatures. Comically, earnestly, lyrically, ecstatically, anecdotally, beautifully, these writers have approached their chosen subjects with an eye to their uniqueness. In so doing, they have primed a space within which those subjects can be respected – can come to seem less seizable and usable by the greedy human self.

In a crucial sense, therefore, the real subject of nature writing is not nature, but a restructuring of the human attitude towards nature – and there can be few subjects more urgent or necessary of our attention than this. The most important nature writing poses profound questions about the durability and significance of human schemes. It offers, in Lopez's fine phrase, a cause for 'incorporating nature into the meaning of human community, in that moral realm'.

*   *   *

I remember late one January, setting out with three friends to climb Beinn a'Chaorainn, The Hill of the Rowan, near Loch Laggan in the Western Highlands of Scotland. The day began magnificently. Galleons of cloud were at full sail in the sky, racing slowly over the blueness. The sunshine was hard and bright, the snow tuning the light to its own white frequency. Walking on, I could feel the blood pulsing warmly in my toes and fingers, and the sun burning on the edges of my cheeks.

From the roadside, the Hill of the Rowan rises to three distinct tops. On its east flank are two glacier-carved cirques. That day the steep cliffs of the cirques were plated with ice, which flashed and glittered in the sunlight as we approached them. We passed first through a copse of pine trees, and then emerged onto open ground, crossing several wide swathes of sphagnum moss. In summer, these would have been tremulous and brimming with rainfall, as wobbly as waterbeds. But winter had hammered them into stasis, and glazed them with ice. Looking down into the clear ice as I walked over it, I could see the moss, dense and colourful as a carpet, yellow-green stars of butterwort dotted here and there.

We began to ascend one of the east-facing ridges of the mountain, which separated the two icy cirques. As we climbed, the weather changed its mood. The clouds thickened and settled in the sky. The light became unstable, flicking from silver to dirty grey. After an hour of climbing it started to snow heavily. Approaching the top of the mountain, we were in near white-out conditions, and it was hard visually to separate the air and the land. It had become much colder. My gloves had frozen into rigid shells, which clunked hollowly when I knocked them together, and a thick scab of white ice had built up on my balaclava where my breath came through it, like a clumsy clown's mouth.

A few hundred yards from the summit the ridge flattened out, and we were able to unrope safely. The others stopped for something to eat. I moved on ahead, wanting to enjoy the solitude of the white-out. The wind was blowing along the ridge towards me, and under its invisible pressure everything was on the move. Millions of particles of snow dust streamed just above the ground in a continuous flow. Rounded chunks of old hard snow were being blown reluctantly along, skidding over the surface of the ridge. And the big soft flakes that were falling from the sky were being driven into me by the wind. They walloped almost soundlessly against my clothing, and I built up a clean white fur of snow on my windward side. It seemed as though I were wading up-current in a loose white river. I could see no more than five yards in any direction, and I felt excitingly alone. The world beyond the whirled snow became unimportant, almost unimaginable. I could have been the last person on the planet.

After several minutes' walking, I reached the small summit plateau of the mountain, and stopped. A few paces away, sitting and contemplating me, hunkered back on its huge hind legs, its tall ears twitching, was a snow hare. It seemed curious at this apparition on its mountaintop, but not alarmed. The hare's fur was a clean white all over, except for its black tail, a small patch of grey on its chest, and the two black rims of its ears. It moved on a few paces in its peculiar gait, its rear legs shunting its hindquarters slowly forward and up, almost over its head. Then it stopped again. For half a minute we stood there in the blowing snow, in the strange silence of the snowstorm. Me with my clown's mouth of ice, and the hare with its lush white coat and polished black eyes.

And then my friends emerged like spectres from the white-out, their climbers' hardware clanking. Immediately the hare kicked away with a spurt of snow, swerving and zigzagging off into the blizzard, delicately but urgently, its black tail bobbing long after its body had disappeared.

I stayed on the top of the mountain for a while and let the others walk on ahead to begin the descent. I thought about the snow hare; about how for an animal like this to cross one's path was to be reminded that it had a path, too – that I had crossed the snow hare's path as much as it had crossed mine. Then my mind moved away from the mountaintop. The solitude I had experienced in the white-out on the ridge had been replaced by a sense of the distance invisibly before me. I no longer felt cocooned by the falling snow, I felt accommodated by it, extended by it – part of the hundreds of miles of landscape over which the snow was falling. I thought east, to where the snow would be falling over the thousand-million-year-old granite backs of the Cairngorm mountains. I thought north, to where snow would silently be covering the empty wilderness of the Monadhliaths, the Grey Hills. I thought west, to where snow would be falling on the great peaks of The Rough Bounds of Knoydart – Ladhar Bheinn, the Hill of the Claw; Meall Buidhe, the Yellow Hill; and Luinne Bheinn, the Hill of Anger. I thought of the snow falling across ridge on ridge of the invisible hills, and I thought too that there was nowhere at that moment I would rather be than there.

Robert Macfarlane

Robert Macfarlane is the author of Mountains of the Mind *(2003) and* The Wild Places *(2007). He is currently writing a book about paths, tracks and stories.*

THE WILDLIFE
TRUSTS

By the 1960s, in response to the widespread devastation of our natural habitats, Wildlife Trusts had been formed across the length and breadth of the UK. Ancient woodlands, wildflower meadows, lakes, mosses, moors, islands, estuaries and beaches were all rescued in an urgent drive to save our natural heritage for future generations.

Today there are 47 individual Wildlife Trusts covering the whole of the UK and collectively we have more than 800,000 members. We manage around 2,300 nature reserves and every year we advise thousands of landowners on how to manage their land for wildlife. We run marine conservation projects around the UK, collecting vital data on the state of our seas and celebrating our amazing marine wildlife. Every year we work with thousands of schools and our nature reserves and visitor centres receive millions of visitors.

Our many nature reserves are the cornerstone for our vision of A Living Landscape - a recovery plan for nature, championed by The Wildlife Trusts since 2006, to help create a resilient and healthy

environment rich in wildlife and provide ecological security for people. We are working with landowners across the UK to create large areas in which wildlife flourishes, also helping to safeguard the ecosystems we depend on for natural services like clean air, clean water and carbon storage.

We are at the forefront of marine conservation in the UK. The Wildlife Trusts are working and campaigning for Living Seas - The Wildlife Trusts' vision for the future of the UK's seas. Within Living Seas, marine wildlife thrives from the depths of the ocean to the coastal shallows. The Wildlife Trusts are making a difference for marine wildlife from the seashore to the corridors of power. Our Marine Bill campaign played a pivotal role in convincing the government to pass new laws to protect our seas. Across the UK we are inspiring people about marine wildlife and carrying out vital research to help protect basking sharks, dolphins, seals, corals and a host of rare and fragile marine habitats.

We couldn't do our work without the support of our members. If you'd like to join your local Wildlife Trust and help us protect your local wildlife and wild places, call 01636 677711 or visit www.wildlifetrusts.org/yourlocaltrust.

INDEX

INDEX

ACKNOWLEDGEMENTS

Illustrations by Carry Akroyd.

Sir David Attenborough, Caroline Allen, Elizabeth Allen, Graeme Andrew, Sarah Ballard, Geoff Barlow, Adam Cormack, Tom Ellis, John English, Jacqui Graham, Vivien Green, Anna Guthrie, Anwen Hoosen, Kat Hollaway, Kate Inskip, Matt Johnson, Sheila Kerr, Julia Kingsford, Jonny Leighton, Anna Lewis, Professor Aubrey Manning, Ellen Marshall, Julian Roughton, Mark Searle, Jane Southcott, Karen Sullivan, Marjolein Wytzes.

AUTHOR BIOGRAPHIES

Michael Allen is Chairman of the Royal Society of Wildlife Trusts and has been devoted to his own local Wildlife Trust in Cambridgeshire through much of his life, latterly becoming Chairman of its Council. On his retirement he was appointed a Vice President of the Trusts.

A life-long birdwatcher and general naturalist, he has led natural history and wildlife tours in many parts of the United Kingdom as well as in Europe and Africa, and travelled in North America, often in pursuit of wild places.

He spent his career at the University of Cambridge where he directed the Madingley Hall Centre for Continuing Education before becoming Director of Studies in English and Bursar of Churchill College. In retirement he has spent much of his time on regional matters in the East of England, where he has served on several committees including for the National Trust and the Heritage Lottery Fund. He was successively Hon. Treasurer and Hon. Secretary of the British Trust for Ornithology and was a founder member of the Bristol Ornithological Club and the Wicken Fen bird ringing group.

Sonya Patel Ellis is an experienced freelance writer on the environment, wildlife and travel.